Kara,

Thanks so much for coming out and hanging out on Pollock Mountain! Hope you enjoy the book

6/2/24

Pot Doc:

A Physician's Search for the Holy Grail of Medical Marijuana

Michael Geci, MD

Blessings

Mike

Chapbook Press

Schuler Books
2660 28th Street SE
Grand Rapids, MI 49512
(616) 942-7330
www.schulerbooks.com

Pot Doc – A Physician's Search for the Holy Grail of Medical Marijuana

www.potdocthebook.com

ISBN 13: 9781948237482

Library of Congress Control Number: 2020909360

Copyright © 2020 Michael Geci, MD

All rights reserved. No part of this publication may be reproduced, stored in a retrieval system, or transmitted in any form by any means—electronic, mechanical, photocopying, recording, or otherwise—except for the purpose of brief reviews, without written permission of the author.

Printed in the United States by Chapbook Press.

Copyright © 2020 by Michael Geci

All rights reserved. No part of this publication may be reproduced, stored in a retrieval system, or transmitted in any form by any means—electronic, mechanical, photocopying, recording, or otherwise—without prior written consent.

Darkness cannot drive out darkness; only light can do that.

—Dr. Martin Luther King Jr.

The spirit of truth will do more to bring persons to light and knowledge than flowery words.

—Brigham Young

Acknowledgments

It's a blessing that I am finally able to write this page, because without the help and support of those below, *Pot Doc* might forever remain just an idea buzzing around my mind.

I am forever indebted to lj for her love, guidance, editorial assistance, and support, Tom Daubert for his patience and guidance in reading a manuscript that was raw, the Guth for her friendship and company on our epic bike rides, Dorothy for believing in me and throwing me a rope, Laura for taking the time and showing me the pond, Rachel for her editorial assistance, Ty for a great cover design, Vivian and Pierre for getting the manuscript into print, and my son, whose patience allowed me to keep moving forward.

And to those mentioned in the book, particularly Nigel, Lori, and especially to Hillari (who made this story possible), I just wish the outcome had been different.

Contents

Introduction

A Mixing Pot

The Pit of Gloom

The Call of Montana

Meeting Pete

Under the Bodhi Tree

Hi, I'm Hillari

MT-148

The Road to Missoula

Taking the East Coast West

Christ is Not the Lord

PFU

Gerald's Grandma

Burned Out

The Science of Cannabis

The Lab

A Logic Vacuum

The Slow Kid Gets Eaten

Losing Bud

What's a Business Plan?

Looking for Arno

An Ad For a Chemist

The Joy of Grateful Patients

Wearing Out My Welcome

Flying Standby

Sam

Trying to Be Legal

A Message from the Board

The Christening: MBA

Christmas in BZN

Rumblings

The MMGA

Birthing the Lab

Full Spectrum Labs

The Grand Illusion

All or Nothing

Into the Darkness

We Got Peaks!

Searching for a Home

Unraveling

Jackpot

Road Trip

A Mouse Trap

Battle Preparations

Broken Promises

Going to California

Where's My Car?

Plant 2 Product Program

The Rev

Wall Street & The Sketchheads

Getting Chunged

The Summit

Freefall

A Listing Ship

A Strain Called Misty

The MMGA Does It Again

The Midterm Tsunami

A Really Good Question

Damage Control: The MTCIA

Hiring Bryan

Pitching Amy

ACS

The War Begins

The Logical Ghost: LC-991

The Calm Before the Storm

Consulting the HR Book

Money Talks

9:12

The Morning After

The Nuclear Option: SB-423

Branding Day

The Lawsuit

My Final Plea

From the Witness Stand

The Verdict

After the Dust Settled

5A

The Final Demon

The Crumbling Wall

Epilogue

Citations

Introduction

My name is Michael Geci (pronounced: GET-see). I've been a practicing emergency physician since 1996. This is the story of how I became a knowledgeable physician regarding the medicinal properties of *Cannabis sativa* (aka, cannabis), and the bizarre relationship the people of the United States, and particularly its government, have with this ubiquitous plant.

Cannabis is a large genus of plants that includes hemp and is frequently called marijuana when used for its recreational perception-altering properties. It grows well in most areas of the world, and in many places, it is considered a weed. Its serrated, compound, multi-lobed leaf is likely the most recognizable leaf on the planet, a symbol of counterculture. Cannabis is a hardy annual that doesn't require fertilizer, pesticides, or herbicides for it to reach heights of close to eighteen feet.

Cannabis is a useful plant. Its fiber makes for hardy textiles that rival cotton and paper; in fact, the first two drafts of the Declaration of Independence were written on Dutch hemp paper. Cannabis seed is one of the most nutritious in the plant world, high in protein, including all twenty amino acids, rich in omega fats, as well as a great source of essential minerals. And most notably, cannabis produces cannabinoids, mysterious organic compounds produced in the sticky trichomes of the ripening female flowers. Cannabinoids have been used for the treatment of countless medical conditions from arthritis to Alzheimer's and everything in between.

If our culture were logical, cannabis would be embraced as a beneficial plant. But unfortunately, logic only taunts us into believing what is possible, not what is reasonable or sustainable. No plant species has suffered for the sins of one of its rogue varietals as much as cannabis. Of the many hundreds of varieties of cannabis, a minority produce a compound called tetrahydrocannabinolic acid (THCA). When heated, THCA undergoes a chemical reaction that transforms the innocuous, non-psychoactive molecule into a decarboxylated derivative, tetrahydrocannabinol (THC), noted for its potent ability to alter human consciousness. Millennia ago, someone had the bright idea of inhaling the smoke of one of the fragrant dried flower buds of THC-laden cannabis (thousands of years later to be called marijuana), and what occurred after that is history.

What inspired that first person to smoke cannabis, we'll never know. What is certain is that the experimenter wasn't able to keep a secret—telling their friends who found the experience to be pleasant enough to tell their friends who tried it, and in turn, they told all of *their* friends, who...eventually told you.

For a hundred generations the story of cannabis had an uneventful history. The plant was used for fiber, seeds, and most recently, its cannabinoids, working its way into being a mainstay in Western medicine—that is, until the 1936 release of the propaganda film *Reefer Madness*. For reasons that would satisfy even the most ardent conspiratorialists, citizens were told that cannabis, in the form of marijuana, would corrupt their minds. Recreational use of the marijuana plant, due to its higher content of THC, became associated primarily with Mexican American immigrant workers and the African American jazz musician community. It was during this time that hemp was renamed "marihuana," and the plant's long-standing history as a cash crop was replaced with a new image: "The Devil's Weed."[1]

In 1930 the federal government founded the Federal Bureau of Narcotics (FBN), headed by Commissioner Harry Anslinger. The propaganda campaign initiated by Anslinger painted cannabis as a seductive drug used to lure White women into the dens of iniquity of Blacks and Hispanics. The fear generated from the FBN propaganda machine precipitated the cultural and political lunacy that influenced twenty-seven states to pass laws against marijuana in the years leading up to federal prohibition. It set the stage for the passage of the 1937 Marihuana Tax Act.[2] Thus began the long federal prohibition of cannabis that is largely still in place today.

Pot Doc is a story about how cannabis changed my life as I naïvely trekked into the wonky world of medical marijuana. It is a story about a wild and crazy time in a state famous for its Wild

West gold rush legacies, like Virginia City and Confederate Gulch. But this time the Big Sky boom wasn't gold, or silver, or copper, or even oil or natural gas. Montana's newest boom was lush green and smelled of skunk.

Pot Doc is also a story about a plant and the irrational way we continue to react to it. It's a story about pain and healing and how we, as citizens, are permitted (or not) by our government to seek the individualized healing modalities that work best for us.

Pot Doc illustrates how rational innovation is stifled by emotion, myth, and prejudice. Evaluating patients to use medical marijuana flipped a switch in my brain: if you were going to call marijuana medicine, you needed to treat it like any other medicine. This book describes my quest to bring an element of quality control into an industry that heretofore had none, by starting an analytical laboratory to quantitate and quantify the cannabinoid content in the medical marijuana sold to patients.

And it's the story of how the US government, acting at the bequest of the State of Montana, essentially shut down my laboratory.

For obvious reasons, a number of the names in the book have been changed to protect the innocent (and those not so innocent) and to defuse needless litigation. This book intends to educate those who are ignorant about cannabis and inspire those who are looking for alternative treatments to many common maladies like seizures, insomnia, anxiety, cancer, and chronic pain.

Fear perpetuates ignorance and prejudice. My journey with cannabis showed me the wicked resistance of the darkness—that the light of truth sometimes takes more time than it ought to shine in all the nooks and crannies where it is so sorely needed.

If *Pot Doc* imparts at least one additional lumen to the cause of edifying the truths and myths surrounding cannabis, then my effort will have been rewarded.

A Mixing Pot

My parents weren't hippies, and I didn't grow up in a commune. I'm a multi-generational American, a mixing pot of ethnicities. My family heritage is rooted in Germany, Italy, and Croatia. I went to a parochial elementary school in a small Pennsylvania town on the eastern edge of the Allegheny Mountains and attended Catholic mass six times a week. I was pre-med at Nebraska Wesleyan University (NWU), the first of my family to attend college. I earned a double major in biology and English. And I voted for Ronald Reagan (twice).

Entering senior year, my confidence that I would be accepted to medical school was high, largely because NWU had such a terrific pre-med program. But the year I applied, less than half of us were accepted. Worse than getting rejected from medical school was my utter confusion of what to do next. I bounced around a bit, working at odd jobs like building roof trusses and working in research labs at the University of Alabama-Birmingham. I felt trapped in an endless series of wanderings until my best friend suggested I try teaching high school. It was a noble job, the pay was decent, and I would have my summers off; a sweet package for a secondary career choice. I went back to school and earned a master's degree in education.

In the summer of 1988, after finishing my first year teaching high school biology and earth science in an Atlanta suburb, I devoted myself to one more attempt at medical school. I took a MCAT review course, spending 10-12 hours a day at the Kaplan center studying for the medical school admissions exam. The exam went well and I was confident that I'd done my best. The rest was up to the various admissions committees that would ultimately judge my applications against the hundreds of others I was competing against. In March, I finally got that long-dreamed-about letter from the admission's committee at the Medical College of Georgia (MCG).

I'd been accepted.

In med school, I was elected our class's academic vice-president, but I never considered myself an activist. I sat on lots of academic committees, seeing how things got done in the world of academia. I petitioned the administration for better learning conditions and made some important contributions, most notably, the program I developed, called The Clinical Mentor Program. The program matches wide-eyed first year medical students with seasoned third year students. The groups meet at least once a month, developing a social and professional partnership. The first years are given their initial taste of clinical medicine, as third years introduce the freshmen to their hospital-assigned patients. After 30 years, the program is still a favorite among MCG students.

What led to my involvement in the world of marijuana was a series of seemingly unrelated events—random dots on a map that led me to Montana and the Alice-in-Wonderland world of the medical marijuana industry. I wasn't a lifelong stoner grinding an ax against the establishment. I didn't follow the Grateful Dead for years at a time (though I did see them twice before Jerry died). As fate would have it, I stumbled onto cannabis, and it stumbled onto me.

Before I became a pot doc, I smoked a little bit of marijuana in college and a little more in med school. My total knowledge of medical marijuana amounted to a few newspaper articles I'd read about patients smoking pot to ease their glaucoma. I thought medical marijuana was a sophisticated hoax to dupe the public into relaxing the rules regarding the recreational use of marijuana.

When I began my quest into the world of "weed," I knew less about marijuana than most of you who are reading this. Yet in the years I was active in the Montana medical marijuana program (2009–12), I learned more about neurochemistry and pharmacology than during my four years of medical school. I learned about politicking and how fairness depends on what piece of the pie comes your way. I learned about friendship and love and the depths of my codependency. And I learned more about my favorite plant than I ever thought possible.

So how did I become a pot doc?

Throughout my life, I've been blessed with a wonderful community of friends. In college, medical school, and during my residency, someone was always around to hang out, lend an ear, or give me a needed hug. I wasn't ashamed to admit that I much preferred a puff off a joint to drinking a cold brew or taking a shot of Jack. Marijuana was readily available, and my friends were generous, although my use was mostly a weekend affair. My network of friends became my tribe—kind folks who helped me cope with the stress and chaos of learning medicine in a big city emergency department (ED). Without my tribe, I doubt I'd have become a doctor.

During the three years of my residency, I enjoyed the sheltered environment of my academic training at Thomas Jefferson University Hospital in Philadelphia. Little did I know how woefully unprepared I was for the reality of working in the world of private practice. In 1996 I completed my residency and moved to Alabama so I could be closer to family—mostly to be near Rachel, my sister's only child. I was the closest thing Rachel had to a dad, as she'd never met her biological father. Once he got the news that my sister was pregnant, he took off, rumored to have disappeared somewhere in Texas.

Upon accepting a staff position at Huntsville Hospital, I bought an old Victorian house on the edge of Gurley, a speck on the map just east of Huntsville, in a rural part of Madison County. The hospital had just built a brand-new ED with a well-trained staff and a terrific pay and benefits package. I thought I'd hit the lottery.

In hindsight, it's embarrassing to admit how naïve I was. Working at Huntsville Hospital thrust me into the real world of emergency medicine. There was no upper-level resident or attending physician to ask for help. On the very first day, it dawned on me that I was it—the go-to physician at the busiest ED in the state. On a regular basis, the department was utterly chaotic and sometimes I felt overwhelmed. I regularly wouldn't have time to finish patient charts, and so they would pile up. Oftentimes I fell asleep dictating charts hours after my late-night shifts were over. My job felt like compressing a lifetime of knowledge into a single, year-long event.

All my life, I wanted to be a doctor. I thought my life would be complete after I received my medical degree. But once I was outside of the ivory towers of an academic medical center, I uncovered an unexpected emptiness. When people find out you're a doctor, they treat you differently. Folks assume you have tons of money and that you're an insensitive, arrogant ass. I tried to hide my career from public view. My hair stayed loosely ponytailed. I refused to wear matching hospital-issued scrubs or don the starched white lab coat. Outside the ED, I shopped at the thrift store and wore faded Levi's and Birkenstocks.

By the end of my first year, I also added to my collection of canines. Honey, the Collie/German Shepherd mix my sister had given me in college now had friends: six rescue dogs and a cat, named Sven. By the fall of 1997, I'd married the woman that I'd met on a trip to Costa Rica. She gave up her high-powered marketing career, sold all her possessions, and moved from Madrid, in order to be with me. We should have been happier, but each of us had much deeper, darker issues that infiltrated our souls, things invisible during our whirlwind six-month courtship.

By the end of my second year at Huntsville Hospital, the hidden political landmines of working in a large for-profit hospital were taking their toll. I'd had enough of them and they'd had enough of me. My wife and I thought a quieter professional environment would be a better fit.

After considering numerous offers, we settled on moving to western Kentucky to join a hospital group that was upgrading its ED, hiring only emergency medicine-trained physicians. That gig didn't last long either as I soon learned that the closed-door, "good ole boy" system of medicine wasn't confined to northeast Alabama. I clashed with a cavalier radiologist over a significant patient safety issue. Unfortunately, he was also the son of the founder of the hospital system. In my letter to the hospital's chief of staff, I was clear that if appropriate action wasn't taken, I was prepared to report the situation to the Kentucky Board of Medical Examiners. Perhaps I shouldn't have been surprised when my contract for the following year was not extended.

It was back to the drawing board to find a more nurturing place to practice. After living the better half of ten years in the South, it was time for a change. My wife and I opted to narrow our search to the Northeast, settling for a quaint college town in upstate New York. We found a old farm on the top of a wooded hillside overlooking a beautiful valley. We fell in love with the place at the top of Crumhorn Mountain.

But the demons caught up with me again. My life revolved around the whims of a work schedule that didn't care about the physiological and psychological damage I incurred when I flip-flopped my circadian rhythms. I worked week-long stretches of twelve-hour night shifts, a handful of days off, followed by a week of day shifts, and then repeated the cycle. The money was great, but the job was burning me out. If I was going to continue to practice emergency medicine, I needed to carve a different path.

Emergency physicians are in high demand, so finding work is not a problem, especially if you are willing to travel. I decided to try my hand as a locum tenens physician. I traveled from hospital to hospital, as staffing needs dictated. I'd work a week at a facility in Kentucky, or North Carolina, or New York, and come home. Although the demands of the ED were similar, now I had control of my schedule. As a locum, I met a lot of interesting people.

During one of my locum assignments on Long Island, a nurse (also a traveler) gave me Lance Armstrong's biography, *It's Not About the Bike*. Throughout medical school, I had cycled with classmates, blowing off the tension generated from countless hours studying anatomy and memorizing arcane biochemical pathways. As a resident, I cycled all over Philadelphia, but cyclists pay a heavy price in the City of Brotherly Love. I was struck by motorists on two separate occasions, fortunately with no long-term sequelae other than an occasional dream about flying through the air with just my helmet.

Reading Lance's book inspired me.

Then one night I was jarred awake by a troubling dream. My toddler son had asked me why I was fat like everyone else. For some reason, that dream haunted me until I marched out to the garage and dusted off my mountain bike. It'd been years since I'd been on a bike. I inflated the boggy tires and sprayed WD-40 on the rust-speckled chain. The change began the moment I got back on my bike—I felt like a kid again.

The road to my house is long and steep. It winds up the east side of Crumhorn Mountain, from top to bottom a mile and a half of cracked asphalt with a grade that approaches 14 percent. After the forty-minute ride into town, I turned off the main road and prayed that I could pedal back up to my home. Out of the saddle, my body labored with each pedal stroke, bouncing like a pogo stick as the front shocks rhythmically absorbed my momentum. I struggled upward in a slow, agonizing forward progress, but was stoked when the last big incline was behind me. As I pedaled into my driveway, I knew that my days of being a slug were over. My love affair with the bicycle was renewed.

I rode nearly every day and eventually bought a sleek, fast road bike. I rediscovered things about myself that I hadn't even known I'd lost. Instinctively, I tracked down causal riders and lumbering tractors making their way back to somewhere. I wanted to be faster.

If I was going to be a stronger rider, I needed to take better care of myself. What I put into my body became as paramount as to how I conditioned it. My alcohol and cannabis intake, although never excessive, ceased altogether. Intuitively, I understood the power of nutrition, but without no formal course in nutrition in medical school, I ordered a couple of nutrition books online.

Medical school taught me anatomy, physiology, and biochemistry, but most importantly, it taught me the skill of independent learning. The nutrition books I read increased my awareness that eating the proper foods and avoiding comfort calories is essential for muscles to build strength and endurance. I saw patterns between health and nutrition, between illness and lifestyle patterns, and the connection between the unity of the mind and the body. I began attending conferences on alternative medicine, with topics like plant-based hormone replacement therapies, herbal medicine, homeopathy, and integrative medicine.

While keeping my day job in the ED, I decided to open a private practice, Whole Health & Healing (WH&H). It was an exciting yet scary leap. I saw patients by appointment only; a few days a week.

In the fall of 2008, I went to Atlanta for a conference sponsored by the Autism Research Institute, a professional group dedicated to biomedical interventions in autism. As a parent, I couldn't imagine the challenge of having a child with such a debilitating and mysterious illness. I dedicated myself to creating a supportive space for families affected by autism. In my karmic scheme of things, it would be a blessing if I could help parents get back a bit of their child's life that autism had taken away.

Prior to the conference, I bought a laptop computer with Wi-Fi. Armed with this new technology, I joined the ranks of the other conference attendees sitting with their laptops open. Having

Wi-Fi and the power of the internet, I found it mesmerizing that all the known information in the world was right at my fingertips. Any questions, I could access the power of the world wide web.

And that's what I did.

While the conference lecturer discussed the clinical applications of using a nicotine transdermal patch for a subgroup of autistic patients, I did a PubMed search. PubMed is the website for the National Library of Medicine under the auspices of the National Institutes of Health (NIH). It's the definitive website for researching any subject in medical science without politics or prejudice. Just type in your subject heading and hit search; within seconds every relevant research article published on the topic pops up. Browsing through the list of abstracts, one caught my eye: an article discussing the use of cannabinoids for treating cerebral inflammation.[3]

I've always had a certain knack for drawing inferences. I knew that cannabinoids were compounds derived from cannabis. After reading that abstract, I had an idea.

Politely, I raised my hand until called upon. I referenced the article regarding cannabinoids and inflammation and asked the speaker's thoughts about using medical marijuana as a treatment option for autistic patients.

"Give a kid a joint?" He snickered. "This isn't something we should be talking about here." He shook his head to a chorus of chuckles.

I was embarrassed before my peers, but a seed was planted.

The Pit of Gloom

On New Year's Eve 2008, my six-year-old son Jacob and I were riding on the lone ski lift at Royal Mountain, a tiny mom and pop resort in the southern Adirondacks. The sounds of skiers reveling were all around while Jacob sat merrily dangling his skis, talking about how fun the last run had been. Cornflakes of snow were drifting down from the grayness above onto the awaiting tongue of my giggling dude. Happiness was all around me, yet I felt flat. As I pondered my inner emptiness, it struck me that the depression I'd struggled with off and on since my divorce took a new twist. I'd lost my ability to feel joy. My life was stuck in the pit of gloom.

At the age of forty-seven, I was divorced and living alone with the four remnants of the pack of rescued canines my ex-wife and I had accrued during the happier moments of our marriage. It'd been a long five years since she took my son and left Crumhorn Mountain. I wondered if this is how my father felt when our mother had taken my younger sister and me away after their divorce when I was eleven. We moved thousands of miles away, had our surname changed from Geci to Black, and had no contact with my dad for the next five years. From my seat now, I marveled how he coped.

Seasons passed in brute fashion. Seven months of mostly dismal weather with an occasional smattering of sunshine, and five months of temperate paradise. I wondered how to survive the loneliness and the family memories in the old farmhouse on Crumhorn Mountain. I reached out to find my place in the community, joining the local PTA, coaching little league and pee-wee football, and regularly attending church, yet my attempts to find a local tribe eluded me. My funk continued to grow, my only option was to change or die. Aside from seeing my son every other weekend, my social life sputtered. Finding a potential partner within the confines of my local social sphere was as likely as finding a Dairy Queen in the middle of the Sahara.

A friend suggested online dating.

Over time, I met a few women—interactions that were brief and vapid. Undaunted, I tried a different site, one that purported using a scientific approach to relationship matching, eharmony. The concept of matching personality types to find a partner made sense. After setting up a profile, I began my search. Although I had set my distance parameters within a hundred miles from home, a woman from Bozeman, Montana, popped up on my screen. My first impulse was to move onto the next profile, but something about her caught my eye.

I clicked on her profile.

Lori seemed like a cool woman. She lived in an awesome place, and her smile was infectious. I took a chance and sent her a note. To my surprise, she wrote back.

And so it began...

The Call of Montana

After weeks of emails and phone calls, Lori Bedford and I decided to meet. Although not on either of our bucket lists, we chose to rendezvous in Reno. It was an odd place for a first date, but I was keen on attending a probiotic conference. We had a fun time, and I accepted her invitation to visit her in early February 2009, coinciding with a wilderness medicine conference I'd wanted to attend.

Lori picked me up at the Bozeman airport, her *Hope We Can Believe In* Obama campaign button still pinned to her pile-lined North Face parka. On the drive to Big Sky, we shared our excitement for a more liberal and progressive America under our new president.

"Did you cry during the inauguration?" Lori asked, expectantly.

"Absolutely. Didn't you?"

"Through the entire speech, I was a wreck. I'm so excited to see him start pulling us back from the abyss."

"There's a lot of things that need change."

"Amen."

As we drove, I stared at the fast-moving Gallatin River. Birthed in Yellowstone National Park, the north-flowing river winds its way through the Gallatin Mountains and the sinuous canyon of thick-layered gneiss, limestone, and shale. Once through the mountains, the Gallatin makes its way to its confluence with the Madison and Jefferson Rivers, where they form the mighty Missouri River.

After the week-long conference, Lori brought me back into Bozeman. Saturday morning, after breakfast, she told me about something on Craigslist that might pique my interest. I peered over her shoulder as she pulled up the page:

In need of a medical doctor to staff a medical marijuana clinic. $100/hour. Call Pete.

"Sounds interesting, but what's a medical marijuana clinic?"

Lori gave me a quizzical look. "You know that Montana is a legal state, right?"

"What's a legal state?"

In short order, Lori informed me that Montana was one of the first states in the country to legalize medical marijuana. The law, called the Montana Medical Marijuana Act, was popularly known as MT-148, a voter initiative that passed in 2004. Any patient who met the law's criteria for any of a half-dozen state-approved medical conditions could either grow up to six female cannabis plants or have someone else (termed "caregivers" or "providers") grow six plants on their behalf. All you needed was a doctor to sign the paperwork. And therein lies the rub. There were just a couple of doctors in the entire state who were willing to evaluate patients for the use of medical marijuana.

"Hmmm." I pondered the possibilities..

Montana is one of those places that you just have to see to believe. Even now, when I hear the name Montana, it evokes emotion—I close my eyes and envision jagged, snow-capped peaks under a deep blue sky that seems as wide as the planet. Montana is a magical place. I think back to the scene in *The Hunt for Red October*, where a wounded Captain Vasili Bordoni, second in command to Sean Connery's Commander Marko Ramius, talks dreamily about moving to Montana as he fades into the afterlife.

Montana is for dreamers, and my dream for Montana hid in the gloominess that I had allowed my life to become.

Meeting Pete

After weeks of bleak upstate New York winter weather, I craved the Big Sky sunshine and bluebird skies. Lori had introduced me to her circle of friends and going back to Montana was appealing.

Then I thought about Pete's ad. *What would it be like to work in a medical marijuana clinic?*

I'd worked hard to become a doctor, and I didn't want to jeopardize my professional reputation by being labeled a "pot doc." As I packed for another dreaded string of night shifts, I pondered where my life was headed. I was at the end of my rope.

So, I went to Craigslist, found Pete's posting, and dialed the number.

The raspy voice on the other end of the line sounded inspired and reasonably articulate. For the next twenty minutes, Pete Jones shared his vision for a medical marijuana clinic.

"It won't be long, and I'll have clinics in every state. And it won't be long after that till you won't even need a stupid-ass medical card to get your medicine." Pete continued his bombastic tirade on the lunacy of marijuana laws and his master plan for cornering the entire US medical marijuana market. After listening quietly, I had a lot to think about. I told him I'd call him back in a week or two.

My first impression was that Pete had been a used car salesman in another life. But with each cold and dreary February day that passed, I felt a burning to return to Montana. I called Pete back. It was time to make a trip back to Bozeman.

Unfortunately, the weekend I planned on meeting Pete, Lori was going out of town. "You can stay at my place," she offered. Although the romantic aspect of our relationship sputtered, we smoothly transitioned into a welcomed friendship. Lori seemed to know everybody in Bozeman and told me about several alternative medicine practitioners in the Gallatin Valley. I contacted a number of them, hoping someone might be interested in incorporating me into their practice group. The co-partners of the Bodhi Tree, a yoga and massage studio on North Seventh, expressed the most interest.

My trip was taking shape.

Joining me was my colleague, Joseph Brown, a charming Jamaican naturopathic doctor. I'd met Joseph during my tenure teaching emergency medicine as an adjunct professor at the University of Bridgeport's School of Naturopathic Medicine, a few years prior. I drove to Connecticut a couple of weekends to teach an introductory course in emergency medicine. There, Joseph and I had become friends and had talked about the possibility of starting an integrative practice together.

My 6:15 a.m. flight from Albany got me into Bozeman mid-afternoon, giving me ample time to get settled and check out the downtown area. It struck me as a little odd that Pete was not at the airport to greet me. Had I been in his shoes, I'd have been there to greet him and show him around a bit. For me, it was common courtesy, a sign of respect. Yet what it turned out to be was the beginning of a recalibration of expectations; I was soon to learn that nothing about the medical marijuana industry, or the people within it, was typical.

After picking up Joseph, I called Pete. We were to meet at Ted's, a new restaurant in the famous Baxter Building on Main Street, at eight o'clock. Joseph and I arrived about fifteen minutes early and found seats at the bar. The place, owned by Ted Turner, had an elegant Old West feel. By 8:30, I was wondering if Joseph and I were going to be having dinner alone.

Just before nine, Pete finally showed. Dressed in ratty blue jeans and a questionably white T-shirt, he reeked of marijuana. In Pete's shadow was his girlfriend, Marci, and Pam Likert, a nurse practitioner from Missoula who had also answered Pete's ad. After introductions, Pete brusquely apologized for being late as the waitress seated us.

Feeling festive, I ordered a bottle of wine and began discussing the excitement regarding Obama's inauguration. Pete shared his interpretation of recent White House innuendos that state medical marijuana laws would be honored, despite the federal prohibition. He was confident that state medical marijuana programs would no longer be under the onerous purview of the Department of Justice (DOJ). After eight years of George W. Bush, we all had high hopes that the country would get back to a more progressive course. Aside from the withdrawal of troops from Iraq and Afghanistan, we hoped a more reasonable marijuana policy was just around the corner, too.

In short order, I learned that Pete Jones had strong opinions about everything. Aside from being loud and abrasive, Pete was also never wrong. I bit my lip for the first hour, but it was clear that there was more than simple gruffness responsible for Pete's behavior. Pete outlined his vision: owning an empire of medical marijuana clinics—first in Bozeman, then throughout Montana. Then Pete's steely gray eyes grew wider. "I want to take this concept across the entire country. I'm going to be the Walgreen's of pot clinics," he huffed.

"All I need is a doctor," Pete said, looking squarely at me. "There's enough patients out there waiting to see a doctor. I could keep you busy for the next six months, Doc. Easy."

I mulled over his comment. Doctors are the bottleneck in any medical marijuana program. Without a doctor's signature, a patient can't receive a card from the state and, therefore, can't use marijuana legally. The equation is simple: Doctor plus patient equals state-issued medical marijuana cards. State-issued medical marijuana cards plus enormous demand for legal medical marijuana equals enviable profits. It was just that simple.

"What about medical records?" I asked.

"What about 'em?" He grunted. "Seeing a doctor to use marijuana is a joke."

"But that's the law."

"The law is fucking stupid and needs to be changed," Pete barked.

It took me little time to figure out that everything would be done Pete's way. Graciously, I tried to illustrate that physicians had a standard of care that supersedes economics. With every angle of our discussion, Pete complained.

"You aren't listening to what I'm saying!"

As a reasonable man, I tried to give Pete the benefit of the doubt. But it was clear he was impaired. Pete had either spent too much time at sustained high altitude or smoked way too much pot in his life. Not surprisingly, he denied any interest in high-altitude mountaineering.

My attention drifted to a side discussion with Pam, Marci, and Joseph. We discussed how to run a proper medical marijuana clinic. We shared ideas, and it seemed clear that operating a professionally staffed facility was doable. But since our ideas weren't sprouted from Pete's brain, they were terminally flawed.

After dinner, I excused myself. And as luck would have it, Pam and I emerged from the restrooms at the same time. Anxious to vent our respective frustrations over Pete's stubbornness, we chatted before returning to our table. Pam invited us to visit her clinic in Missoula.

Returning to our table, there were two empty seats.

"Hey—where's Pete and Marci?" Pam asked.

In a reggae meter, Joseph smiled. "Pete left a few minutes ago. He said you guys were conspiring against him. And off he went."

Pam and I looked at each other and rolled our eyes.

Under the Bodhi Tree

The next morning, Joseph and I met with the partners of the Bodhi Tree, Catherine and Kali. The pair had recently opened the cozy, cottage-style house on North Seventh Street. They were offering the services of an acupuncturist, a massage therapist, an herbalist, and a mental health counselor. The place was painted in soothing pastels of green and yellow and was warmly decorated with a mellow granola vibe. Joseph and I shared our vision for integrating a medical practice. We offered them the opportunity to have licensed physicians in their space, giving their facility a more comprehensive health care offering.

Before our meeting, Kali had shared that she was a recovering cocaine addict and alcoholic. I was sensitive that offering medical marijuana certifications might conflict with her recovery and assured her that my intentions were honorable and professional. My plan was to bring my New York integrative practice, Whole Health & Healing (WH&H), to the Bodhi Tree. Patient appointments would be professionally scheduled, and all medical marijuana patients would need valid medical records before their physician statement would be signed. My intention for the clinic was no different from my role in the ED. *Primum non nocere*: first, do no harm.

Despite my presentation, both women were concerned that their wellness center would turn into a pot shop.

"We don't want you to be seen as a ...pot doc," Catherine said hesitantly.

We all laughed.

The sound of "pot doc" made me cringe. I committed, at that moment, to do everything within my power to dispel the notion that I was simply dolling out pot cards to anyone who walked through the door. Although eager for a change in my life, I wasn't desperate. I held board certifications from the American Board of Emergency Medicine and the American Board of Integrative and Holistic Medicine. I had also earned fellow status from the American College of Emergency Physicians. I'd paid my dues to become an enlightened, well-trained physician, not some fly-by-night "pot doc."

But Catherine was right. There would be people who would see me in a negative light, no matter what I did. After some thoughtful discussion, we agreed to market WH&H to emphasize my integrative medical approach, rather than my open-mindedness regarding medical marijuana. We decided that a public presentation on the biomedical interventions for autism would be a great way to introduce my practice to the Bozeman community. I decided to come back in April to give the lecture.

After the appointment, Joseph and I drove up to Missoula to visit Pam's family medicine clinic which she'd opened about six months prior. She confided that the practice wasn't meeting her financial expectations and conceded that unless something changed, she wouldn't be able to keep her doors open through the end of the year. Pam envisioned patients seeking medical marijuana as an untapped demographic, suggesting a cannabis clinic could save her practice.

Pam proudly toured us through her space, a warmly lit area with three fully equipped exam rooms, a private office, and a spacious reception area. The place was tastefully decorated and felt like a doctor's office, less the soft rock music and the 1969 Martin D-28 by her desk. Pam was also interested in learning about integrative medicine. "I'm excited about the synergies we could create as a team."

I agreed.

Montana gives nurse practitioners significantly more clinical freedom than many states, allowing them to own their own clinics and see patients independent of a physician's purview (as required in many states). What cemented our professional relationship was the provision in MT-148, stating that only an MD or a DO could sign a physician statement. Regardless of our chemistry, Pam needed a doctor to open her clinic to medical marijuana clientele.

Under the Bodhi Tree

After the office tour, we drove downtown. Missoula seemed like the place where all the hippies went who didn't move to Boulder. Nestled between the Bitterroots and the Sapphire Mountains, on the wetter western slopes of the continental divide, the city maintains a youthful, vibrant energy. The area has a robust arts scene in addition to being an outdoor wonderland. The Clark Fork River cuts the town in half, and nearly thirty-three thousand acres of the Rattlesnake Wilderness is on the northeast edge of town. There are more hot springs, paddling, hiking, and cycling opportunities within two hours of town than anywhere else in the country. Missoula seemed like a perfect fit for me. We went to a park and I watched the kids on the playground. I thought about how cool it would be to have my son grow up here.

Pam and I agreed to develop a medical marijuana clinic that could serve as a model for other clinics in Montana. The excitement we shared bordered on intoxicating. Just a week ago, I was feeling lonely and depressed, holed away in my upstate New York mountain retreat. And now, I was forging alliances and discussing business partnerships in this magical place called Montana.

Even as Joseph and I drove back to Bozeman, discussing the fabulous opportunities that were swirling before us, always, in the back of my mind, I wondered just how much time I could spend away from my son. Jacob had just turned seven, so living a dual-state life was going to be a challenge. Tensions between his mother and I waxed and waned in an endless cycle. I feared her accusing me of abandoning him to follow a pot of gold. For me, the calculus was about balance. How could I spend enough time in Montana developing my practice and yet still be a good father? I spent endless hours pondering this question.

What sealed the deal for me was the next day's drive to Moonlight Basin, on the backside of Big Sky Ski Resort. I'd only been skiing once in the past ten years, but the winter before I started my residency, I was a certified ski bum. I finished my coursework in medical school early, and rather than taking additional courses, I chose to go to Colorado. I stayed with a friend who lived outside of Vail and landed a sweet job as a host at Piney River Ranch, a restaurant tucked away at the base of the Gore Mountains. The Ranch was only accessible in the winter via a fourteen-mile snowmobile trip. The gig earned me an unlimited ski pass at both Vail and its sister facility down I-90, Beaver Creek. By the end of the season, I was skiing chest-high powder like a pro.

Making our way toward Moonlight stirred a memory of my departure from Vail as I drove toward Philadelphia to start my residency. That morning in 1993, I clearly remember heading east over Vail Pass. The stereo blasted the hypnotic driving power chords of Bob Mould. As I left Colorado, I wondered when I'd be back in the Rockies. As Joseph and I drove toward the towering image of Lone Peak, I felt the energy. I flashed back to the song, "The Act We Act" and the stirring distortion of Mould's guitar. A smile crept across my face. I'd finally come full circle.

Joy is a beautiful thing.

After a day of skiing at Moonlight, I knew that I had to try my luck in Montana. I felt blessed to have another chance to be happy. On the way back to Bozeman, Joseph turned to me.

"Michael...I like this place a lot, but it's just not a good place for me. My daughter is in New York and would hate it out here," he smiled tenderly.

I was disappointed but understood. On the day of our departure, Joseph marveled at the depth of blue in the sky. He said the color reminded him of the lagoon he swam in as a child on the south coast of Jamaica. After we cleared security, Joseph took my hand and held it firmly. "I wish I could come here and help you, Michael."

"I know."

A brilliant smile slowly rippled across his face. "This is a good place for you, Michael. I feel that. Good-bye, my friend." Joseph turned and made his way to the gate with the elegance of a diplomat. He would have been a terrific partner.

On the way back to Albany, I thought about the evening with Pete Jones. I called him during my layover in Minneapolis. I thanked him for inviting me to dinner and asked him why he left so quickly.

"Listen, Doc. I'm sorry we just got up and left like that."

"So, why did you leave?"

His gravelly voice sounded like it was coming from an old phonograph. "You guys were fucking wasted on wine. I can't deal with drunk folk, Doc."

"*Drunk?* We had a single bottle between five people. No one had more than a glass."

"Well, maybe *you* weren't drunk."

"Nobody was drunk." Then I thought I'd express the obvious. "You were the only person stoned the other night."

"Well, Doc, let me tell you something. From the time I wake up to the time I go to sleep, I am as medicated as I can be. It helps me keep my mind focused and dulls the pain." In the background, I heard him hack and spit. "And you know what else, Doc? I just hate being around people who drink. My dad used to drink. He'd beat us boys whenever he got drunk—wasn't much fun. But he's dead now. So I guess it don't much matter."

"Sorry to hear about that, Pete. We all have our stories about drunks."

"Rock and roll, Doc. I hear ya."

It was a rare moment of disclosure from this marijuana fanatic. Despite my compassion, developing a business relationship with Pete wasn't an option. Controversy was something that I didn't need, and Pete Jones was its poster child.

Having lived with a drunken stepdad, I could relate to Pete. I sensed a vulnerability that I thought I could nurture. I sincerely believe that every person has potential for universal transformation, but the reality is that some folks are just way too fried for any kind of radical metamorphosis. It's like a hard-boiled egg—it'll never be runny again, no matter how hard you try or how much you wish it would change back to what it once was.

I told Pete that I'd email him when I'd be back in Bozeman.

"People are gonna get filthy rich, Doc. If we all just worked together, we could make a killing."

"Let me think it over."

"Well, don't think about it too long, Doc. I'm fuckin' tired of suing all the state pricks by myself. You got to be more understanding of what I'm trying to do here. Think about it, Doc. I want to work with you, but whoever I get as a doctor, they gotta see it from my point of view, too. There ain't any rules for how this all gets done, cuz I've already looked into it. I can bring you all the patients you can handle. Think about it and give me a call, Doc."

"I'll give it some thought. I promise."

I had a lot going through my mind, but one thing I knew for sure was my commitment to run a medical marijuana clinic with integrity. It seemed prudent to operate under the premise that someday my charts were going to be audited. WH&H was going to be managed scrupulously. While it was probably true that I could have made a lot of money churning out physician statements in a pot mill, if the clinic wasn't something that I could show off with pride to my son, I wasn't interested.

When I arrived back in New York, Pam and I fine-tuned how the clinic would operate. She was excited by the overwhelming response to the clinic ad she had placed in the Missoula *Independent*. Initially, we agreed that each new patient would require a fifty-minute appointment. We were forging new ground, so we wanted our efforts to withstand scrutiny. Once Pam and I had agreed upon our clinic guidelines, I called Pete.

"Fifty minutes? Doc, are you fuckin' serious, dude?" Pete replied. "And you want me to just bring my patients to you for free? I have twenty-five patients waiting right now. It seems to me we don't have the same idea of how this clinic oughta work. Listen, Doc, I met with another doctor this week willing to work for The Healing Circle. What do you think of the name—THC? Pretty clever, don't you think?"

I chuckled at how quickly Pete shifted gears. "Listen, Pete; it's important that the doctor runs the clinic and that the clinic doesn't run the doctor. The clinic has to be in a professional space, not run out of some abandoned trailer or hotel conference room. And the idea of me giving you a kickback for the patients you refer is simply illegal. I spoke to my attorney about it. The practice is called fee-splitting. I have a medical license that I would like to keep."

"Listen, Doc, best of luck to you. You do it your way; I'll do it mine."

"Thanks, Pete. Take it easy."

"You know I will, Doc. Take care."

In another life, I was sure Pete would have been a legendary gunslinger. There was predictable fallout from nearly every interaction he had with others. If Pete was in the room, you knew it. He was the first to threaten legal action whenever he felt his constitutional rights were infringed, and there was no doubt he was going to make a lot of money in this green marijuana gold rush.

Over the years, no one I knew ever said anything positive about Pete, but he always treated me with respect. For me, Pete Jones was simply the first of many crazy characters I was to meet whom I wouldn't bring home to meet my mother.

Hi, I'm Hillari

Living in Montana changed my life.

Although the thought of permanently moving to Montana crossed my mind numerous times, my innate obligation as a father overrode any other feelings. At the risk of sounding maudlin, I simply couldn't leave my son for long periods of time. I loved him more than anything and wanted to continue to shape his life in ways that I wished my father could have shaped mine. That said, every time my flight descended through the mountains to land at Bozeman's Gallatin field, I felt an uncontrollable swell of emotion. Seeing the Bridger Mountains overlooking the city reminded me I was back in the place that felt like home.

During the next three years I took monthly trips leaving New York for at least a week to come to this place that infused my soul with hope and joy. Being in Montana, I felt supported in ways that I hadn't felt since I was a resident back in Philly. The endless blue sky, the mountain-riddled horizon, the warmth and kindness of the friends I met—all helped heal my soul.

I kept a journal. I took it everywhere, taking notes. I thought it might come in handy if I ever decided to write a book.

With my Montana medical license now in hand, I planned to transplant WH&H and start a clinic in Bozeman. Lori suggested temporary housing and connected me with one of her trustifarian friends. Bill is a trust fund baby–a supported adult pursuing life with reckless abandon as long as he didn't overspend his generous annual family endowment. Bill rented me a room in his quaint house a few blocks from downtown, across the street from a small park. The living arrangement with Bill seemed perfect; he was rarely there, preferring to spend the majority of his time either traveling, or on his small ranch outside of Bozeman. I took an empty bedroom upstairs. The basement was rented to a bluegrass musician/MSU student named Mike Singer. The evening of my arrival, I was touched by a note Mike left for me on the kitchen table. I was eager to find a sense of community, and his "welcome" note was symbolic. He always treated me like a long-lost brother.

On my birthday, I showcased my new practice with a community lecture at the Grandtree Hotel. Despite a twenty-four-inch snowstorm the evening before, an impressive crowd showed up. The talk, *Current Biomedical Interventions in Treating Autism*, went off without a hitch. During the question-and-answer period, a physician stood up and introduced himself, commending me for a well-constructed presentation.

Jerry Taylor is a naturopathic physician who was living in Helena. A former Indiana wrestling state champion, Jerry is tenacious by nature, eking out a living practicing naturopathic medicine while supporting his ever-pregnant wife and growing Latter-Day Saint family of six.

Afterward, Jerry said that he had heard a rumor from a supplement rep during the Atlanta ARI conference that a doctor was giving an autism lecture in Bozeman. Jerry was determined not to let a charlatan come into his state and destroy the work he was doing to secure medical help for families and affected children in need. He said that he had just driven more than five hundred miles through the late-spring snowstorm to hear my lecture and vet my acumen. It was the beginning of a terrific friendship and professional association.

Catherine and Kali had set up a post-lecture reception at the Bodhi Tree. I talked to dozens of people, but the most memorable person introduced herself with a tap on my shoulder.

"Hi, I'm Hillari."

Catherine had told me that Hillari was a massage therapist and herbalist who had just started working out of the Bodhi Tree. "Hey. I'm really glad to finally meet you. Catherine told me you might be interested in helping me with my new clinic."

"I'd love to talk to you about it," she smiled sweetly.

I was enamored.

Some things in life are certain. Death and taxes immediately come to mind. Despite my love of western Montana, if not for the relationship I developed with Hillari and her invaluable assistance, this story certainly could not have been written.

Hillari radiated kindness, recognized my vulnerability, and nurtured my soul, giving me the love that I needed rather than the love I wanted. Without Hillari's help and unwavering support, I certainly wouldn't have been able to maintain a practice in Montana, nor would I have survived the numerous minefields I navigated as I became more involved in medical marijuana.

Hillari took the burden of running the clinic off my shoulders. She seamlessly did all the little things. When I arrived in Bozeman each month, the clinic was ready to go. Hillari was a godsend—an angel with a spirit as big as the sky above her family's homestead along the Gallatin River. Over the next few months, she and I spoke or emailed each other multiple times a day. Hillari became my friend, my workmate, my healer, and my confidant. I trusted her implicitly. She sparked a long-absent fire inside of me. And maybe most importantly, she laughed at my jokes and made me feel like I mattered.

One of Hillari's notes etched in my mind:

i hope you are well. montana is beautiful and waiting for you. i will see you in a couple of days.

Hillari became my rock, and I adored her. Had a romantic moment presented itself, I would have seized it, but it never did. I thought about being more direct, but I was afraid of what she might say. Hillari resuscitated my life, and I accepted that it was much more important to have her on my team than in my bed.

With some reluctance, I let my fantasy fade into the Bridger skyline.

MT-148

On November 2, 2004, Montana voters approved the Montana Medical Marijuana Allowance Initiative, by the largest margin for a citizen initiative in state history, passing by 61.8 percent. Once enacted into law, the initiative, renamed MT-148, made Montana the tenth state to pass legislation to legalize marijuana for medical use.

So how did Montana, not considered a bastion of progressive liberalism, become one of the first states to embrace medical marijuana?

Like most social movements, it began with a single person standing up to injustice. Like Rosa Parks, Robin Prosser was a woman who had had enough. Ms. Prosser was a talented concert pianist/composer who became debilitated by a progressive autoimmune disorder. Under the care of her physicians, she tried every combination of conventional drug therapy. Nothing worked.

Ms. Prosser's life became a nightmare of intractable pain until she tried a specific strain of marijuana (other strains had no effect). Her pain suddenly became manageable. She was able to play the piano again. And perhaps most importantly, she was able to take care of her young daughter. Because of federal marijuana laws, Prosser faced the option of living her life in constant incapacitating pain or being characterized as a criminal by using a contraband plant. Cannabis not only afforded her significant relief of her pain, but it also allowed her to live her life as she'd known it before her illness.

In 2002 Ms. Prosser began a sixty-day hunger strike that garnered national attention, shedding light on the plight of thousands of others like her who found that using marijuana was the only effective remedy available. Her actions empowered others in the state to take up the cause of medical marijuana. Former chairman of the University of Montana Chemistry Department and then House Democrat Ron Erickson proposed a bill in 2003 that was very similar to MT-148 but was killed by a Republican caucus on the House floor.

With the defeat of Erickson's bill, the effort to pass a medical marijuana program in Montana reemerged as a citizen initiative, I-148. The initiative was supported and funded by the Medical Marijuana Policy Project of Montana (MPP), with most of the money coming from the founder of Progressive insurance company, Peter Lewis. The leading author of the text was Karen O'Keefe, an MPP staffer who worked closely with spokesperson Paul Befumo, and Tom Daubert, founder of the patient advocacy group Patients and Families United. I-148 was intended to give legal protection to patients to use medical marijuana who were suffering from cancer, multiple sclerosis, AIDS, and other serious illnesses.

Aside from Ms. Prosser, another patient that garnered the attention of medical marijuana advocates was Scott Day. Scott was born with a rare congenital disease, mucopolysaccharidosis, an enzyme-deficiency disease which, over the course of his life, spawned diverse and severe physical pain and other serious health problems. He found that using marijuana eased the pain he'd lived with his entire life.

Beside absolving patients from the constant fear of serving six months in prison and being fined for using marijuana as a medicine, I-148 also allowed patients to grow their own marijuana. The initiative also allowed patients the option to buy their cannabis medicine from a state-registered local grower, termed a provider or caregiver. The initiative also had the support of the Montana branch of the National Organization for the Reform of Marijuana Laws (NORML). As the 2004 election approached, both Prosser and Day were featured on billboards across the states, encouraging citizens to vote for the initiative.

Appropriately, Ms. Prosser became the first registered medical marijuana patient under the MT-148 provisions. By the end of the law's first year, there were only 176 enrolled. By the end of the third year, only 576 patients had visited a physician and secured permission to use medical marijuana legally. The paucity of participants and the relative anonymity of the medical marijuana program kept the reality of medical marijuana off the public radar. Except for a few hundred registered patients, a few dozen licensed growers and providers, and a handful of staff members in the Department of Public Health and Human Services (DPHHS) office in Helena, few people remembered MT-148.

Yet, even with the protections offered under MT-148, the draconian measures of US federal drug policy took their toll. In March of 2007, federal authorities were tipped off that a package to Ms. Prosser containing marijuana was being shipped from her legally assigned provider. The package was confiscated, and although there were no arrests, Prosser's marijuana provider feared further legal action and discontinued supplying her with marijuana.

In July, she penned an op-ed piece in the *Billings Gazette*, pleading with Montana politicians and her fellow citizens to speak out against the actions of the Drug Enforcement Agency (DEA) and improve the lives of people like her.

"Give me liberty or give me death," she wrote. "Maybe the next campaign ought to be for assisted-suicide laws in our state. If they will not allow me to live in peace, and a little less pain, would they help me to die, humanely?" Sadly, before another provider, Richard Flor, could grow her cannabis strain to harvest, Ms. Prosser could endure the wait no longer and took her life on October 18, 2007.[4]

In the wake of September 11th and while George W. Bush was president, government bureaucrats threw civil liberties out the window in the name of protecting the homeland. Marijuana was still on the frontlines of the "war on drugs." Under the Bush administration, most people were afraid to come out of the closet about their marijuana use, even if it was deemed medical. Additionally, many Montanans felt uncomfortable that the state kept a database registry of those permitted to use marijuana legally.

Prior to the 2008 presidential election, only 1,119 patients had been issued their medical cards to use marijuana. As the debates between Barack Obama and John McCain led us toward the November election, there wasn't a single medical marijuana dispensary anywhere in Montana. The prevailing political thinking was that medical marijuana was a dead issue, and there was no pressing need to change the political status quo—and had John McCain been elected, those folks would have been correct.

But Barack Obama was elected president, and everything changed.

MT-148 was an imperfect piece of legislation. The initiative was designed to help a small group of deserving patients, and at the time, nobody seemed overly concerned about its imperfections. The bill was never intended to be scalable. And according to Daubert, because of the political landmines associated with marijuana, making the law more functional on a larger scale was impossible. Daubert tried unsuccessfully to amend MT-148 in the 2007 and 2009 legislature. Montana legislators felt that there was no need to tinker with a law that affected just *one-tenth of 1 percent* of the State's population. The motto of many legislators seemed justified: *If it ain't broke, don't fix it.*

But everything about MT-148 changed after Obama was elected. From 2005 to 2008, the rate of growth of patients who opted to take advantage of MT-148 hovered at about 10 percent. Within the first year of Obama's presidency, the program's growth shot up over 500 percent, exceeding 12,000 patients. The exponential growth was fueled by the perception by many Montanans who felt they were witnessing an historic shift in the way the federal government viewed medical marijuana.

As evidenced before 2009, on a small scale, MT-148 was a tenable law. But as more patients got their medical marijuana card, so grew the demand for marijuana. There was an abrupt shift in the economy of scale. Suddenly, issues that never arose with less than a thousand patients now became glaring problems as tens of thousands of Montanans were now cardholders, purchasing marijuana legally. Within the vague text of MT-148 were innumerable ways of interpreting what was considered legal and what wasn't.

The key to a patient receiving their medical marijuana card was obtaining a signed physician statement. The physician statement required a licensed Montana physician to give written verification that the patient met one of the state-approved conditions for medical marijuana use deemed appropriate by DPHHS. Before the end of 2009, there were eight qualifying conditions that the physician could check. Physicians could mark as many as appropriate. Of the qualifying conditions listed, *severe or chronic pain* was the one used most frequently:

a) Cancer, glaucoma, or positive status for HIV or AIDS

b) Chronic or debilitating disease or medical condition or its treatment that produces one or more of the following:

c) Cachexia or wasting syndrome

d) Severe or chronic pain

e) Severe nausea

f) Seizures, including but not limited to seizures caused by epilepsy

g) Severe or persistent muscle spasm, including but not limited to spasms caused by multiple sclerosis or Crohn's disease

h) Other

Once the physician statement was signed, the patient mailed the form into the DPHHS with a check or money order and waited for the staff at the Helena office to approve the application. There was a 99 percent approval rate if the physician signed the statement. Once the department approved the application, they sent the patient their state-approved medical marijuana card, often referred to as a "green card." Valid for a full calendar year, with the green card, the patient could grow up to six marijuana plants or seek out a caregiver who could grow six marijuana plants on behalf of the patient.

Of some concern for me, all of the qualifying conditions deemed appropriate for medical marijuana use by the state were enacted without any input by qualified physicians, including input from the Montana State Board of Medical Examiners. Unfortunately, there were no guidelines provided by the board to physicians receptive to medical marijuana. The only guidance given to physicians was that there needed to be an "appropriate" doctor-patient relationship established. This issue was to become the eight hundred–pound gorilla in the room.

Once I began my practice in Montana, if patients had any of the previously mentioned conditions, and had medical records for documentation, I happily signed their physician statement. If a patient had a condition not listed within the physician statement guidelines, I would search PubMed and review any research that might substantiate the patient's request to use medical marijuana. In cases where I checked option *h* (*other*), I would include a list of research references supporting medical marijuana as a reasonable therapeutic option. DPHHS initially honored these exceptions.

Midway through 2009, the ability of the DPHHS staff to individualize the application process was made impossible due to the sheer deluge of applications. By the summer of 2009, makeshift clinics were set up in conference rooms of local hotels, and hundreds of patients in a single day would see a doctor. The staff at DPHHS went from processing less than ten applications a week to suddenly more than six hundred a week.

The atmospherics of medical marijuana in Montana didn't change de novo. In the early months of the Obama presidency, a speech given by the Assistant US Attorney General David W. Ogden hinted that states with medical marijuana programs would not be scrutinized by the DOJ. Officially, on October 19, 2009, the Ogden memo was released.[5] This document stated that in states with medical marijuana programs, individuals compliant with state laws would be free of the legal microscope of the DOJ and the DEA.

Under the Obama administration, many Montanans (like Pete Jones) felt a palpable excitement that federal marijuana oversight was relaxing. Many foresaw the floodgates of a medical marijuana marketplace bursting wide open. Many felt that 2009 marked the beginning of the next Montana gold rush. Many believed that the marijuana express was leaving the station, and if you weren't on board the train you were going to miss out on the economic opportunity of a lifetime.

Like the news of Confederate Gulch, the most lucrative gold-mining area ever discovered in Montana, pot fever spread like a massive western wildfire.

The Road to Missoula

The morning after my autism lecture, I was on the road by six, driving to Missoula, where Pam and I were going to host our first medical marijuana clinic. I arrived just before nine, after a beautiful ride up I-90. The raw beauty of the vast bluebird sky set against the snow-capped mountains overwhelmed me. I checked my pulse to be sure that I hadn't been transported into some sort of dreamland.

Somewhat to my surprise, the day was packed. Most of the patients were middle-aged, middle-class men and women who complained of chronic pain issues. They were seeking to use medical marijuana because they were fed up with the ball and chain of prescription opiate use. I was also surprised by the degree of disability many of the patients endured; a number of patients were using a cane or crutches or were being escorted in wheelchairs by friends or spouses. Gaunt men hobbled into my office, sharing their stories of bodies ravaged by trauma, and eager to show their surgical scars to prove it. By 7:00 p.m., we'd seen our last patient and were exhausted, yet I wanted to conference with the staff to discuss the clinic's operation.

How could we streamline the process? How could we be more efficient? Did we seem professional enough?

The consensus was that things had gone smoother than anticipated. Well pleased, I tossed my pack into Pam's truck and we made our way to the house she was sharing with her boyfriend. While Pam cooked dinner, I sat on the deck overlooking the valley, playing her '69 D-28.

On Sunday, we started promptly at 9:00 a.m., again with a full waiting room of patients. Our second day proved to be a bit more troublesome. A local medical marijuana provider named

Rick Rosio brought in a van full of patients and wanted to pay for the entire group with a single business check. Apparently, the patients were going to sign up with Rosio as their caregiver if I signed their physician statement. I spoke to Pam, and she agreed that we wanted to eliminate any appearance of a conflict of interest between the patient, the physician, and an individual caregiver. I told Rick that patients would have to pay for their appointments individually. Despite his protest, we stood our ground, establishing our boundaries about how the clinic would operate.

Although there was an implicit expectation that every patient would receive a signed physician statement, we made it clear that patients would need medical records to document their qualifying condition. Though most of the patients that weekend qualified, two did not.

One twenty-something patient complained of chronic pain and brought dental records documenting his wisdom teeth extracted eight years prior.

"You still have chronic pain from having your wisdom teeth pulled eight years ago?" I asked.

The guy looked stoned. "Ah...yeah man. The dentist must have left something in there, like a root or something, cuz they ache a lot."

I reached for the examination light. "Open your mouth, please."

His teeth were perfect. He had some of the best-looking gums I'd ever seen. "Do you floss?"

"Uh-huh. Twice a day."

I considered my words. "If you're having this much discomfort with a set of teeth that are as nice as yours, you need to see your dentist. You might have something serious causing your pain, like lymphoma."

Suddenly the haze that rimmed around his glassy eyes cleared. "Seriously, man? You think I might have lymphoma?"

"I doubt it, but I can't say for sure. That's why I can't sign your physician statement. If your mouth hurts this bad, then you need to see your dentist to make sure there's nothing more serious going on. I don't want you using marijuana to mask the pain of something that might be potentially life-threatening."

I shook the man's hand and wished him luck.

The second person not to qualify was a thin eighteen-year-old woman whose chief complaint was insomnia.

"Why do you think you need to use medical marijuana?" I queried.

"I have a hard time falling asleep sometimes," she said shyly. "Smoking pot before I go to bed helps me relax."

"Why do you think you can't sleep?"

It took her a moment to formulate a response. "Because I get stressed out sometimes, you know, with school stuff and being in a relationship."

"Have you tried any other techniques or other types of medicine to help with your insomnia? You know, like chamomile tea, meditation, or taking melatonin?"

"No."

I glanced through her chart and made a few notes.

"I see that you don't have any medical records to support your claim of insomnia. I'm sure the secretary told you that medical records were an absolute requirement unless there is some sort of exceptional circumstance. Did the secretary speak to you about bringing medical records?"

She nodded.

"Do you think your insomnia constitutes an exceptional circumstance?"

The woman's face relaxed as her unlaced sneaker began to scuff at the side of the chair. "No, not really."

I leaned back in my chair and took a sip of water. "It's not my intention to be mean. I want to be as liberal as I can. In good faith to the people of Montana who voted for this law, what you have as a complaint doesn't justify me signing your physician statement. I feel it's really important to protect the credibility of the program, not to mention my own professional integrity."

The young woman adjusted her slumped shoulders and looked away.

"Do you think that you really meet the qualifications for your medical marijuana card?"

The young woman nervously tugged her linen blouse from beneath her purple-blotted yoga pants and blushed, slowly shaking her head. "Not really."

"Thanks for understanding." I felt a weight lifted when she walked out the door. Denying her physician statement established a boundary that in my WH&H clinics, you had to have a qualifying condition *and* medical records, or you wouldn't receive your certificate.

An hour later, another unexpected issue came up.

At the end of our appointment, an elderly grandmother of fourteen asked me straight-faced, "Where do I get my medicine, Doctor?"

After a few moments of thoughtful contemplation, I looked at her. "I'm really sorry, but I don't have a clue where you can get your medicine. We don't' sell it here, and they don't sell it at a pharmacy." I hesitated for a moment. "Maybe you could ask the woman at the front desk."

The question caught me off guard. I had no idea where patients could reliably buy marijuana. And how weird was that? My job was to sign a form allowing patients to use medical marijuana, but I had no idea where the patients could buy their medicine, let alone vouch for its quality. There was no official Montana state registry, no listing of licensed dispensaries from which the patients could reliably purchase their cannabis. For the long-time user, finding marijuana wasn't an issue, but for those patients who were new to using marijuana, finding a reliable source was a problem.

Fortunately, this wasn't the way other medicines were prescribed. Can you imagine going to your doctor's office for blood pressure medication or an antibiotic and being told, "Good luck finding your medicine. Maybe you could ask your neighbor or friends. Come back if you're getting worse."

Everything about medical marijuana ran counter to what I had been taught during my two decades practicing Western medicine. In the conventional world, the sequence of medication dispensing follows this path: The provider takes a history of your complaint(s) and examines you and may want to run a few tests in an attempt to confirm a diagnosis. He or she then writes the prescription(s) for the ailment(s). The patient goes to the local pharmacy to have the medicine(s) dispensed.

The pharmacist is a professionally licensed individual with a degree in pharmacy. They are smartly dressed and discuss the possible side effects of your new medicine with any of your other medications. The pharmacy is clean and secure, and *all* the medicine is accurately labeled and identified by the dosage of the drug(s) ingested. In the pharmacy, medicine is treated like medicine.

Not so with medical marijuana.

There were no Montana pharmacies that sold marijuana. I had no clue which caregivers were honest and reliable, nor any clue about what the impact their marijuana would have on the patient. Providers had no idea of the potency of the marijuana they were growing; they grew and sold it like they'd done for decades on the black market. It was the classic case of *caveat emptor,* buyer beware. Can you imagine the chaos if pharmaceutical medicines were sold like this?

Why was medical marijuana treated differently?

It seemed to me that if you were going to call marijuana a form of medicine, you needed to treat it like a medicine. When I asked a couple of pharmacists about it, they were adamant; they didn't want to dispense it. The state board of pharmacy was against the idea too. It was frustrating that there was nothing medical about marijuana in Montana. But one thing was obvious, if marijuana were genuinely going to be elevated to the level of a medicine in the eyes of other doctors, it needed an element of quality control.

Then a light flickered in my mind. And the idea of starting an analytical laboratory for marijuana testing was spawned. It was surprising that something so obvious like marijuana quality control had yet to be adopted. There was much work to be done.

Pam and I were giddy that our inaugural clinic had gone so well. We were proud that we'd created an environment where patients could have a reliable and professional venue in which to secure their physician statement. After all the money was counted and the clinic expenses were paid, we agreed that we would put the money in a separate account and divvy it up later. No contract. We sealed the deal with a handshake. When I left Missoula, one thing was clear: we would have another weekend clinic in May.

Taking the East Coast West

Although a bit of an iconoclast, I don't see myself as radical. I feel strongly that a citizen's liberty should, in most cases, prevail over the state's interest. I believe we should be tolerant and embrace the ideals that our founding fathers described in the Constitution. Life, liberty, and the pursuit of happiness isn't some arbitrary phrase. As an emergency physician, I see health care as a fundamental right, a necessity for a modern, progressive culture. How can you pursue life, liberty, and happiness if you are sick, injured, or disabled?

The doctor-patient relationship is sacred and shouldn't be subject to state approval. Citizens should have the ability to seek the type of medical care and healing treatment(s) they feel will best suit their individual physical, spiritual, emotional, financial, and familial needs. A patient's health care options should be based upon the patient's private relationship with their physician or health care provider of choice.

Among the oddest things about the Montana medical marijuana program was that the state issued a political mandate to doctors. The State, not doctors, dictated for which conditions medical marijuana could be used. No other medical procedure, herbal, OTC, or prescription medicine carries such governmental edicts—except abortion.

With the exception of marijuana, the state leaves issues of health care to the Department of Health or the state medical board. In all other circumstances, except marijuana, licensed physicians make personal medical decisions for each patient, privately. Does the state tell doctors which pharmaceuticals are appropriate for their patients? No way; physicians wouldn't stand for it, nor would the general public (or big pharma).

I also found it a bit Orwellian that the state would require all medical marijuana patients to be placed on a computer database registry. Only patients taking prescription medicines that are significantly more dangerous—substances like opiates or benzodiazepines—are subject to such tracking. Although philosophically troubling, these issues didn't stop me from evaluating patients for appropriate medical marijuana use.

Extending my New York WH&H practice to Montana was logical—plus having both office locations on my business card made for some interesting conversations. Mind you, I was still working six to ten shifts a month in the ED. The intention was to spend at least a week a month in Bozeman seeing patients, and when in New York, I could also see patients at my WH&H location.

I started WH&H in 2006, well before any whiff of medical marijuana. Cycling had spurred my interest in nutrition, and after reading enough textbooks and attending enough conferences centered around integrative and alternative medicine, my knowledge base reached a critical mass. I passed the national board examination for integrative and holistic medicine and found a practice space a few miles from my home—a large first-floor studio with lots of light.

A few friends helped me decorate and paint; then, on a cool September evening, I had an open house. I was surprised by the impressive turnout. Starting a solo alternative medicine practice in rural upstate New York was a bit daunting and the economics were troublesome because it was a cash-only practice. Not accepting insurance kept a lot of people away, and who could blame them—I would be reluctant to pay out of pocket when I was also paying for health insurance. The practice grew, but too slowly for me to stop working in the ED. But thanks to medical marijuana, the growth of WH&H wasn't an issue in Montana.

May was the inaugural WH&H clinic at the Bodhi Tree. Although Hillari had been instrumental in getting the clinic off the ground, she was away. Luckily, Lori offered to help. She arrived early, lit some sweet incense, and made sure everything was ready.

One of my first patients was a rail-thin Gen-Xer dressed in pressed designer jeans, a silk shirt, and brown Italian shoes. His black aviator sunglasses sat atop his waxed scalp. He was as likable as a puppy, with an edge that gave you the impression that he had relatives in the mafia. Anthony Gallo, and his enthusiasm for medical marijuana, was impressive.

After a thorough review of his medical records and a brief exam, I signed his physician statement.

"Thank you very much, Dr. Geci," he said, shaking my hand. "You don't mind if I call you Doctor Mike, do you?"

"That would be fine."

Anthony smiled like a kid on Christmas morning. "This is one of the most memorable days of my life. Because of you, I can no longer be sent to jail for using marijuana." He kissed his signed physician statement. "Thanks a million, Dr. Mike!"

Later, after my lunch break, Lori told me that one of my morning patients had come back to speak with me. Anthony excitedly waved as I walked into the reception area. "Hey, Dr. Mike! I wanted to show you something."

Always curious, I obliged his request, and we stepped out onto the sunny Rhododendron-lined patio.

Anthony beamed. "How would you like to see the medicine I grow?"

"*Medicine you grow?*" Then it dawned on me. I was wondered what "medical" marijuana looked like. "Sure, let's see what you've got."

In a flash, Anthony whipped out a brown paper bag from his daypack. "Check it out, dude."

Inside the bag were several clear plastic baggies filled with what appeared to be the biggest, best-groomed marijuana buds I'd ever seen. I carefully eyed them with suspicion. "This looks like pot."

"It's my *medicine*!" Anthony was quick to point out.

For some reason I was expecting medical marijuana to look different. To be honest, I'm not sure what I expected it to look like. Perhaps it should have been in a large pill container, clearly labeled, *Medical Marijuana*. But it wasn't. Anthony's aromatic stash looked similar to the pot I had smoked in college.

"This is your medicine?" I asked incredulously.

"Sure is, buddy. Didn't I tell you I was a grower, too?"

"I'm sure I didn't ask you that earlier."

Anthony primped himself, a Cheshire cat grin pasted across his face as he handed me a thickly packed baggie. "So what'ya think?"

I feared Anthony would label me a total idiot. "Of what?"

"Dude...of my medicine," he said proudly.

I was confused and did little to hide it. "But, what's in it?"

"I don't know," he shrugged. "But it's really good! You want to try some?"

"No thanks." I looked at Anthony in disbelief. "You mean you *really* don't know what's in this pot you call medicine?"

"I know it's kick-ass weed, dude. That's all I need to know," he said with a swagger.

"Doesn't anyone test their medicine here to see what cannabinoids are in it?"

Anthony looked at me as though I had just beamed down from another planet. "Are you trying to play some weird doctor mind game with me?"

"No, not at all. But if you're going to call something medicine, you need to know what's in it. Just like every other medicine. It's pretty simple."

I thought back to the grandmother in Missoula who'd asked me where she could purchase medical marijuana. Now, after seeing Anthony's marijuana, I was convinced of the need for an analytical laboratory devoted to marijuana quality control. It seemed so obvious.

Medical marijuana needed a measure of quality control so patients could know what cannabinoids they would be ingesting. And more importantly, if other physicians were going to embrace the idea of medical marijuana, they would need to know the dosage of the medicine they were recommending.

The medical marijuana industry had no objective quality control measures; that vacuum needed to be filled by a passionate professional, someone who could shine the light of truth into the darkness of the formerly illegal and underground marijuana marketplace. And for some reason, I thought that person was me.

Little did I know just how vigorously the darkness would oppose the light.

Christ is Not the Lord

If I thought Pete Jones was weird, I was just scratching the surface compared to what I found when I met Jason Christ (JC). Little did I know I was dealing with the Walter White of medical marijuana. He singlehandedly lit the fuse that ultimately caused the entire medical marijuana industry in Montana to implode. Without JC, this story would likely have had a happy ending.

My introduction to JC could only be explained by the euphemism: *Truth is stranger than fiction.*

It was early May, and I was making preparations to take my son to France to visit some friends I'd made during a three-week medical relief trip to Indonesia after the devastating 2004 tsunami. I met Michael and Fatima on a beach in eastern Bali and we became instant friends. They'd invited me to visit on several occasions. While I was packing I received a phone call.

"Hello, Dr. Geci?"

"Depends on who's calling?" I said suspiciously, wondering how this person had figured out how to pronounce my last name correctly.

"Sir, this is Jason Christ. I'm a software engineer who is setting up a statewide database for patients to find doctors willing to evaluate them for medical marijuana."

"How did you get my number?"

"It's a small state, sir."

Perhaps a little red light should have flashed in my head, but I was eager to speak to knowledgeable people about the Montana medical marijuana world. I listened to his spiel. Like Pete Jones, JC sounded polite, respectful, and enthusiastic. He conveyed gratefulness that I might be willing to help him manifest his vision of opening medical marijuana access to other needy patients. JC said that he had been a medical marijuana patient for more than a year and detailed the difficulty and frustration he experienced finding a physician to evaluate him. His mission was to change the system so others wouldn't have to suffer like he did. He made a compelling case.

"Doctor, it took me over ten months to finally get an appointment with a doctor to sign my physician statement."

"That's unfortunate."

JC replied with measured emotion. "It was needless suffering, Doctor. I wouldn't want anyone to experience my pain. I want to change things."

I knew that physician skepticism toward medical marijuana was high, in part because the marijuana was being sold in ziplock baggies. Most doctors thought the whole DPHHS program was a scam—a simple back-door approach for recreational marijuana. JC was not subtle in suggesting that any doctor willing to help him could make a fortune. I knew he was right; the DPHHS website kept statistics on the demographics of the program. There were only a few doctors in the entire state who had signed more than a dozen physician statements. It was obvious why JC was interested in me.

He must have sensed my naïveté. In laborious detail, he described being ping-ponged from one doctor to another, trying to find a doctor who would sign his physician statement, until he found Dr. Chris Christensen, a craggy, irascible physician who operated Big Creek Family Practice in the Bitterroot Valley. Christensen offered a medical marijuana clinic one weekend a month and was booked eight months in advance. JC went on to describe his newly developed computer network, where patients could access a web-based appointment system to find a doctor and schedule an appointment promptly.

"I want to partner with a knowledgeable doctor so I can help appropriately coordinate patient referrals to a cannabis-friendly doctor."

From my perspective, JC's idea seemed like a good one. But there's always a rub. "How much are you going to charge for this service?"

"It'll be free."

"*Really?*" I didn't try to hide my surprise.

The concept of a nonprofit electronic system connecting patients with cannabis-friendly physicians was lofty. I spent considerable time during my first summer in Bozeman, tinkering with the idea of a cannabis-based (and funded) alternative health clinic, offering indigent patients therapeutic massage, yoga, acupuncture, and nutritional counseling. I called it the Bozeman Health Co-op.

"Absolutely, Doctor. It's my way of giving back to the community," JC explained solemnly. "It's my mission to channel patients to doctors so that they won't have to go through the same type of hell that I had to endure trying to find a doctor willing to sign my physician statement."

"Wow...that's really noble of you."

"Thank you for listening, Doctor."

Whoever was on the other end of the phone was very smart.

JC then went on to detail his "pathetic" GI condition which had afflicted him for many years, methodically depicting his numerous misdiagnoses within the Western model of medical care. He scorned his unnecessary surgeries and "poisonous pharmaceuticals" that were prescribed by a greedy and corrupt medical establishment ripe with corporate collusion.

"Only cannabis relieves the pain," JC said with a cracking voice.

His story was moving. I've seen many ER patients ravaged by horrible gastrointestinal (GI) diseases such as celiac disease, Crohn's disease, diverticulitis, irritable bowel syndrome (IBS), and ulcerative colitis. I've treated patients whose lives have been upended by surgical complications, colostomies, infections, GI bleeding, perforations, and intractable pain. I wondered what combination of these dreadful conditions JC must have endured. Finally, my curiosity got the best of me.

"Jacob, if you don't mind me asking...what's your diagnosis?"

There was an uncomfortable pause. I began to imagine the worst.

"Hemorrhoids."

In the twenty years I had been practicing emergency medicine, I'd never heard of hemorrhoids being so devastating. I've had them myself and can vouch that they can be a literal pain in the butt, but it was hard to imagine them causing such heinous symptoms. JC's story was beginning to feel strangely familiar. Perhaps he was just another odd pothead.

I tried to ignore my misgivings about JC's story because I wanted to grow my new practice. I also wanted to bring medical marijuana access to everyone it was intended to help. JC's system was a good idea, but it had some major bugs that needed to be worked out.

"I'd be happy to help you fine-tune your model," I offered, being clear I was working with Pam and the women at the Bodhi Tree. "We're actively scheduling patients for the May clinics in Missoula and Bozeman."

JC interrupted with an eerie enthusiasm. "I can assume immediate responsibility for the entire scheduling process in both places."

I hesitated. "Well, for the time being, everything needs to be cleared through Pam and Catherine."

JC protested. "But I am creating a network that will be much more efficient, Doctor."

"No. There's not enough time. I'm leaving the country for a couple of weeks. It'd be better for the time being to leave well enough alone. Maybe we can implement your system in a month or two after I get back from France."

There was no time to bring JC into the fold. It was essential to nurture the relationships I'd already begun to develop—people I'd met in person and, most importantly, people I trusted. To allow JC to usurp all the work Hillari, Catherine, and Pam had done to support me seemed crazy and irresponsible. JC seemed too eager; his enthusiasm bordered on creepy obsessive. He was blindly focused on the gigantic responsibility of scheduling and supporting a statewide clinic system—and most peculiarly, doing all the work for free.

I told JC that he would have to be patient. I would consider traveling to other cities around the state if the need justified. JC assured me that there were tens of thousands of Montanans who wanted their green card. I said I'd consider his proposal.

The morning before leaving for Paris, I called Hillari, Catherine, Pam, and JC to make sure that everyone was on the same page. Everyone was fine with the clinic trajectory.

What could go wrong?

The trip to France was fantastic. My son and I took daily trips to fascinating places, and with the graciousness of my friends, we immersed ourselves in the French lifestyle. After our adventure,

I dropped off my son at his mother's, returned home, unpacked my backpack, and sorted through my pile of mail. Then I listened to the messages on my blinking answering machine.

My heart skipped a beat when I heard the third message.

"Michael, this is Catherine. What have you done? Please call me as soon as you get this!"

Her voice was frantic and ruffled. *What could have possibly happened? Maybe we should have stayed in France*, I thought as I dialed her number.

Catherine informed me that not only had JC booked the entire May clinic at the Bodhi Tree; he'd already overbooked it—threefold.

"Michael, I am so upset. I haven't wanted a cigarette this bad since I quit six years ago. And did you see the article in the *Chronicle*, Michael? Have you read that yet?," She asked in a panic. I pulled the article up online.

"Oh my God," I whispered.

JC had somehow managed to get a front-page article in the *Bozeman Chronicle*,[6] highlighting the problem of inadequate patient access to doctors sympathetic to medical marijuana. The journalist interviewed a frail white-haired woman dependent on home oxygen who wanted to use marijuana to ease the suffering from her chronic obstructive pulmonary disease (COPD). She told the reporter that she couldn't find a local doctor willing to consider medical marijuana for her condition.

Until now.

The heartwarming story concluded by saying that Dr. Geci would be hosting a medical marijuana clinic on May 24–27 at the Bodhi Tree Wellness Center. "Please call Jacob at Montana Care Network (MCN) for an appointment."

Catherine was beside herself. "The phone has been ringing off the wall with people calling for an appointment to see the "pot doc." What are you going to do about this, Michael?"

It was clear that boundaries were alien to JC. After I convinced Catherine that I was not in cahoots with JC, I called him. I explained that medical marijuana clinics needed to be run professionally and not perceived as mere soup lines for people to use marijuana without a proper medical evaluation. I emphasized medical ethics and the clinic's core principle: to protect the rights of patients with legitimate medical conditions to use cannabis.

But my call fell on deaf ears.

It was clear that the article in the *Chronicle* was no accident. I was livid that JC had been so arrogant. I told him that I was not going to be able to work with him under these conditions. Then he began using language that would embarrass a sailor. In an attempt to hurt my feelings, he questioned whether I had a valid medical license.

It was time to flush JC from my life. I felt fortunate that he had declared his pathology early. He was clearly unstable.

I promised Catherine that I would do the damage control for JC's antics. Step two, after my call to JC, was to write an op-ed piece in the *Bozeman Chronicle*.

In the piece, I explained that the Bodhi Tree was an integrative center for health and healing. While I was open to evaluating patients for the appropriate use of medical marijuana, our clinic was not "a rubber stamp operation to justify a lifestyle." I outlined my criteria for evaluating patients and emphasized the necessity for medical records to document each patient's condition. I also made it clear that the Bodhi Tree "does NOT, under any circumstances, endorse any caregiver or caregiver organization." I also took a swipe at the reporter. Had the reporter double-checked their sources she would have learned that nothing Mr. Christ said in the article regarding the clinic was factual.

In the aftermath of the *Chronicle* article, I felt the need to reach out to the medical community. Hillari helped me coordinate a mass mailing of my WH&H brochure to local physicians, including oncologists and pain specialists. Fellow physicians needed to know that there was a professional setting where medical marijuana would be treated with dignity and respect.

Catherine appreciated my attempt at damage control. And so, with the gift of hindsight, this is where the end met its beginning.

I witnessed the tortured mind of JC before most Montanans knew his name. Within his macabre intellect sprouted the seed that produced the time bomb that would decimate the entire medical marijuana program. By the fall of 2009, nearly every person in Montana who read a newspaper or watched TV would have recognized Jason Christ. His antics evoked a sense of fear and betrayal for many Montanans. I found it ironic that his surname gave him an existential predilection to become a martyr.

JC taught me the need to walk away from people with evil energy. I thought I could outmaneuver his negativity with my intellect, compassion, and kindness. I was wrong. Sometimes that level of negativity can overwhelm you. JC had an innocent charm that cleverly masked his dark side. I ignored my gut and tried to convince myself that JC was approachable; I just had to find the key to unlock that friendlier, kinder side of him. But there was no key. JC proved to be a greedy and manipulative person with a soul taunted by demons.

JC's strategy was clear. His misguided genius saw the enormous economic potential of being the agent that funneled patients to see a physician. Any preteen can do the math. In his May clinic, JC claimed he had processed 170 patients. At $200 a patient, that's a cool $34,000 for a day's work. His offer of a 50/50 split with the physician still made the day enormously profitable.

According to the 2010 US Census, Montana is the sixth smallest state in population, with just over a million people. If only 10 percent of Montanans opted to get their card (and that was a very conservative number), that's about $20 million a year in potential revenue that MCN looked to capture. JC saw the gold mine. MCN was sponsoring clinics at hotels in Billings, Bozeman, Butte, Great Falls, and Helena. Word spread quickly. Soon the MCN clinics were servicing thousands of patients a month.

In July, I attended a pain management conference in Bozeman, and as luck would have it, the MCN had a clinic at the hotel across the street. During the conference lunch break, I went to check it out.

The parking lot was packed. At the hotel entrance, a pair of thirty-something men silently held large handmade placards. One read "Medical Marijuana Is a Joke." The other declared "Pot Ruins Communities and Schools." I nodded to the demonstrators as I walked in.

Inside, hundreds of people were milling about. The energy was carnival-like. It was hard to spot people who looked debilitated. There was an emaciated woman slumped in a wheelchair and a couple of people limping around on crutches, but most didn't look sick to me. The one conspicuous thing was the smell of marijuana.

The clinic was more like an assembly line than a physician's office. As soon as a patient exited the room where the doctor had signed their physician statement, they would begin mingling in the lobby. The lobby was lined with about two-dozen tables staffed by marijuana caregivers eagerly signing up patients.

Every caregiver was selling the best pot at the best price. Everyone was wheeling and dealing.

Sign up now and get a free ounce of marijuana!

Several patients told me that their total time with the physician was less than five minutes. I was shocked. This clinic was a mockery to the intent of MT-148 and an insult to WH&H.

I wandered around the various caregiver booths. Some were familiar, like Montana Cannabis, Sensible Alternatives, and Mary Jane's Kitchen, but most were new: Wild West Meds, Big Sky Botanicals, and The Medicine Man. Madison Avenue would have been impressed.

Unexpectedly, one of the dreadlocked MCN assistants at the registration desk asked me if I needed any assistance. Perhaps the pressed slacks and shirt and tie caused me to stand out. Maybe she thought I was a cop. I introduced myself and asked if I could meet with JC.

To my astonishment, JC appeared. He was taller than I had expected, reminding me of Brando playing the deranged Colonel Kurtz from *Apocalypse Now*. He glided toward me, carefully cupping his trademark shepherd's pipe, the large glass bowl still smoldering. His smile grew broader as he drew closer. I smiled and held out my hand, but he brushed past and hugged me.

"Hello, Jacob. It's nice to meet you in person."

"The pleasure is all mine, Doctor," JC said with a slight bow of his head.

"Quite an operation you're running."

Nodding, JC cast a sardonic grin and excused himself. I walked around the lobby waiting for him to return. A few minutes later, another cute granola girl tapped me on the shoulder.

"Would you mind leaving, sir?"

Leave? "Why should I leave? I'm having a conversation with Mr. Christ."

"It's a conflict of interest to have you here, Doctor."

I looked at her in utter disbelief. *Conflict of interest?* A cold chill ran up my spine. I'd seen enough. It was time to get some fresh air.

As summer rolled into fall, the MCN clinics were creating more than a stir. Thanks to the roving MCN clinics, the rate of enrollment into the DPHHS program was rising at a logarithmic pace.

With the release of the Ogden memo in October, the Obama administration created the illusion of marijuana tolerance. And now it seemed that marijuana was everywhere. Storefronts and dispensaries were popping up all over Bozeman, as well as in small towns and cities across the state.

It seemed clear that most growers who jumped on the bandwagon early in 2009 had been illegally growing marijuana for years. Many recognized the opportunity in front of them.

Suddenly, the legal demand for marijuana was skyrocketing. And like the zombie apocalypse, every grower in the state came out of the woodwork. It was disheartening to see so many unwashed and haggard, droopy-eyed men and women looking more like outcasts from an *Up in Smoke* remix than flag bearers for the growing medical marijuana movement.

PFU

After my first clinic in Bozeman, I met with Tom Daubert, the director and founder of Patients and Families United (PFU), a nonprofit that served as the sole political action committee for the advocacy of legislation sympathetic to medical marijuana use in Montana. As a co-author of MT-148, he was as familiar with the law as anyone.

"I would have liked to have spoken to you earlier, but I just about died from a very serious viral illness. There's a lot to discuss." Tom had been surveying the shifting political landscape surrounding MT-148 for the past six years. "Since Obama has taken office, everything is changing rapidly. Too rapidly, I fear." His concern was that people across the state were under the illusion that the federal government would not meddle with state-approved medical marijuana programs.

Daubert is one of the most well-spoken individuals I've ever met. His thick salt-and-pepper beard, jovial charm, and grandfatherly affect is more aligned with jolly St. Nick than a pudgy, middle-aged marijuana lobbyist. Daubert's Quaker upbringing and disarming way always made me feel that everything was OK, even when the sky looked like it really was falling. Princeton-educated, his soft-spoken demeanor masked his enormous political sophistication. He served as the western region press secretary for Colorado senator Gary Hart's 1984 presidential bid. I felt honored to be speaking to him.

Tom shared his insights about how the marijuana explosion would likely impact the upcoming 2010 midterm elections. He feared a harsh political reprisal from the ongoing negative media coverage. Television and newspapers painted a picture of pot fever spreading like a plague, leaving a palpable path of destruction in its wake. He chronicled stories from papers across the state about the explosive growth of the industry. If it wasn't a story about Jason Christ and the MCN, then it was a story about some other boneheaded Cheech and Chong devotee who was making ridiculous statements or doing preposterous stunts. In the distance I could see the storm clouds forming.

I wanted to help PFU flourish because the political battles that lay ahead would be long and bitter. I wanted to forge an alliance with Tom. Hillari had fielded lots of calls from patients who'd been referred by Daubert, and I wanted to return the favor. Helping to increase the membership for PFU was important for protecting the emerging pro-cannabis constituency. For my part, at the conclusion of every clinic appointment, patients were informed about PFU and the importance of becoming a member. WH&H was responsible for hundreds of new PFU members.

Daubert validated my efforts to advocate for patients. He was the maestro that had helped orchestrate MT-148 into a reality. I was thrilled to be helping the cause. But like most everyone else I met in this industry, he had a darker side. It wasn't long after our first meeting that I learned that Daubert was one of the four partners in Montana Cannabis—at one time, the biggest medical marijuana grow operation in the state. I was caught off guard by the revelation; it seemed like a conflict of interest.

Despite my reservations about his role in Montana Cannabis, I trusted Daubert. With its monthly newsletter, PFU was the focal point for the dissemination of information and the voice of one of the most underrepresented yet passionate block of voters in the state—patients using medical marijuana.

Montana is one of four state legislatures in the United States that convene every *other* year. With the upcoming legislative session more than a year and a half away, building a strong coalition of supporters was essential. Although Daubert had succeeded in getting a medical marijuana regulatory improvement bill out of both House and Senate committees in 2007 and 2009, it was defeated on the House floor by Republicans. Daubert had reservations that the 2011 legislative session would be friendlier, yet we both felt that we'd ultimately prevail in the battle to reform MT-148.

For my part, I thought we'd win because we were the "good" guys.

Daubert and I also became allies because I understood what was at stake if MT-148 was repealed. He didn't think I was certifiably crazy, like so many of the other people he knew in the industry. And although some perceived me as a carpet-bagging doctor from New York, looking to cash in on the growing ganja gold mine, Daubert never doubted my sincerity, nor my motives. I shared genuine concerns that patients have an opportunity for a safe and well-regulated cannabis medicine program. We kept in touch because we each brought something valuable to the table: information.

Later that summer, I offered to drive up to Helena to have lunch with Daubert at the Hawthorne Pub one afternoon. I was eager to share with him my evolving idea of cannabis quality control testing. Daubert was one of the few people who understood the implications of cannabis quality control. I was anxious to get his thoughts regarding the commercial interest in an analytical testing laboratory.

"It's is the most legitimate way of making the distinction between medical and recreational marijuana," I said. "And it's the only way to truly legitimize the industry."

Daubert smiled. "That's a terrific talking point." Then he ordered another Guinness and changed the subject to the most recent MCN clinic that took place in Billings.

It was hard to hide my disgust. "These clinics are like some sort of pot carnival."

Tom crooked his neck to sip the creamy foam from his Guinness and calmly nodded. "I heard they saw five hundred patients this weekend."

"How can one doctor see five hundred patients in a weekend? This is an absolute mockery of the citizens' initiative. No one would have voted for this."

Daubert seemed amused by my incredulousness. "I know. But this is what we have. Christ is in the papers all the time, toting that goddamn shepherd's staff of a pipe."

"Haven't you talked to him?"

"Oh c'mon, you know what he's like. He's crazier than Pete Jones by a Montana mile," he chuckled. "He won't listen to anybody. And sure as hell not me."

"I'm thinking about reporting him to the State Board of Medical Examiners. If he doesn't have a doctor, his clinics can't operate."

Tom mulled over what I'd just said with a long sip. "You ought to report him, but I doubt that the state board has any leverage over Christ. He'll just find another doctor."

And that's exactly what happened. Once the state board received my letter of complaint and requested a hearing with Dr. Patricia Cole, the first MCN doctor, Christ fired her. The next MCN clinic had another doctor that was flown in from out of state to staff JC's traveling carnival clinics.

Daubert was a critical connection in my decision to continue to dig myself deeper into the stew. We emailed each other regularly, sharing news and ideas. I loved reading his wistful prose and can only appreciate now how prophetic his words turned out to be:

(Regarding the) 2011 lobbying [effort], unless I have the good fortune of dying before then, I can't imagine a world without my lobbying. At the same time, it seems to me that the medical MJ scene is spiraling far beyond any ability I might hope to have to control it or possibly even represent it. My guess is that, unlike the 2009 session, by 2011 there may be a lot of fractionation within the ranks of existing patients and caregivers.

Tom validated many of my feelings. As time passed, he and I grew friendlier. I wanted him to embrace me as wholly as I embraced him, but that never happened—maybe because he was a professional lobbyist.

Gerald's Grandma

For most of my medical career, when I heard someone say, "medical marijuana," my first thought was the word "pot." The word evoked images of hippies blissfully dancing to the Grateful Dead, passing around a joint, and having a blast. Yet, as my interest in medical marijuana grew, my perception of cannabis was undergoing a radical shift. The more I read about the science of cannabinoids, the more I understood the importance of the path I'd taken. And yet, despite all my assiduous studying, what taught me the most about the power of cannabis came from talking to my patients I saw in clinic.

During one of my early clinics, a frail-looking woman told me about her chronic back pain. She traveled more than three hours to see me and said her grandson (who had driven her) was growing marijuana for her. She carried a bulky manila envelope neatly stuffed with her medical records—documents testifying to decades of medical care for her constant back and joint pain dating back to a major car accident in the eighties. The woman underwent numerous surgeries and an array of other therapies, all of which were ultimately unsuccessful. At the bottom of the pile of documents was a list of her medications.

"Do you take all of these medicines?" I asked.

The woman's eyes narrowed. "What medicines?"

"These medicines," I said, handing her the copy of the list of prescriptions she'd been prescribed.

The woman looked at the sheet, then scoffed. "Naw. I don't take none of them anymore. I think they made me more sick."

As I reviewed the medication list, I was surprised to find that her family doctor had been prescribing 360 Percocet a month for the past 10 years, averaging 12 pills a day. That seemed like an awful lot of opiates. The list also included a diuretic that I presumed was to treat her hypertension, and a statin, to manage her cholesterol. I glanced at her vital signs. They were normal.

"I don't need none of 'em since I started using the marijuana," she said unapologetically.

"Really?" I had heard rumors that patients could wean themselves off narcotics if they used medical marijuana, but this was the first patient I'd met who had actually done it.

The woman slowly nodded.

"I know this may sound like a weird question, but if you have a family doctor who has been writing you all of these prescriptions for pain, why didn't you have him fill out your physician statement?"

The woman sounded annoyed. "Cuz he don't believe in this medical marijuana jazz. I asked him about it and he just told me flat out, 'No!' He said he don't want nothin' to do with it. Then he told me not to bring it up again or I could find another doctor."

We sat in the sunlit room and looked at each other in silence. I'd had other patients tell me that they were afraid their doctor would "fire" them if they found out they were using medical marijuana. I found it sad that so many physicians were unwilling to consider cannabis as an alternative therapy.

"Let me be honest with you, Doc. When my grandson, Gerald, first told me about using marijuana for my aches and pains, I thought he was a looney tune. He said to me, 'Gram, I can get you some marijuana that won't make you high or make you feel like a drug addict.'" The woman bowed her head. "And I trusted him. Ain't nobody want to smoke my medicine."

"Why's that?"

"Cuz it won't get you high," the woman said brightly. "My grandson says he bred it that way cuz he knows I never liked feeling high. So, I listened to him because he wanted to help me. He's a good boy—been living with me since he was a child. And you know what, Doc? It really helps. Using this marijuana he grows me has been a godsend."

Gerald's Grandma leaned forward. "I never thought I'd live to see the day when I wouldn't have to feel like a criminal because I use marijuana. That's why I want my card. I don't wanna stay awake at night, wonderin' if the police are gonna raid my place and haul my grandson off to jail."

What a shame.

Another physician statement I was proud to sign.

Burned Out

Perhaps you've been wondering: Why did I give up a perfectly good job as an ER doctor to get involved in medical marijuana?

Like most things in life, getting from point A to point D can take numerous twists and turns. The result is all about timing. After a dozen plus years of working in emergency departments across the eastern United States, I felt like a hamster stuck on its wheel. I felt like I'd lost control of my life, yielding it to the person who made the physician schedule. I sometimes worked six night shifts in a row, and by midway through the third one, I could feel the warmth of my personality withering like a parched potted plant in the August sun. Sure, I had four or five days off afterward, before another stretch, but over a period of years, I was never able to fully recover. I was burned out. I was the poster child of physician burnout, before the word became such a popular catchphrase.

But it was more than that.

Since I was a kid, I wanted to be a doctor. I went into emergency medicine because I wanted to save lives. I fantasized about becoming a peacetime Hawkeye Pierce, a hero wearing scrubs. But I wasn't in it the heroics. For me it was all about karma. I just wanted to be a good doctor and to feel I was making a positive difference in someone's life. I wanted to be the "cool doctor" who fixed the problem with acumen, sensitivity, and a sense of humor. I wanted patients to feel like they'd had a good ER experience with me as their doctor. I wanted to placate their fear of bright surgical lamps, unpronounceable terminology, and sharp needles with my laid-back style and competence.

But something went wrong.

Over time, my job felt like I was working at McDonald's. Instead of serving Big Macs and fries, I was the guy who was expected to doll out pain meds and antibiotics to assuage the neuroses of the masses. For me, the ED was like working in a boundaryless environment, yet I was the only one expected to respect others' boundaries. Patients, their families, nurses, and staff could say and do just about whatever they pleased without repercussions. Yet if I'd done something out of line, forget it—just find a new job.

And if you thought that having to be 100 percent perfect in every diagnosis of every patient wasn't pressure enough, ED physicians are monitored constantly-by hospital, state and federal administrators. Every data point is measured; patient triage times, patient wait times to see the doctor, every physician order, from blood work to CT scans was accounted for and compared to other ED physicians across the country, as well as door-to-disposition time of every patient, how long did the patient linger in the ED before they were either discharged or admitted to the hospital. Sadly, more importantly than providing a good outcome, patient satisfaction scores were more valued than their clinical outcomes.

In an attempt to maintain my sanity, I discounted the administrative auditing of my performance measures. Instead, my frustrations were compounded when the nursing staff questioned my orders (or worse, just flat out didn't carry them out). I embraced a well-thought out nursing question, but more often than not, the questioning exposed the nurses lack of clinical understanding of the potential complexity of the patient's problems. And over time, this too was exhausting.

Keep in mind that the human drama within the ED takes place in an assembly-line environment, moving patients like hungry customers at a drive-thru restaurant. It's stressful being the emergency physician. Your job is to manage the patients seeking medical care, evaluating, treating, and assigning them a final disposition in a timely fashion. But what made the job one-hundred times worse was navigating the not-so-subtle pressure of the staff (nurses) to simply move bodies. In and out. Patients became bed numbers. To cope, I tried to tune out the distractions, staying focused on the methodical and robotic approach I'd been trained to employ—battling the demon of complacency, while still considering the possibilities of life-threatening diagnoses with every patient.

"Just get 'em out of here. I need the bed for the next one," the nurse would often say. "There's six patients in the waiting room. Why are you doing a workup in Bed 5? She's got bronchitis and just wants a work note and an antibiotic." Of course, the nurse failed to consider the blood-tinged sputum, the increasing shortness of breath, and the ever-looming possibility that the patient might have something more serious, like a pulmonary embolism, a condition that could easily be fatal if I missed the diagnosis.

I also tried ignoring the universal comment: "He's just a drug seeker. I'm not giving him any pain medicine." Of course, the nurse ignored the fact that the patient had a long-documented history of kidney stones and was now urinating blood with a low-grade fever. Clinical data often had little bearing on things as many nurses had preconceived notions about what was wrong with a patient. My job required me to politely dismiss their prejudices and evaluate each patient objectively; still the barrage of whispered nursing innuendos slowly wore me down.

Additionally, even if you saw the patient in a timely manner, smiled appropriately, made the right diagnosis, and even scheduled a follow-up medical appointment, sometimes the patients (or their family members) still complained. There's nothing that hospital administrators hate more than having to field patient complaints directed toward the physician staff. I had an ER director tell me once, "I'd rather have a mediocre doctor who didn't get complaints than an excellent doctor who generated them."

This wasn't what I'd signed up for.

Granted, I'm truly grateful for the opportunities that have been bestowed upon me being an emergency physician. I have been blessed to have worked with some of the most intelligent and dedicated people I've ever met. I'm honored to have had the fortuity to treat so many wonderful patients. But still, the ED became parasitic. I told myself years before that if something else came up, I was going to leave this ER gig in a heartbeat.

Although I was certainly ready for a career change, what ultimately drew me to medical marijuana was my fascination with its science.

Aside from climate change, I feel few things are more misunderstood by the general public than the science of cannabis. It's important to give you, the reader, an insight into what sparked my passion about cannabis. The medicinal molecules made by cannabis influence many aspects of human physiology, and sometimes profoundly so. Once I learned these concepts, I quickly came to appreciate the breadth of the plant's clinical applications. My only conclusion was that the solid body of science refuted the notion that using cannabis/marijuana as a medicine was just some sort of snake-oil remedy.

I'd like to put special focus on the *Addiction, Pregnancy,* and *Psychiatry* sections of the following chapter—for it's in these areas that I find the biggest controversies and confusion with cannabis. It is primarily in these three sections where the nuance of cannabis as a medicine and marijuana as a powerful and potentially dangerous drug intersect.

There's sometimes a fine line between the medical use of marijuana and its recreational use. No drug is completely harmless. None. Cannabis, regardless of what the dispensary salesperson may say, is no exception. The public needs to be clear about the potential dangers of using marijuana, especially in a reckless manner.

What did I learn about cannabis that I found so interesting?

The Science of Cannabis

Cannabis sativa is thought to have originated from central Asia and is known as one of humanity's oldest cultivated plants. It is the genus and species name of a large family of plants that, to a novice, all look similar. The *Cannabis* genus includes three subspecies or varieties, named *indica, sativa,* and *ruderalis.* Also found within the *Cannabis* genus is the innocuous sibling of marijuana, hemp. Closely related to cannabis is its plant cousin, *Humulus lupuli,* better known as hops, one of the principle ingredients in beer.

Just as there are numerous strains (varieties) of grapes and tomatoes with different flavors, colors, and fruit morphology, not all strains of cannabis are the same either; not every strain will get you stoned. Cannabis strains that induce a psychoactive response (i.e., alter your state of consciousness, or get you "high") are colloquially called marijuana. The molecule responsible for the buzz or the "high" that's made marijuana famous (and illegal) is due primarily to the presence of THC. Strains of marijuana may alter consciousness quite differently, depending on the concentration of THC. Additionally, the psychoactivity is also due to the spectrum of other cannabinoids and terpenes produced by individual strains.

Due to the extensive amount of cannabis breeding over the past several decades, finding a pure indica or sativa strain is rare. At most dispensaries, budtenders will tell you that indica strains produce a more body-centered, sedative experience. Sativa strains, on the other hand, are purported to generate highs that are described as heady, providing a more cerebral experience.

Interestingly, cannabis produces nearly five hundred different chemical compounds. The most notable are called cannabinoids.[7] As per the US Department of Agriculture, (USDA) cannabis containing less than 0.3 percent THC can legally be called hemp; strains with higher levels of THC are considered as marijuana.

The other important class of organic compounds found in cannabis is the aromatic terpenes, which are responsible for the distinctive aromas of many cannabis strains. Terpenes are essential oils found throughout the plant world and their medicinal properties have been well studied. Ultimately, the combination of cannabinoids and terpenes found in each cannabis strain dictates its medicinal or recreational use.

To summarize, all marijuana and hemp may be accurately referred to as cannabis, but not all cannabis is necessarily marijuana.

The 0.3 percent THC cutoff for cannabis to be considered hemp is a rather arbitrary cutoff, as cannabis with a THC concentration of less than 1 percent would have very little psychoactive effect and thus minimal "recreational" value. Still, if you are growing hemp and your plants are producing THC at a meager 0.89 percent, the government can confiscate your entire crop, impose a hefty fine, and possibly add jail time, even if the grower's intent was to grow the cannabis for seed or fiber.

Unfortunately, the cannabis/marijuana labeling nomenclature is vague in much of the scientific literature. When reading the cannabis literature, THC-rich strains are oftentimes referred to as cannabis just as often as they are termed marijuana. Perhaps, it's best to note that if a person *isn't* confused by the cannabis labeling nomenclature, then they're not paying attention.

The distinction between cannabis and marijuana is important because a lot of patients who are seeking to use marijuana as a medicine don't want to use strains that significantly alter their perception of time, space, or reality.

For generations, marijuana has been bred to get the user as high as possible. For many, including myself, the idea of using marijuana as a medicine seemed like some Wall Street penny-stock scheme. But that opinion began to change when I started to review the scientific literature and discovered how cannabis works as a medicine.

What makes cannabinoids so unique and interesting is that they are highly fat-soluble molecules that have an affinity for one or more of the various cannabinoid receptors found in the body. Cannabinoids bind to a large number of other, non-cannabinoid receptors, too. Cannabinoid receptors are concentrated everywhere in the body, except in the cells deep within the respiratory center of our primitive forebrain (the medulla oblongata).[8] Due to the relative paucity of cannabinoid receptors in the medulla oblongata, cannabinoids do not depress the respiratory drive to the point of completely inhibiting spontaneous respiration. Without significant receptors in the brain's respiratory center, cannabinoids avert the lethal side effects of alcohol, benzodiazepines (prescription drugs like Valium, Ativan, and Xanax), and opiates (like heroin, Percocet, fentanyl, and Oxycontin) that cause respiratory depression, asphyxiation, and death.

Cannabinoid receptors are crucial in mammalian physiology. Scientists have dated cannabinoid receptors back to sea squirts—primordial organisms that appeared on the Earth a mere six hundred million years ago.[9] At present, there are two cannabinoid receptors that have been discovered and studied: the cannabinoid-1 receptor (CB-1) and the cannabinoid-2 receptor (CB-2).[10]

In a nutshell, the CB-1 receptor is found throughout the brain and nervous system, as well as throughout most of the cells in your body. When you smoke a joint (inhaling THC), the CB-1 receptor is stimulated, and you'll likely feel a sense of euphoria, your mouth gets dry, your eyes are bloodshot and glassy, and you get the munchies. Alternatively, the CB-2 receptor is mostly found on the cells composing the immune system. When the CB-2 receptor is stimulated, the immune system is modulated.

The two main cannabinoids that have been studied are THC and the now mega-popular CBD. Textbooks could be written regarding both substances, but briefly, THC binds with modest affinity to both CB-1 and CB-2 receptors to elicit its various effects. Interestingly, CBD has been shown to have negligible binding to either the CB-1 or CB-2 receptors. CBD effects the body in ways that are very different from THC.

Cannabinoid receptors act like all receptors, as cellular communication tools, yet they are very different from other cellular receptors, such as histamine, dopamine, and serotonin. Cannabinoid receptors have been amazingly preserved through evolution as an essential part of the endocannabinoid system (ECS).

The role of the ECS has been simplified to eat, sleep, relax, protect, and forget. The ECS plays an essential role in maintaining homeostasis, or balance. Without homeostasis, biologic chaos ensues. The ECS is involved in every aspect of human physiology; it is intimately involved in sleep, learning and memory, emotions, pain perception, immune function, vascular tone, appetite, bone growth and regulation, fertility, embryo implantation and gestation, and vision.

The ECS is ubiquitous, a neuro-modulatory system that plays important roles in central nervous system (CNS) development, synaptic plasticity, and the response to endogenous and environmental insults. The ECS comprises the receptors and transporters to which endogenous cannabinoids (endocannabinoids), as well as plant-based and synthetic cannabinoids, bind and activate, and the enzymes responsible for the synthesis and degradation of endocannabinoids. Endocannabinoids are the body's naturally produced cannabinoids, not unlike how endorphins and enkephalins are the body's naturally produced opiates.

The ECS is critical in major physiological processes like appetite, pain-sensation, reproduction, mood, memory, neuronal growth and differentiation, energy balance and metabolism, stress response, thermoregulation, and the immune response. The ECS acts as a bridge between the body and the mind, orchestrating complex actions of our immune system, nervous system, and all of the body's organs.[11] The cannabinoids in cannabis have significant impacts on the ECS.

At the beginning of my Montana journey, I was completely ignorant about cannabinoids and the ECS, not because I was a slacker in medical school, but rather because the ECS wasn't discovered until after I graduated in 1993. Back then, next to nothing was being published about cannabinoid therapeutics. The notable exception was a CB-1 antagonist (which blocks the receptor) called rimonabant. The drug was marketed as a miracle weight-loss drug. It made sense that blocking the CB-1 receptor would inhibit the urge to eat since the munchies is such a common side effect of using marijuana. And to the pharmaceutical company's delight, rimonabant worked like a charm—people lost weight.

But something unexpected happened during the clinical trials. Those patients taking rimonabant who were suffering from mild to moderate depression began to kill themselves.[12] Within a short period of time, Bayer withdrew the drug from the market, and the pharmaceutical debut of manipulating the ECS was a catastrophe.

The debut and disaster of rimonabant was a wake-up call to the delicacy of manipulating the ECS. I took note. If rimonabant could have these types of effects on patients, then it stood to reason that marijuana might also have profound effects, too.

Once I'd committed to evaluating patients to use medical marijuana, I learned as much about the plant as possible. I visited the PubMed website regularly, reading the latest papers on the ECS and the therapeutic potential of cannabinoids.

Listed below is a brief encapsulation of the clinical applications of medical marijuana, including the use of CBD. My investigative research re-enforced my hunch that medical marijuana could be a significant therapeutic tool for physicians. It quickly became clear to me it wasn't simply some stoner fabrication.

Oncology/Cancer

Few words strike fear in someone's soul like the six letters c-a-n-c-e-r. The antitumor properties of cannabinoids were first described in the early 1990s when Munson showed that THC inhibits the cell growth of lung adenocarcinoma cells in vivo.[13] Suffice to say that the mechanisms and pathways in which cannabinoids inhibit tumor growth is complex and still being elucidated.

There are several major pathways in which tumor growth is inhibited by cannabinoids.

Apoptosis refers to the programmed death of an organism's cells as part of its natural cell cycle of growth, development, and death. In most cases, cell death gives rise to new cell growth. The hallmark of cancer is unchecked cell growth—that's why most cancers form masses or tumors. Many strains of cannabis produce cannabinoids that promote apoptosis in many different human cell lines.[14]

If the normal process of apoptosis fails, the malignant cell begins to divide indefinitely, becoming an immortal growing mass of cancerous cells. Fortunately, this expanding ball of tumor cells can't get very large unless it's able to stimulate blood vessel growth, termed *angiogenesis*, into the expanding glob of cancer cells. Without angiogenesis, a tumor can't connect to the host's vascular supply. Without a consistent flow of blood and nutrients into the mass, it is impossible for the tumor to grow and spread. Cannabinoids have been shown to inhibit angiogenesis.[15]

Provided that the body's normal mechanisms for apoptosis is usurped and the tumor is able to stimulate angiogenesis, the next step in the progression of cancer is perhaps the most feared. Cancer cells often migrate and spread from the primary tumor site. Once these cells break off, they travel and adhere to other distant cells, invading their space in a process known as *metastasis*.[16] Once a tumor has metastasized, the prognosis for the patient worsens dramatically. Cannabinoids have been shown to significantly limit the ability of certain cancer cells to metastasize. Tumor lines such as breast, colon, lung, pancreatic, prostate, and brain (the dreaded glioblastoma multiform) have been shown to be receptive to cannabis-based treatments.[17]

When the signs and symptoms of cancer, such as a palpable mass, fatigue, unexplained bruising or bleeding, shortness of breath, or pain, finally present themselves and the diagnosis of cancer is made, patients are referred to a cancer specialist, the oncologist. Patients look to their oncologist to save them from certain death by using treatments aimed at killing the cancer cells—modalities like surgery, radiation, and chemotherapy; cocktails of toxic drugs designed to kill the tumor cells.

Millions of cancer patients suffer from the pernicious effects of chemotherapy-induced nausea and vomiting. THC acts to modulate the vomiting center of the brain and thus is quite effective at inhibiting the nausea and vomiting induced by chemotherapy. Marijuana is also well-recognized for stimulating appetite (the munchies).[18] Without proper nutrition and caloric support, cancer patients succumb more quickly to their disease.

Provocatively, it has been suggested that we have all had cancer, and perhaps there are cancer cells that are present within our bodies at all times, not unlike weeds in a garden. What keeps this tumor load manageable and in check is our immune system. Ultimately, cancer wields its ugly head when our immune defenses falter and fail, allowing tumor cells to enjoy unchecked growth.

Immunology/Inflammation

The immune system is our guardian angel. Period.

Animals without an immune system perish quickly. Our immune system keeps us from being devoured by the hostile world of microbes. Invisible threats such as bacteria, fungi, parasites, and viruses are all eagerly awaiting an opportunity to overwhelm and turn us into compost. Without a healthy immune system, each of us succumbs. An overwhelming majority of our health issues are related to imbalances in the immune system. Cannabinoids, such as CBD, have been effective in safely rebalancing the immune response in such disorders as arthritis, psoriasis, Crohn's disease, irritable bowel syndrome, multiple sclerosis, Huntington's disease, autism, Alzheimer's, and Parkinson's disease.[19]

CB-2 receptors are found almost exclusively on immune cells. Both THC and cannabinol (CBN) bind to the CB-2 receptor, as well as the terpene essential oil beta-caryophyllene, a substance found not only in cannabis but also in cloves, rosemary, hops, and echinacea.[20]

Psychiatry

In no specialty of medicine does the use of cannabis offer so much potential and yet introduce an equal measure of controversy as psychiatry. Since the advent of the modern pharmaceutical industry, doctors have used powerful psychotropic drugs to sedate patients suffering from a host of mental health disorders like bipolar disorder, depression, and schizophrenia. Although many patients enjoy a higher quality of life due to the appropriate use of these drugs,[21] a significant number have suffered devastating side effects from tardive dyskinesia (repetitive, involuntary grimacing and lip smacking) to suicide.[22] In 2011 Medicaid spent $8 billion for anti-psychotic drugs such as Abilify, Seroquel, and Zyprexa.[23]

As a safer alternative to psychotropics, CBD has been shown to be effective in the treatment of acute psychosis, as well as depression, insomnia, and anxiety,[24, 25] without the debilitating side effects of psychotropic pharmaceuticals.

Psychiatry is the first area where I saw a clear delineation between the potential benefits of using cannabis (e.g., CBD strains) and the possible risks of using high-potency marijuana. Although it's an unpopular subject to breach, one of the most controversial topics about marijuana use is its ability to cause psychosis, especially in vulnerable teens and young adults.

Colorado was the first state in the country to legalize recreational marijuana use in 2012. In a recent study evaluating marijuana-related psychiatric problems, the rate of adolescent emergency department and urgent care visits to a children's hospital in Colorado rose more than 2.5-fold over the period of 2009 to 2015.[26]

Numerous studies have suggested that early marijuana abuse during adolescence can have significant negative impacts on long-term emotional and cognitive development.[27] The *New York Times* recently ran an op-ed piece written by two prominent physicians, Kenneth L. Davis and Mary Jeanne Kreek, who discussed the dangers of adolescent marijuana use. They quoted numerous studies strongly suggesting that we rethink the notion that marijuana (i.e., THC) is a harmless drug. A key distinction is that the marijuana available twenty-five years ago had an average THC content of 3.7 percent, whereas now that number is 18.7 percent.[28] Studies propose that the dangers of marijuana center around its THC potency and, secondarily, the chronicity of use. Many of the early studies with marijuana, advising that it was a relatively benign substance, were done using strains of marijuana that pale in comparison to the THC potency available now.

The *Times* piece also noted recent studies suggesting the negative impact of adolescent marijuana use on cognitive development,[29] executive function (the ability to plan organize and complete tasks),[30] processing speed,[31] memory,[32] attention span,[33] and concentration,[34] as well as significant decreases in IQ.[35] Fortunately, some data suggests at least some of these impairments may not be permanent, but even with up to six weeks of marijuana abstinence in teens and young adults, deficits in learning and working memory were still detectable.[36]

Although I have reservations about marijuana legalization, I am completely behind the notion of full decriminalization of marijuana. I applaud the recommendations of Drs. Davis and Kreek, who suggest that marijuana should not be recreationally available to adults younger than the age of twenty-five, as a precautionary measure to ensure that their brain develops naturally without the interference of exogenous cannabinoids, especially THC.

This recommendation is based on sound science that clearly shows that the endocannabinoid system is intimately involved in brain and nervous cell differentiation, migration, and maturation. And one of the most potent modulators of the ECS is THC.[37] The influence of THC on the brain depends on numerous factors, including the dose of the drug, the duration of drug exposure, the age of first exposure, as well as the genetics of the individual. There is clear evidence that the human brain undergoes significant maturity well into the mid-twenties, and if an individual is exposed to THC, it may alter that individual's ability to maximize his or her cognitive and psychosocial potential. There are data suggesting that once an adult brain has fully matured, the effects of THC on neurocircuitry do not seem nearly as ominous as they do for an adolescent.[38]

What is at stake are the minds of our children. Adolescence is a vulnerable time for brain development and as such should be respected and protected as best possible. The unregulated use of THC by our youth may have far-reaching and dire long-term consequences.

Are governments so desperate for marijuana tax revenue that the legal age for marijuana consumption can't be based on the results of years of neuroscience research, rather than the arbitrary numbers that states have used for alcohol and tobacco sales?

For me, this is also a personal issue. I have a teenage son and I have seen some of his friends spiral downward after they began using marijuana regularly. It's a sad thing to watch.

The aforementioned *Times* article also made reference to a view that's been scoffed at for years: the idea that marijuana is a "gateway drug," a substance that can lead a person to experiment with other more serious and dangerous types of controlled substances.[39] Perhaps people thought that calling marijuana a "gateway drug" was simply part of the failed war on drugs—another piece of the government's propaganda machine against marijuana. To be honest, that's what I thought. But during my extensive research, I changed my mind. There is emerging evidence of a genetic component to addiction, with links to marijuana use and opiate addiction.

Critics who attempt to slow down the momentum for marijuana legalization are harshly criticized in the press. I was aghast to read the comments from readers responding to Drs. Davis and Kreek's article. Unfortunately, it appears the political binary of "you're either with us or against us" has infiltrated the discussion regarding marijuana, too. Prudence and facts no longer matter; intelligent and thoughtful debate seems to have assumed the same fate as the landline and the phonograph.

Science doesn't have a political agenda. Although there are certainly examples of scientists fudging data to support an ulterior motive, far and away, scientists seek out the truth in whatever outcome the truth presents itself. To suggest that high-potency marijuana doesn't have the potential to inflict serious adverse effects on an adolescent's neurological and psychological development is to simply ignore the science; it's akin to dispelling human responsibility for climate change.

In my mind, we should err on the side of caution and consider adolescent marijuana use as a public health risk. Aside from the increasing mental health risks of high-potency marijuana use, the elephant in the room is the use of THC concentrates—highly purified THC-rich products such as "shatter", "wax", and "butter". These products approach 90 percent THC and in my opinion represent the "crack" of marijuana products. If you think I'm an overprotective father, YouTube "dabbing weed" and the effects of free-basing THC concentrates.[40]

Outside of adolescence, cannabis can be a safe and effective treatment for mental health disorders. Patients suffering from post-traumatic stress disorder (PTSD) have found that strains of cannabis help mitigate haunting and agonizing traumatic memories.[41] It's estimated that more than forty thousand veterans suffer from PTSD,[42] and many say that marijuana has saved their lives. The DEA has given its blessing to a study looking at the effects of medical marijuana on PTSD—the first randomized, controlled research in the United States.

Addiction

Perhaps the biggest secret about marijuana is that it is not an addictive substance. Few things will spark the ire of marijuana advocates faster than bringing up the subject of addiction. But denial is based on fear and ignorance, not science.

Although we're all susceptible to addictive behavior to some degree (e.g., sugar, caffeine, and electronic gadgets), some of us are at greater risk for addictive behaviors than others. Recent research sheds light on the importance of oxytocin in perpetuating addition. Our propensity to addiction is largely due to a combination of individual genetics, our daily stress burden (especially in childhood),[43] and how we were raised by our mothers, which has a critical impact on the density of oxytocin receptors in the brain.[44] Although the road to addiction is a complicated path that no one sets out to travel, there is growing evidence that from a genetics perspective, the behaviors of addiction start with a biochemical defect in an important neurological pathway involving reward, namely the neurotransmitter dopamine.

Dopamine is the major neurotransmitter in the brain responsible for pleasure,[45] and dopaminergic neurons are modulated by the ECS.[46] Dopamine is critical in the regulation of the expression of reward, which is perceived as pleasure. With the exception of the LSD and mescaline-like hallucinogens, the single pharmacological property that all addictive drugs share is the stimulation of the dopamine receptor and the drug's ability to enhance dopamine levels in the brain.

Individuals with highly addictive, drug-seeking behavior have been shown to possess a pathological flaw surrounding the dopamine-synthesizing enzyme, tyrosine hydroxylase, found within the dopamine axons of the brain's reward circuitry, an anatomical place called the striatum.[47] In essence, drug abuse is regulated by dopamine levels in the striatum. A person feeding a drug addiction does so unconsciously to elevate levels of dopamine within the reward center in order to maintain a certain pleasurable effect.

The science of genetics has exploded in the last twenty years. A powerful factor influencing genetic expression is called epigenetics—the science of the changes that take place in DNA expression after birth. These changes can permanently modify DNA. Epigenetic changes represent a change in phenotype (how the gene is expressed; e.g., eye color) without a change in genotype (the actual DNA nucleotide sequence for eye color), which affects how the cell's transcriptional machinery actually reads the genetic information.

It's been clearly shown that drugs (both recreational and pharmaceutical) and chemical toxins can have long-term and even generational impacts on the individual and their offspring. The classic example is the drug diethylstilbestrol (DES) which was prescribed to pregnant woman between 1940 and 1971 to prevent miscarriage and premature labor. DES was later linked to the incidence of clear-cell carcinoma of the cervix in the offspring of mothers exposed to the drug.[48]

Epigenetic changes in adolescent rats exposed to marijuana enhance morphine-induced sensitization, demonstrating physiological alterations associated with reward and stress in first-generation female offspring.[49] Additionally, there is an association between THC, nicotine, and opiates in inducing *narp* gene expression in drug withdrawal.[50] The *narp* gene encodes a secreted protein seen during drug withdrawal. Chronic THC use causes an increase in *narp* encoding.[51]

An understanding of the biologically essential nature of the functioning of these reward circuits gives rise to the notion that addictive drugs "hijack" the brain's reward circuits. The theory suggests that addictive drugs activate these reward circuits more strongly than natural rewards, thereby diverting the addict's life to the pursuit of drug-induced pleasure at the expense of the normal pleasures and rewards one would obtain in an otherwise drug-free life.[52]

The rat model for addiction also demonstrated clear neurobiological adaptations to addiction, showing that adolescent THC exposure contributed to opiate vulnerability in adulthood.[53] Not unlike other drugs of abuse, marijuana stimulates the brain's dopamine signaling apparatus, with studies confirming that THC increases dopamine levels in the striatum.[54] This pharmacological mechanism of THC stimulating dopamine release within the addiction centers of the striatum suggests that marijuana, especially in the form of THC concentrates, puts individuals susceptible to addiction at risk.[55] In addition, THC, like heroin, increases dopamine levels by exerting similar effects through a common mu-1 opioid receptor mechanism located in a different part of the striatum.[56]

I remember growing up and being told that marijuana wasn't addictive. Back then, most of the research about marijuana and addiction was pretty soft. The conclusions were based on data using marijuana considered anemic compared to today's standards. Currently, marijuana plants are being bred to produce THC concentrations at over 30 percent, and marijuana concentrates can contain THC levels as high as 90 percent.[57]

Studies suggest that the higher the concentration of THC, the greater the incidence for abuse and for adverse side effects, with one study citing an 8 percent rate of dependency with chronic marijuana users, while alcohol dependency was reported at 12 to 13 percent and cocaine dependency at 15 to 16 percent. College students using butane hash oil, a type of marijuana concentrate, show a higher rate of cannabis abuse.[58] The DSM-5, the mental health care "bible" of disorder classifications, considers chronic marijuana use as cannabis use disorder (CUD),[59] although I prefer the terminology marijuana use disorder (MUD), so as to not impugn those using high-CBD strains of cannabis.

If the truth really sets us free, then we should try to look at the issue of marijuana addiction objectively.

Cardiovascular

I distinctly remember the day I stumbled upon the article that profoundly changed my opinion of cannabis as a medicine. I was doing a PubMed search and came across the Durst article.[60] In this landmark study, researchers led by Dr. Ronan Durst induced a heart attack, also called an acute myocardial infarction (AMI), in two groups of rats; one was given CBD, while the other group received placebo. The results were nothing short of astounding. Durst's study showed a 66 percent reduction in the infarct size between the CBD-treated rats versus the placebo group.

The study was an epiphany. Heart disease is the number one killer in the United States—one in four Americans die from cardiovascular disease. From my perspective as an emergency physician, decreasing the morbidity and mortality of an AMI by two-thirds would be as revolutionary a treatment modality as the introduction of the clot-busting drugs known as thrombolytics. Interestingly, the clinical success of thrombolytics ushered in the biotech revolution. It seems reasonable that cannabinoid therapeutics could be the next revolution in health care.

Neurology

People with seizure disorders are trapped in a world of uncertainty. Most epileptics have little warning about what will trigger their next seizure, or when it will happen. Oftentimes epileptics have recurrent seizures because of their noncompliance with pharmaceutical epileptic medicines that often have troublesome side effects.

Dravet syndrome and Unverricht-Lundborg disease are rare and severe forms of pediatric epilepsy that cannot be controlled by conventional medications. Children suffering from these disorders often have hundreds of seizures a day.[61] A CBD strain named Charlotte's Web is currently being tested at several medical centers across the United States, including Stanford and Columbia.

The FDA has granted Orphan Drug Designation (ODD) to a highly purified extract of CBD called epidiolex.[62] The ODD arose from the Orphan Drug Act and provides special status to a drug or biological product ["drug"] to treat a rare disease or condition. Cannabis has been used to treat certain types of seizure disorders just as effectively as pharmaceuticals, minus the uncomfortable side effects.

Medical cannabis has also shown great promise in the treatment of one of the most devastating neurologic conditions known—stroke or cerebral vascular accident (CVA). Once a CVA occurs, the best hope for recovery is mitigating the ischemic damage to the brain. As with heart attacks, CBD has been shown to decrease the postinflammatory/ischemic changes that occur as the result of an acute stroke.[63] Cannabis can also minimize the long-term damage caused by traumatic brain injury.[64]

Sleep is an essential component to good health. Sixty percent of Americans report occasional insomnia. Cannabis use has a positive effect in promoting sleep.[65] Of all the stories that patients volunteered during my clinic time in Montana, I would estimate that 80 percent talked about how marijuana helped give them their best sleep in years.

Not coincidentally, the hallmark symptom of marijuana withdrawal is insomnia.

Ophthalmology

Millions of people suffer from diabetic retinopathy—a progressive microvascular disease of the retina, the focal point of vision in the eye. Eighty percent of all long-term diabetics develop diabetic retinopathy. It is the leading cause of blindness in people ages twenty to sixty-four.

Macular degeneration is the leading cause of blindness in adults older than the age of fifty. The administration of CBD as an ophthalmologic drop has been shown to significantly decrease the damaging effects of both macular degeneration and diabetic retinopathy.[66, 67]

Pregnancy

Pregnancy is a revered state of being.

How many women do you know that become fanatical about their lifestyle and diet when they discover they are pregnant? The most devoted mothers-to-be give up coffee, cigarettes, alcohol, and drugs (including marijuana). They dedicate themselves to eating a better diet, exercising, and trying to positively maximize the environment of the life growing inside of them.

But some women ignore this maternal impulse.

From the moment of conception, when a mother's DNA fuses with a father's DNA, creating a single-celled fertilized egg known as a zygote, until birth, when the child emerges into the outside world as one of the most complex multicellular organisms on the planet, the human infant undergoes an enormously intricate and labyrinthine development. At no point in your life are you more vulnerable (and more protected) than when you are in the dark, warm, liquid confines of your mother's uterus—a place doctors call in utero. The developing fetus is utterly dependent on the mother to provide a safe and stable environment for its growth and development. In many respects, the fetus's world is a mirror of the mother's; it's well-accepted that a multitude of maternal factors, like pharmaceutical medicines, drugs, toxins, stress, and nutrition, impact the normal embryological development of the fetus.

According to the Frameworks Institute, the early years of life matter because early experiences affect the architecture of the maturing brain. The quality of an individual's neurological architecture, all the billions of neurons and the subsequent trillions of possible synaptic connections with each other, establishes either a sturdy or a fragile foundation for the future development and behavior of each and every child.[68]

The use of high-potency marijuana (especially THC concentrates) directly impacts and changes the ECS.[69, 70] In animal models, prenatal exposure to THC permanently changes the cortical circuity of the brain.[71, 72] Just what those changes represent in the long term we can only speculate, as scientists are only now beginning to look at THC's long-lasting consequences on the adult children of mothers who used marijuana during their pregnancy. We are beginning to understand how prenatal exposure to THC stimulating the embryonic CB-1 receptors has a profound effect on the developing brain and CNS.[73] I've heard mothers say that they used marijuana throughout their pregnancy and feel that their kids are fine.

But do we *really* know for sure?

The data suggests that a child has a better opportunity to be brighter, more attentive, less susceptible to depression, anxiety, psychosis, cognitive deficits, and addictions if they are not exposed to prenatal marijuana.[74] THC is neurotoxic in areas of the brain rich in CB-1 receptors—areas of the brain like the hippocampus (memory, learning, and emotion), the amygdala (emotions, emotional behavior, and motivation), striatum (which coordinates multiple aspects of cognition, including motor and action planning, decision-making, motivation, reinforcement, and reward perception), and the prefrontal cortex (physiologic constructs of memory, perception, and diverse cognitive processes).[75, 76]

Marijuana use has also been shown to be an independent risk factor for pre-term labor. Continued use through twenty weeks gestation is independently associated with a fivefold increase in the risk of pre-term birth.[77]

Prenatal exposure to THC affects the genetic information of the unborn child. Perhaps the most alarming data regarding the epigenetic effect of marijuana use suggests an increased incidence of acute non-lymphoblastic leukemia (ANLL),[78] and neuroblastoma,[79] reminiscent of the transgenerational epigenetic cancer risk seen with DES.[80] This data suggests that the prenatal use of marijuana may carry significant risks of morbidity to the offspring. Obviously, more research is needed to elucidate the true risks of prenatal marijuana exposure.

It's been well demonstrated that women ingesting substances such as alcohol, opiates, and even pharmaceutical medicines like thalidomide are directly responsible for such neonatal morbidity as fetal alcohol syndrome, drug withdrawal, and phocomelia (limb malformations). Due to governmental restrictions in cannabis research, we remain ignorant of the full scope of effects that THC has on the prenatally exposed child.

And finally, in response to marijuana use during breastfeeding, a 2018 study notes that THC was found in breast milk up to six days after the mother's last use, while CBD was not reported to be detected.[81] The study indicates that others who use marijuana during breastfeeding expose their infants to the potential toxicity of THC.

Pain Management

By far, most of the patients I evaluated in my WH&H practice suffered from chronic pain. I found many articles supporting the use of cannabis in the treatment of chronic pain.[82, 83] Of the hundreds of patients I evaluated, some stated that cannabis took their pain completely away, while most stated that using cannabis was a pleasant distraction from the nagging burden of their chronic pain problem.

After two decades of working in the ED, I've seen plenty of pain. Each patient's pain perception is unique. Pain is complex; it can be psychic, traumatic, thermal, emotional, physical, mental, burning, sharp and stabbing, gnawing, squeezing, unbearable, piercing, unrelenting, soul bending, and spiritual. Pain is relative and complicated. At a pain conference, one lecturer reported that up to 85 percent of women with chronic pain were abused as children.[84]

In the context of pain, the body remembers what the mind forgets. And the use of cannabis for pain management is about permissive forgetting.

Thus, after months of reading the medical literature, I committed myself to change the public's grossly misinformed perception of medical marijuana. During the summer of 2009, found the mind-set of the growers and caregiver community was focused on THC and producing the most potent marijuana possible. When I mentioned CBD, I uniformly got a blank look. Then, when I suggested that the real market for medical marijuana would be in growing CBD-rich strains, people looked at me like I was from outer space.

My research had turned me on to something I thought was really important and potentially game-changing. When I graduated from the Medical College of Georgia, I took the Hippocratic oath. For me to stay silent about the medical benefits of cannabis was to be complicit with a medical establishment not willing to look objectively at the benefits that medical marijuana could provide to millions.

I felt that the first step toward changing that antiquated mindset and breaking the silence was to start a lab.

The Lab

It was evident to me that if medical marijuana had any chance of becoming accepted by other physicians, there needed to be a reliable element of quality control. Few physicians (outside of California) were going to embrace the "take two hits and call me in the morning" approach to cannabis use.

For the seven years I spent in medical school and residency training, I subjected myself to the dogma of American medical doctrine. I was taught to believe in the religion of empiricism; simply put, if we can't see it, feel it, define, or measure it in some concrete way, it simply doesn't exist.

Doctors are trained to love data—quantifiable and tangible information. Doctors love numbers, especially when they amount to points on a graph that suggests a predictable trend. Those numbers can be any of the innumerable things that we can measure in our patients, like weight, hemoglobin concentration, serum cholesterol, or the number of milligrams of a drug in a pill. Doctors need numbers to calculate dosage because that's how every physician in the United States is taught to medicate their patients. This made my idea for a medical marijuana lab dizzyingly simple. Knowing the cannabinoid content was critical to properly dose cannabis.

It was a no brainer. I needed a lab.

During my premed studies at Nebraska Wesleyan University, I earned a minor in chemistry. I loved to visualize the interaction of chemicals on a molecular level. I was mesmerized by the relationships within the periodic table of elements, although it didn't necessarily make for great conversation at fraternity parties.

One afternoon, I dusted off my copy of Fessenden and Fessenden's *Organic Chemistry* (2nd edition) and began to review the chapter on analytical methodology. Reviewing my college organic chemistry text turned up a short list of relevant isolation techniques such as thin-layer chromatography (TLC), high-pressure liquid chromatography (HPLC), gas chromatography (GC), and mass spectrometry (MS). I pondered which methods would work best for measuring cannabinoid content in cannabis; it proved to be a deep wormhole.

In the United States, all medicine, over-the-counter (OTC) and prescription, is labeled with a dosage of the active ingredient(s). Quality control is essential in the pharmaceutical industry because of patient safety concerns. Many medicines have a relatively narrow therapeutic window; if the safe dosage window is surpassed, the results could be lethal. Numerous pharmaceutical drugs like opiates, digoxin, warfarin, and even OTC medications like Tylenol, can be fatal if the maximum recommended safe dosage is exceeded.

And aside from dosing considerations, since the 1982 Tylenol tampering and the resultant seven deaths from potassium cyanide poisoning, pharmaceutical companies placed enormous emphasis on quality control, going to great lengths (e.g., child-proof bottles and shrink-wrapped containers) to keep medicine safe from contamination and criminal tampering. Physicians, as well as the general public, take great solace in trusting that the medicine is accurately dosed as labeled and unadulterated.

In 2009, at the beginning of my journey, this simply wasn't the case with medical marijuana. From my perspective it was a classic example of caveat emptor.

By early summer, I'd met enough patients, growers, and providers to know that buying cannabis was a crap-shoot. The only index of quality control was how high the "medicine" got you. But many of my patients didn't want to be high, especially the older ones who believed that cannabis could ease their chronic pain and offer them a better quality of life.

During clinic visits, when grandmothers asked me where they could buy cannabis, I felt a gnawing impotence. I had no idea where they could find cannabis that might ease their symptoms. And if I couldn't tell them, who could?

I became obsessed with the concept of cannabis quality control. I felt alienated by my groundbreaking idea that no one else seemed interested in. There was no mention of quality control in MT-148; it was a solely voluntary act. The key was convincing growers and dispensary owners that it was a necessary expense and would ultimately improve profit margins. If not, I'd be wasting my time.

Although the idea of quality control may sound boring, it's essential, especially when the product is marketed as a medicine. At its most basic level, quality control is about trust. People gravitate toward certain products and brands because they like what the product provides and trust that the quality of the product will be consistent. When you drink a Coke, you trust that it will taste the same as the Coke you had last week or last year. Nothing about medical marijuana engendered trust—other than it'd probably get you high.

Quality control is important with cannabis is because it's a plant with a myriad of strains. The cannabinoid content and potency of every cannabis plant is different unless it is cloned and grown under controlled conditions.

Cannabis can be grown from seeds or propagated as clones. Most growers prefer clones, because the genetics are identical to the "mother," plant, it's merely a rooted cutting from a stem. In contrast to a clone, a seed-germinated plant may have significant genetic variability from the "mother". This variation in the cannabinoid content and potency may be insignificant or considerable. In short, not all cannabis is the same.

It's easiest to compare cannabis to wine.

White wine varietals include such types as chardonnay, chenin blanc, French columbard, muscot, and pinot blanc, with each of these varietals having a distinctive flavor. The geographic location, the terroir, of where the grapes are grown also has an influence on the final product, as differences in micro-climate and soil ecology affect the flavor characteristics.

Similar distinctions apply to cannabis. Indica strains of cannabis include such varietals as Ice, Afghan, Skunk, Purple Kush, and Northern Lights and vary considerably in their cannabinoid and terpene potency from their sativa cousins with names like Sour Diesel, White Widow, AK 47, Blue Dream, and Jack Herer.

Similarly, the terroir for cannabis is also important. Cannabis grown in the Coastal Range of northern California (e.g., the Emerald Triangle) will be distinctive from cannabis grown in central Kansas. Furthermore, an indoor-grown Northern Lights strain grown under ideal temperature, humidity, lighting, and carbon dioxide concentration will have an increased cannabinoid potency compared to an outdoor-grown sibling subjected to the whims of Mother Nature.

Pollinated cannabis will produce seeds. For annuals, as opposed to perennials, species survival depends on seed production. Once fertilized, flower buds focus their energy to make the next generation of seeds, leaving less energy for cannabinoid production (which are thought to be a plant defense mechanism against insects). Cannabis plants are prolific seed producers that are highly prized by animals and birds due to their dense nutritional and caloric content.

Humans take a different view of cannabis. The potency (and the price) of pollinated (fertilized) cannabis is dramatically reduced, so growers take great pains to keep the female plants separate from males. Marijuana connoisseurs pay up to $500 per ounce for premium sinsemilla-grade marijuana because it is by far the most potent marijuana flos available. As the plant ripens, the unfertilized flower buds (termed sinsemilla) swell, producing robust trichomes with a higher cannabinoid content than pollinated flower buds.

From my perspective, with so many growers producing cannabis under wildly different growing conditions it was impossible to expect any reasonable type of quality continuity. Perhaps quality control wasn't an important factor in the recreational world of cannabis, but if cannabis was going to make the transition to the medicinal world, quality control was fundamental.

Quantitation of cannabinoid profiles would allow patients the opportunity to decide what strains worked best for them. For example, a strain with a 12% THC:3%CBD content would impact a patient substantially different than a 24% THC:0.5% CBD strain.

Yet, before the thick, aromatic sinsemilla buds can sell in dispensaries, the plant must first be processed. The sticky, cannabinoid-rich flower buds coalesce along the primary and secondary stems, forming large bundles of buds called colas. Once the plant is fully mature and ready for harvest, all of the accessory and fan leaves are trimmed off the colas to expose the delicate trichome-laden buds, often referred to as "nuggets." The colas are hung to dry in a cool, dark room with proper ventilation. Professionally trimmed flos requires a trimmer to have good eyes, patience, a steady hand, and a sharp pair of fine-point scissors. Because the market value of manicured flos is so high, edibles (also called cannabis-infused products, or CIPs) are made from the pounds of trim produced during the trimming process. The trimmed buds are cured in containers for roughly three weeks, with periodic "burping" of the jars. When the cannabis is fully cured, it's ready for sale.

The pharmacology of cannabinoids is dependent of how the cannabis is ingested. When cannabis is smoked or vaporized, the cannabinoids are directly absorbed through the capillary alveoli of the lungs and pass directly into the bloodstream. Inhalation bypasses the liver's metabolic machinery, termed first-pass metabolism, producing the fat-soluble compound Δ-9-THC, which is rapidly absorbed into the fatty tissue of the brain, stimulating the CB-1 receptors. Smoking marijuana produces its euphoric effects within seconds because the dose-response curve is steep. The harm of smoked marijuana is limited because individuals can only inhale so much THC before they are overcome with early symptoms of toxicity—namely, nausea, diaphoresis, palpitations, and lightheadedness.

Although the acute toxicity from THC inhalation is limited because the overall dose ingestion is relatively small, the potential for abuse is higher. Remember that dopamine is the molecule of pleasure and addiction. The higher abuse potential of inhaled high-potency marijuana (and THC concentrates) is the result of higher levels of THC binding to CB-1 receptors, releasing greater quantities of dopamine in the brain's reward center.

The issue of marijuana toxicity is very different with edibles.

Perhaps the most compelling case for dosing cannabis are CIPs. Many patients prefer ingesting cannabis in the form of edibles. CIPs take a myriad of forms, like brownies, candies, chocolates, or gummies. Eating CIPs cause the cannabinoids to be slowly absorbed through the gut and metabolized in the liver. It may take up to an hour before a patient gradually feels the effect of the cannabinoids.

Typically, toxicity from edibles or CIPs occurs in persons expecting the rapid onset of euphoria they would get with smoking. Due to the slower absorption of THC through the GI tract and a substantially less steep dose-response curve, a person won't feel the anticipated "buzz" or "high" for at least thirty to sixty minutes after consumption. Without experiencing the acute euphoria, the naïve CIPs consumer will often eat more, thinking that the product is weakly infused. This is a recipe for an unfortunate experience. Cannabinoids that are orally ingested undergo first-pass metabolism in the liver. Orally ingested THC is transformed by the P450 liver enzymes into 11-hydroxy-THC, a compound that has a longer half-life and is more psychoactive than Δ-9-THC.[85]

Having clearly labeled and dosed CIPs is essential because many cannabis bakers tend to make their products concentrated. Imagine eating several tasty cookies and not knowing they were laced with enough THC to sedate an adult elephant.

The patients I have treated in the emergency department for marijuana toxicity are there because they smoked pot laced with some contaminant (e.g., PCP, opiates, or synthetic cannabinoids) or because of a CIP overdose. Invariably, patients think they are losing their minds, experiencing symptoms of temporary psychosis that may last several hours. Or more rarely, the patient succumbs to cannabis vomiting syndrome, intractable vomiting that's not amenable to traditional antiemetics. Fortunately, acute THC toxicity is amenable to conservative treatment: a few kind words of assurance, darkened lights, a bag of Doritos, and the TV tuned to the Comedy Channel.

Having cannabis tested for cannabinoid content practically eliminates accidental THC toxicity. Without analytical testing, it's impossible to identify the strength of the oil or butter used to extract the cannabinoids from each batch of trim. Without knowledge of the cannabinoid content and concentration, the only way to know the potency of the CIP, is through trial and error.

Several local herbalists found MBA's analytical techniques a vital offering to accurately dose their cannabis products and make them safer. One of MBA's first customers was a New Jersey transplant who'd been makings herbal medicines for years. Shawn, a surfer turned herbalist, spent hours with Nigel to get the maximum effect from his tinctures and candies.

And then another invisible issue: contamination. With the exception of medical cannabis sold in the Netherlands, all cannabis is biologically contaminated—it's just a matter of the degree. Dutch cannabis is unique because they subject it to gamma irradiation[86] and, frankly speaking, zap the bejesus out of it.

On some level, all cannabis is contaminated with large populations of microorganisms. Gamma radiation is universally lethal. Nothing on the planet survives the penetrating high-energy photons emitted from a Cobalt 60 isotope-producing ionization exposure. In living cells, it irreversibly damages DNA and other cellular structures, rendering it sterile from viable mold, bacteria, spore, or viruses, without imparting radioactivity. For the average healthy individual, contamination is not an issue, but for patients undergoing chemotherapy, or who otherwise have a compromised immune system, contaminated cannabis has been shown to cause serious morbidity and even death.[87]

Gamma irradiation only ensures that the medicine is free from infectious contamination. It doesn't protect the plant from environmental contamination like heavy metals, pesticides, and herbicides. With rare exceptions, all indoor-grown cannabis is subjected to some sort of chemical/pesticide cocktail.

With no state regulations or oversight for cannabis grow operations, there was a Gaussian variation of growing techniques and operations. This creates huge variations in the quality of the cannabis being sold as medicine. I visited numerous grows; some were clean and tidy, while more often, they looked like man caves with cannabis growing among towers of empty pizza boxes and beer cans. Considering the variations of growing operations, it seemed reasonable that the lab should consider analysis for molds, pesticides, and heavy metals. Implementation would significantly increase the cost of testing.

My observations convinced me that patients deserved an objective means of choosing where they would buy their cannabis. Quantitative analysis would open the medical marijuana industry to the guiding force of quality control. Patients had the right to know what was in the medicine that was costing them up to $300/ounce.

A Logic Vacuum

Since my journey into the world of medical marijuana began, one thing that seemed consistent was the lack of logic surrounding most matters associated with the plant. It was as if the plant, and everything associated with it was lost in a logic vacuum.

Perhaps the most striking example of this vacuum is the indifference shown by the Nobel Prize selection committee in recognizing the sentinel breakthrough of cannabinoid science. Dr. Raphael Mechoulam, the godfather of medical cannabis, cracked one of the most elusive mysteries in biology in 1964 when Drs. Mechoulam and Yechiel Gaoni at Israel's Weizmann Institute of Science finally isolated the psychoactive cannabinoid molecule in cannabis, THC[88] (a mere 150 years after the discovery of morphine). A few years later, they then elucidated the structure of CBD, as well.

After the discovery of the first cannabinoid receptor in 1989, Mechoulam's team discovered the first endogenous cannabinoid in 1992, a molecule he named anandamide, from the Sanskrit word *ananda*, meaning "sacred bliss." Armed with the knowledge of cannabinoid receptors and the discovery of anandamide, scientists began in earnest to study the role of the ECS, one of the most important discoveries in biology in the past hundred years, began in earnest.

While researching the medical literature, I was astonished to learn the untold potential medical benefits associated with the cannabinoids of cannabis. I discovered GW Pharmaceuticals, an English company licensing Sativex, a cannabis extract with 1:1 ration of THC to CBD for the treatment of the muscle spasticity in multiple sclerosis. Another GW Pharma drug, Epidiolex, a purified form of CBD, received FDA approval in June 2018 for the treatment of two rare, serious childhood epilepsy syndromes—Lennox-Gastaut and Dravet.

Under the Controlled Substance Act (CSA) of 1970,[89] the US government has categorized *every* cannabinoid found in cannabis as a Schedule I substance. Schedule I substances are considered dangerous, without medical benefit, and are forbidden from being prescribed by physicians. Yet opiates, painkillers that were responsible for more than seventy-thousand American deaths in 2018, are listed as Schedule II substances and are readily prescribed by doctors. Additionally, because of its Schedule I designation, all benchtop and clinical research of cannabis products are strictly regulated. As a consequence, scientific investigation into the properties of cannabinoids have been stymied. Despite a mass of scientific evidence strongly suggesting cannabis is an enormously beneficial plant to the contrary, we remain locked in a political cold war mentality with this hardy angiosperm.

Still, the cannabis logic vacuum deepens. The following detail should silence all critics. Despite the DEA's assertion that cannabis has no medicinal value, the US Department of Health & Human Services filed for a patent for the use of CBD as a neuro-protectant agent on February 1, 2001, and on October 7, 2003, patent #6,630,507 was issued.[90]

Yet, with the yin, so come the yang; cannabis has a dark side.

I attended an herbal medicine conference outside of Asheville a few years ago. I spoke with David Winston, a renowned Native American herbalist (fluent in Cherokee). When I asked him about cannabis, his lips tightened. "The Cherokee regarded the plant as deceptive. They felt its medicine was too strong, too unpredictable."

"Really."

Slowly, he shook his head. "They just didn't trust it."

That remark ruminated with me for a long time. How could an entire culture not trust a plant? Cannabis is a beautiful plant; it's easy to grow and has lots of benefits. But now I think I understand why the Cherokee felt this way about marijuana. THC can change your reality; it can bring bliss into your bliss-less world, but it can also falsely distort your perception of realism.

I have friends that call marijuana the "great enhancer." It augments the sensory experiences of sound, sight, touch, and taste. If you don't believe me, try listening to Pink Floyd's *Dark Side of the Moon* after a few hits (or brownie bites) of a hardy sativa strain.

But for those vulnerable to its seduction, marijuana can be a hook subtlety wrapping itself into the life of the user like a tenacious vine. During my time in Montana, there were numerous patients and growers I knew that embraced the "wake and bake" approach to marijuana use, yet none of them felt like they had a problem with marijuana dependence or addiction.

Of course, the rub is that humans have been seeking ways to alter their consciousness since the dawn of time. We alter our respective reality (and brain chemistry) with substances that are legal like alcohol, prescription opiates, and tobacco, as well as a host of other illegal substances like cocaine, LSD, psilocybin, and street opiates like heroin.

I sought to be a proponent of cannabis. I wanted people to know that it could be just as important medicinally as it has been recreationally. I wanted to join the growing chorus of advocates attempting to dispel the notion that this plant is diabolical.

The Slow Kid Gets Eaten

Summer in Bozeman is a warm weather paradise. It's clear why it's consistently listed as one of the best places in the country to live by *Outside Magazine*. Hillari scheduled my summer clinic so she could take long lunches to run errands and check on her young son, Kia. The ninety-minute block was perfect to take a bike ride.

When I began making regular trips to Bozeman I bought a used yellow and charcoal LeMond Buenes Aires road bike. After spending the morning seeing patients, I'd cycle north, up into the windy expanse of Bridger Canyon. On my bike, I didn't have a care in the world. Descending back into town, I eagerly anticipated my afternoon clinic, mellow folks looking to me to allow them to use cannabis legally. I didn't miss the relentless grind of the ED one bit.

One particular bluebird afternoon, as I pedaled out of town, I was oozing joy. I felt moved to call my son's mother, telling her I was enjoying the coolest day of work in my life.

"That's lovely, Michael, but I'm up to my knickers in work. I can't talk. Goodbye."

The silence at the other end of the line was deafening. The contrast between my newfound bliss and her antipathy characterized our decade-long relationship. In spite of our best efforts we'd lost the ability to align with each other, my hot was her cold, her black was my white. I clung to an imagined strand of hope that something more still connected us besides our son. She was the only person who could truly understand my transformation and I wanted her to know. Her brevity was a painful reminder that she really didn't care. Although the heaviness didn't last long, it marred an otherwise perfect day.

The ride past Bridger Bowl is a cyclists' delight. The snow was still clinging onto the Bridger's peaks and craggy north faces. The vegetation gradually shifted from scrub grass and Ponderosa Pine to sloping fields of Black Cottonwoods and Douglass Fir. The alpine transition began at about 6,200 feet, just below Battle Ridge Pass, where the road disappears into the upper Bridger range toward White Sulphur Springs. As I made my way to the apex, I marveled at the handiwork of the muskrat and beaver, stalling the lazy creek that wound its way through the high-elevation patches of Choke Cherry, Quaking Aspen, and Box Elder.

For years, I'd felt my life leaking out of me. Now I was infused with joy, thrilled by the success of WH&H and blessed to have a part-time medical practice in a vibrant Montana mountain community. Bozeman had once been a sleepy cow town, but now it was catering to the wealthy elite and the commoner, the logger and the tree hugger, the redneck Republicans and the bleeding-heart Democrats. I loved being there.

I wanted to fit in. Find my tribe. I wanted my own place, and buying a house was something that would connect me deeper into the Bozeman community. Lori scolded me about being so impetuous.

"Why do you want to be burdened with a second mortgage payment, Michael? Medical marijuana on this scale is brand new. This could all fall apart tomorrow. Why don't you wait and see how things play out?" She pleaded a version of the same story every time I told her about a house I was considering purchasing.

I was torn. I knew Lori was right, but I thought that if I had a house in a nice neighborhood, maybe my son and his mother would move here. If she could see a significant period of stability regarding the business maybe we could patch things up and be a family again. It was a chaotic period. I look back now, and my head still swirls.

When I was back in New York I spent as much time as I could with Jacob. When I was away, I called him daily. I tried not to look at the world in absolute terms. Relativism provided my excuse for my absence.

Dads had to work.

I thought of the sacrifice that service members make when they're deployed. Mothers and fathers are separated from their families for long periods of a time, sometimes well over a year. I was gone eight to twelve days a month. It seemed like a reasonable compromise.

The vibrancy of those early summer days in Bozeman provided a scenic backdrop for all sorts of ideas to surface. My naturopathic friend Jerry Taylor and I mulled over my grand idea, a health cooperative that would be funded primarily by revenues generated by a medical marijuana dispensary, but we couldn't find an affordable space. I kept the concept of a cannabis-based health cooperative in the back of my mind.

Jacob spent the first part of his summer vacation with me. I thought exploring Western Montana would make for a great trip. Fascinated with airplanes since he was a toddler, he was as excited about flying on a Boing-777 as he was about camping in the Montana Rockies.

The first leg of our vacation was a long weekend of canoeing, camping, and fishing with Jerry and his kids on the Missouri River, paddling through the Gates of the Mountains section of Holter Lake, north of Helena. Jacob had a blast playing with Jerry's kids, and it was great hanging out and feeling like a part of their family. Sunday afternoon we said our good-byes and drove up to one of my favorite places, Glacier National Park. We made it to West Glacier with a couple of hours of light left, so we did the logical thing after a long tiring journey; we got ice cream.

Within minutes of entering the West Glacier entrance of the park, I noticed a line of cars up ahead. "Hey bud, check it out."

In the rear-view mirror I could see his attention shift from his dripping chocolate cone.

We slowed down, and I asked a bystander what was going on.

"Grizzly sow and her cubs walking along the shore. Stay in your car," the tourist warned.

Jacob's eyes widened.

"You want to see a grizzly bear, bud?"

"We're not going to get too close, are we, Daddy?"

"Absolutely not."

"OK! Let's go see them, Dad."

I pulled off the road to the opposite side of where the foot traffic had congregated. I told Jacob not to close his car door in case we needed to get back into the car in a hurry.

"Are you serious, Daddy?"

"We're just being extra cautious. It'll be fine."

As we walked across the road, more than a hundred people were lining the side, staring and pointing down to the bears who were sauntering along the pebble-strewn shore of Lake McDonald. The parked tour buses were loaded with retirees. The youngest person in the crowd couldn't have been any younger than seventy.

"Hey, Dad, do you think the bears will want my ice cream?"

"Maybe Bud. But I don't think you'll have to worry about the bears."

Jacob looked up at me, between licks, "Why's that, Daddy?"

"Look at the folks around us."

Jacob scanned the parade of geriatric onlookers and giggled. One of our favorite TV shows was the BBC's *Walking with Dinosaurs*, so the connection was apparent. "The slow kid gets eaten, right Dad?"

"Absolutely, Bud." We both laughed.

Jacob and I had a great time hiking and car camping throughout the park. Aside from the grizzlies, we saw bighorn sheep, mountain goats, and moose. Every evening we cooked by the fire and finished the night with s'mores. It was a trip I hoped he'd never forget.

Another notable event that summer of 2009 was the growth of the clinics, both in Bozeman and with Pam's clinic in Missoula. Even as the MCN carnival clinics grew, I stayed determined that WH&H would maintain its professional integrity. Medical marijuana was not a scam, although the media feed to the general public certainly painted a different picture. Sensing the coming political storm clouds of the MCN carnivals stiffened my conviction to be a patient advocate.

My clinic model was simple: Do the right thing. Every patient had their vital signs measured, with their pulse rate, blood pressure, pulse oximetry reading, and weight recorded on the chart. Once the patient had finished filling out the health assessment forms, they received a thirty-minute appointment. Spouses or significant others were welcomed, and appointments often ran longer than scheduled. My routine was to review the patient's records (many of them bulging with documentation), query their medical history, and then perform a modest physical exam. Most of the patients had been illegally using cannabis for years. Without fail, they said cannabis had changed their lives, making their pain or disability more manageable. Cannabis kept them happier.

Losing Bud

When I wasn't in Montana, I was working six to eight shifts a month in the ED at a cozy bedroom community hospital about an hour northwest of New York City. My days off were spent trying to catch up on being a dad and coaching little league. I also tried to keep up with the seasonal needs of the farm: tending the garden, mowing the grass, and gathering wood for the winter. It all took time. As summer turned to fall, and with winter just a few months away, another variable presented itself: what to do with the dogs?

Leftover from our original pack of thirteen, Alex, Bud, Bart, and Barney were living with me when I started my Montana adventure. Alex was a black-and-white patched Brittany Spaniel/Retriever mix and the sole female. Bud was my canine soulmate—a sleek black lab-malamute mix who jealously demanded my attention. Bart was a nearsighted bulldog and lab combo who loved gliding down the snowy hill behind my house, paws up as he snaked his spine back and forth, effectively scratching his back on the carpet of icy crystals beneath. Barney was the smallest of the group, a Chow-Keeshond mix who was glad to be part of the pack. Alex was the senior member and wanted to just lie in the sun, not to be pestered by the antics of "the boys".

At first, my neighbor would care for the dogs. A lifelong farm boy who came back to upstate New York after a stint in the Army, Rick was a stout man who built a modest home just down the road from me. A sheriff's deputy and a Pentecostal minister, he taught me the way of being a good neighbor. Rick had been a confidant during my divorce and became the latest of several surrogate fathers I'd adopted throughout my life. As nice as Rick was, once winter rolled in, I would have to find someone else to care for them.

Dogs infiltrate my earliest memories. I love them. When I was a kid we always had a dog, yet I couldn't understand why we couldn't keep them longer. Without reason, my dad would always get rid of it. It was sad, but it seemed that running free on a farm seemed a better life than being chained to the dog house in the back yard. Fortunately, it didn't occur to me until much later just what "taking it to the farm" really meant. Then, sometime later, we'd get another one. For continuity's sake, they all had the same name, Cookie. We stopped at Cookie VI.

My sister gave me a dog when I left for my junior year of college. Honey was a German Shepherd/Collie mix that went everywhere with me. When I finished my residency and bought my first house, I went to the local shelter with a friend and proceeded to find her a friend. I just felt a connection with some of them. I could feel them speaking. "Pick me!"

When my wife left with my son, there were 13 dogs, a cat, 10 goats, and a flock of chickens. I was overwhelmed. Downsizing was a survival necessity. With the exception of Alex, Bud, Bart, and Barney, I placed all the animals in good homes. Alone with my remnant pack, my depression grew. The dogs tried to help, nudging me affectionately, but my tank was empty, I barely had energy for myself.

Chasing my Montana dream shifted something deep inside me. I felt a glimmer of hope that this journey would free me from the chains of my isolation and years of gloom. Then one afternoon I came in from the garden and noticed Bud didn't seem himself. Always eager to go outside, he'd not only learned how to let himself out the back door, he also was big enough to scratch at the door handle and let himself in. I wished he'd learned to have shut the door, though. He seemed fine in the morning, however now he was lethargic. I had to help him up off the floor, and when I did he couldn't stand by himself. His nose was warm and dry, his breathing was weak and rapid.

I knelt down beside him.

"What's the matter, Bud?"

His eyes rolled to meet mine. Bud's chocolate brown eyes had turned to a pasty faded yellow. He was jaundiced. I knew my pal was really sick. I got the phone book out to find a vet that was open on a Saturday.

I carried him to my car and laid him carefully on a blanket.

Although I wasn't a vet, I knew that Bud was in a really bad way. I drove to my son's house on the way to the vet. I thought he'd want to say goodbye. Jacob and I both cried. His mother suggested that if I ever took the dogs for checkups this could have been avoided.

I held Bud's head in my lap as he limply laid across the stainless-steel exam table. We waited for the vet to see us. As I rubbed his favorite spot behind his ears, his breathing suddenly became erratic as his entire body tensed and quivered. And then he was gone.

The vet came in and offered her condolences. I was mute. Then she gave me a $350 bill.

Afterwards, my son's mother agreed to let the remaining dogs stay with her and Jacob. On one level, it was a relief that they were gone, but for months I could hear their barking when I pulled into my garage, the eerie silence was haunting.

What's a Business Plan?

I was a reporter for the school newspaper in both high school and college, so I knew how to dig for information. As I mulled over the idea of an analytical cannabis lab, I wondered if there were other such labs in the United States. Then Providence prevailed. Making my way through the Minneapolis–St. Paul airport to my connecting flight to Bozeman, I caught sight of a provocative magazine cover. There, on the September 2009 cover of *Fortune*, was a lovely Mary Louise Parker, clad in a white T-shirt emblazoned by a cannabis leaf, with the tagline, *Is pot already legal?*[91]

Eagerly, I read the fascinating story of Steve DeAngelo, the hippie canna-glam guy, and the face of Harborside Dispensary in Oakland. The article detailed his innovative medical marijuana dispensary and made mention of the lab used to test the cannabis he was selling. I took a shot in the dark and sent him a message on Facebook.

To my considerable surprise, Mr. DeAngelo responded. Being at the forefront of the California marijuana industry, Mr. DeAngelo was a busy guy. He referred me to his cordial assistant who politely informed that I'd have thirty minutes of his time and wouldn't be permitted to ask questions that weren't submitted beforehand.

Hearing from Mr. DeAngelo was the latest in a series of epic changes. I was bordering on disbelief by the doors that were opening to me, doors I didn't even know existed six months prior; all since I began this fortuitous botanical adventure.

Intuitively, I wondered about the need for legal advice in opening a cannabis lab. My accountant (also an attorney) recommended an intellectual property attorney. Devin Morgan had recently moved into the area from Baltimore. I made an appointment.

On a breezy September afternoon, we met for lunch. Devin is a good-natured soul with a razor-sharp acumen and a sense of humor that belied his profession. His boyish looks and easy smile put me at ease as I outlined my idea. After listening patiently, he systematically dissected my proposal and got right to the point.

"As best as I can tell, working with cannabis, in any form, is illegal under federal statute, and you risk losing everything at any time."

"Really?" I frowned.

Devin nodded. "Absolutely. Now, how about business insurance?"

There was a brief pause. "I hadn't thought of that."

"Municipal and state permits and licenses?"

"Umm...I guess I hadn't thought of that, either."

"How about a budget?"

I shook my head.

"And what about a business plan?"

Silence. I was an idea guy. I took a single business class in college—Economics 101. I carefully weighed my next comment.

"What's a business plan?"

Devin clasped his hands and smiled. He discussed the value of a business plan. He said that great ideas are a dime a dozen; as common as guitar players in Nashville. Devin made the point that unless the idea is nurtured, cultivated, and harvested, it's as worthless as watching reruns of *Jerry Springer*. He agreed to take me on as a client. Although I didn't appreciate it immediately, Devin was there to protect me—setting up all the contracts, reviewing all the legal documents, and imparting a realistic perspective of the virgin ground I was plowing. He understood the countless complexities a start-up company represented and appreciated that entrepreneurs were cut from a different cloth.

Over the next several years, we met monthly at his home and discussed the endless challenges I faced trying to carve out my niche in the medical marijuana industry.

Looking for Arno

After months of combing through PubMed, it was clear that THC was simply the tip of the iceberg. Cannabis had several other cannabinoids that also offered significant medicinal potential. Like every explorer and scientist who dreams of making a groundbreaking discovery, the allure of finding a rare strain, rich in some novel cannabinoid, tugged at me like gravity on Jupiter.

The universe repeated its mantra. I needed a lab.

From my research, it seemed that the most effective method for cannabinoid analysis would be HPLC. But I was a physician, not a chemist, I needed validation.

I called a few large analytical chemistry labs like Quest and LabCorp, asking if they performed cannabinoid analysis. Several of the sales representatives had never heard of cannabinoids. One rep said his company would need to look into the legality of testing medical marijuana. Within a week I received the follow-up call.

"Dr. Geci, our company would be happy to do the testing, but it will be a little pricey."

"Hmmm. How much is a 'little pricey'?"

"A thousand dollars per sample, sir."

"One thousand dollars? Per sample?"

"Yes sir, that's the number," he said hesitantly.

No one would pay that kind of fee—even if they were flush with marijuana money. Frustrated by the lack of information I was able to glean from traditional chemical wholesalers, manufacturers, and labs, I began writing to principle authors of research papers published in the area of cannabinoid analytical chemistry.

One afternoon, my heart began to race when I noticed an email from Leiden University, in the Netherlands.

Dear Michael,
This may be your lucky day...

Justin Fishdick was an American graduate student working on his doctorate in chemistry. His particular interest in cannabinoid analysis earned him a place into the laboratory of Dr. Arno Hazekamp, one of the world's leading authorities on cannabinoid analysis. Justin told me he it would be a few more years until he finished his Ph.D. Kindly, he offered to put me in contact with his boss.

I was stoked.

I had come across Dr. Hazekamp's work in numerous papers. Finding someone who could hook me up with him was a fantastic stroke of luck. I'd been to Amsterdam a few times and knew firsthand about the coffeehouse culture. No country has had as tolerant a policy toward cannabis as the Netherlands. It was a no brainer. Fifty years ago, if you wanted to learn about wine, you went to France. If you wanted to learn about cannabis, you asked the Dutch.

Without delay, I wrote him an email.

Arno, as he is affectionately known within the cannabis world, turned out to be a likable beanstalk, emanating warmth and kindness. He's the poster child of a genius-nerd, having maintained a remarkably clean reputation navigating within the midst of hoodlums and paranoid capitalists that dominate the cannabis industry. Arno has worked within the Alice-in-Wonderland world of medical cannabis since 2001. By his own acknowledgment, he is the leading authority on the chemical analysis of cannabinoids. Arno and I wrote back and forth. He told me that he came to the United States several times a year to visit his girlfriend (now his ex-wife) living in California and said he would be happy to help me.

Several considerations delineated my decisions regarding the lab. First, I didn't want to perform the chemical analyses myself. I'm a doctor, I take care of patients, I wasn't interested in learning to be an analytical chemist, too. I needed a chemist who would embrace the challenge and potential of my idea.

Secondly, I clung to my commitment to ensuring that my laboratory would be the gold standard for the industry, at least in the United States. My lab would be a world-class facility, scrupulous and beyond reproach. I couldn't settle for anything less.

As fall deepened, my professional relationship with Arno inspired a deeper friendship and trust. Arno described himself as a lone wolf in the wild, who, for years, had been calling for the standardization and implementation of quality control testing with all cannabis products.

Anticipating that all the pieces for the lab would eventually fall into place, I invited Arno to Bozeman to help set up the lab. He was eager to give a guest lecture at Montana State University (MSU). Leveraging a partnership with the university would be a terrific asset, capping the wild idea that I had to make Bozeman the medical marijuana research center of the United States.

Finding Arno changed everything. He was the academic VIP that would give my lab credibility. The pieces of the puzzle were coming together.

Now I was ready to find my chemist.

An Ad For a Chemist

It was clear what I needed.

Aside from buying the equipment, the most critical ingredient for the lab was finding the right chemist. I wanted a stable partner to help me navigate through the murky waters of the medical marijuana industry. Finally, one September night while I sat at home and pondered my next step, I rode a breeze of inspiration. I went to Craigslist, opened an account, and penned an ad for a chemist.

The ad was brief:

Chemist needed for start-up botanical analysis laboratory: Minimum educational requirements of a MS in chemistry, with a doctorate degree preferred. Focus will be on cannabinoid analysis.

My first response came within hours. A young man said he took a year of chemistry in high school and really liked plants.

Really? Did you even read the ad?

It was days before anyone who was a legitimate chemist replied. There were a lot of people who wanted to be chemists, though, with several responders assuring me that they were "quick learners." Within a week I had accumulated enough responses that I could begin to cull out the wheat from the chaff. After reading them over, I resonated with one.

Hello,

My name is Nigel Plumer. I am an analytical chemist focused on soil chemistry. I am proficient with analytical instrumentation and techniques and understand how cannabinoids (and their derivatives) need to be qualified and quantified.

Techniques that I have used that I would consider applicable to your needs would include HPLC, GC, TLC, spectroscopic techniques (UV/Vis and IR), and other colorimetric techniques

documented throughout the literature. I find this type of work fascinating and would be excited to discuss further opportunities.
Best,
Nigel

Nigel had everything I needed. I wrote him.

Our fit was instantaneous and powerful. Nigel and I began to email each other several times a day. Coincidentally, he'd accepted a two-year National Science Foundation postdoctoral fellowship at MSU at the beginning of January. Nigel would be working with the acclaimed Antarctic climate scientist Dr. John Priscu. Not surprisingly, Plumer had been selected from a very competitive list of highly qualified postdoctoral candidates.

Nigel and I shared our respective dreams for the lab. His game-day enthusiasm was inspiring. Most impressively, even before I formally hired him, Nigel dug right in. He sensed our collaborative energy, too.

Nigel formally interviewed the next time I was in Bozeman. We met at the co-op for breakfast. When he topped the stairs and walked toward my table, Nigel could have been mistaken as a local Bridger ski bum with his scruffy red hair and beard, rather than a recent doctoral laureate from the University of Idaho. I chuckled. There was no mistaking his contagious exuberance, speaking in short measured bursts, and maybe what I liked most about him was his keen, sardonic wit.

Since we were in Bozeman, the crux of our interview was the thirty-four-mile loop past Bridger Bowl up to Battle Run Pass. Nigel said he hadn't ridden this distance in a couple of years but was certainly up for the challenge. I'd been cycling seriously for over a decade. In 2004, less nine months since I'd had the dream about being a slug and getting back on my bike after over a decade, I raced in the Etape de Tour, the largest international cycling race in the world. The Etape takes place on the first rest stage of the Tour de France. The year I raced, I was in the best shape of my life; riding the 147.3 miles from Limoges to Saint-Flour while climbing an estimated 12, 000 feet in elevation through the French Massif Central mountains. Crossing the finish line ranks right up there with the birth of my son and reading my acceptance letter to med school.

Aside from a few well-deserved pants on a couple of long climbs, Nigel rode with me, pedal stroke for pedal stroke. By the end of the ride, I knew I had my chemist, but I still wanted some independent validation. Before I gave Nigel my final decision, I set up a dinner meeting with a small group of friends.

The first person on the list was Hillari. The other person I invited was Shannon Bishop. She's Anthony Gallo's partner (the patient who'd shown me his "medicine" during my first Bozeman clinic) and the mother of his one-year-old son. Shannon is smart, practical, and at the time was an account manager for a local investment firm. Shannon is also driven to meet the family expectations for success, as her father was one of the first scientists hired at Amgen, a company synonymous with the biotech revolution.

The dinner went fabulously. Everyone loved Nigel and thought we'd make a great match. I offered him the job the next day.

Neither of us fully envisioned the journey we were embarking upon, but our objective was making the lab a model for medical cannabis testing labs across the country. We were infused with a passion to be on the cutting edge of something special.

Nothing else mattered.

Nigel became the lab. He understood we were creating something both revolutionary and pretty damn cool. Our kinship was brotherly. I couldn't have found a better partner.

Since Nigel was beginning his fellowship at MSU, we utilized his connections within the university. Collaboration was something that we both wanted to cultivate. We had met with the chairman of the Chemistry department, Dr. David Singer, in hopes of developing a working relationship between our lab and MSU chemistry department.

Nigel's job was to put my vision of a lab into reality. Once we decided on the equipment purchases, the next step was to find a location. Finding a space for the lab proved infinitely more problematic than I could have ever imagined. Nigel and I looked at dozens of spaces in the area. Ideally, the lab and the clinic would be in a single large, dividable space. We found spaces that worked great for a lab but wouldn't work for a clinic, and vice versa. And when we found a space that would work for both businesses, the owner would pull the plug because they didn't want their space to be associated with marijuana. Even as a clean-cut, professional team we couldn't shake the stigma. It didn't matter that an MD and a Ph. D tandem were dedicated to transforming the image of the cannabis industry, the answers we got were universal.

"No."

We looked for months.

Despite the rejections, we pressed on. The space issue was temporarily settled when Nigel's wife, Audrey, a gentle soul who found time to teach yoga while raising two small kids, suggested we set up the lab in the unused room adjacent to their garage.

"I can't tell you how much I appreciate this, Audrey," I said humbly.

"Nigel hasn't been this excited in years," she smiled.

We were off to the races.

Nigel found a great deal on our HPLC machine, an Agilent 1100 HPLC with auto-sampler and digital-analog detector (DAD). Leasing a device was not an option. The company required a year's worth of documented cash flow before considering any leasing agreement. The lab was a start-up, so there was no cash flow. The only option was to buy the machine outright. Fortunately, the WH&H clinics were cash flow positive, allowing me to finance every aspect of building the lab.

I was living out a dream. Nigel and I tried not to think too far ahead of ourselves, but the magnitude of what we were creating had enormous implications. When I was a kid, I longed for a brother. And now, through the weird machinations of an outlawed plant, I had finally found one in Nigel—my brother from another mother.

During one of our meetings back in New York, Devin had cautioned me that my greatest weakness in developing the lab was my utter reliance on Nigel. I understood the risk. At one point I said that if the relationship between Nigel and me dissolved, there would no longer be a lab. I had invested so much in him, both emotional and economic capital, that the idea of starting over, with someone else, was simply inconceivable.

I trusted Nigel with everything. If more than fifty dollars was involved, Nigel discussed it with me. Everything was moving along as planned—all we needed were clients and a space.

Word of the lab spread. In the marijuana world, unless you were grade school buddies, everyone is suspicious. Rumors abound. Everyone was curious. I fielded calls from numerous providers and dispensary owners asking me about partnerships. I recognized the importance of maintaining my professional integrity and autonomy; I was cautious not to align myself with anyone in the industry other than Nigel.

Once the HPLC was purchased, the next hurdle was to find cannabinoid standards. One of the foundations of analytical testing is having a known standard to compare against what you are measuring. A standard is a highly purified and exactingly quantitated sample. A precise amount of the standard is pipetted into the machine, which measures the sample and plots the measurement as a curve. Next, you run the sample, measure the area under the curves, then do a few nifty calculations, and you have your answer. Without pharmaceutical-grade standards, the lab couldn't open.

Six months into this canna-venture, my gestalt warned that our customers wouldn't care about the accuracy or integrity of our certifying data. To them, the potency of their products was all that mattered; higher THC meant increased profits. They just wanted a number for their customers. For them, it was all about marketing.

For Nigel and me, it was all about doing good, clean science.

The Joy of Grateful Patients

I clearly remember the patient looking down at the floor, trying to stifle an unexpected tear. I had just handed him back his medical records along with his signed physician statement.

"I'm so tired of feeling like a criminal, Doc. And now I don't have to live in fear that the police are going to come knocking at my door some night." With a trembling hand, he reached out for mine and firmly grasped it. "Thank you, sir."

I was speechless. Nothing like that ever happened in the ER.

Working in my clinic, I witnessed the personal side of medical marijuana—the side that most politicians, policy makers, and critics never see. The patients I was evaluating were salt-of-the-earth folks. These weren't citizens growing pot for the black market or looking to cash in on the unfolding canna-boom. These were ordinary citizens who just wanted freedom from the stigma of using a plant that helped them live a more normal life.

At first, I brushed off the thanks that patients offered me. I guess it made me a little uncomfortable because all I was doing was signing a piece of paper, but to them, that piece of paper was freedom. I reckoned that I'd been so jaded by the years of slogging away in the ED, where too often patients feigned sincerity to manipulate me into giving them the drugs they wanted. Hearing the patient's perspective about medical marijuana caused me to rethink my own ideas about the plant. I began to believe that I was participating in a true social movement.

Although I've used marijuana recreationally at times, I never felt like a criminal. I've always thought it was silly, and just downright dumb, to outlaw a plant. There were lots of laws that didn't make sense and were enforced for the benefit of a chosen few; most rules related to cannabis were no exception. I wasn't hurting anyone with the small amount cannabis I possessed; I wasn't selling it, nor was I marketing the marijuana to kids in the form of a cool cartooned camel, like the folks at R.J. Reynolds have done for so many years.

During my clinics, I had numerous interesting conversations with patients. Their stories were often sad, occasionally horrifying, and always sincere. An overwhelming majority of the patients wanted to use cannabis for treating their chronic pain—a complaint that many right-wing "Christian" legislators and law enforcement officials lauded as being "ridiculous." There was a popular expression among the opponents of MT-148: If you have a hangnail, you should get your green card for chronic pain.

Of the hundreds of chronic pain stories told to me, one always comes to mind. Joseph is a ruggedly handsome young father who explained his unexpected tragedy to me during a morning clinic visit. One summer afternoon, a few years prior, he was four-wheeling with his preschool-age son who was seated securely behind him. The child hung tightly onto his dad while they were tooling around on an abandoned logging road deep within the Gallatin National Forest. They were winding their way along the curvy and narrow one-way mountain road, when suddenly a fully loaded logging truck appeared out of nowhere. To avoid a direct collision, Joseph swerved off the road and down the steep embankment. In an instant, he made a decision.

"I saw how steep the embankment was and thought that I might be able to just drive down to the next switchback below me...but then the brakes failed." Joseph glanced at me with glistening eyes. "I chucked my boy off and thought he'd fare better rollin' down the hill than riding that damn four-wheeler with me."

A long pause gripped the room.

"What happened next?"

With a broken smile, he shrugged. "I really don't know. The next thing I remember was looking up at my son. He had a stick in his hand, pointing it at my face."

"Why are your bones sticking out, Daddy?" Joseph whispered, holding back the tears.

The medical records documented that he'd been emergency airlifted to Billings, the sole tertiary care hospital in the state. While there, Joseph underwent numerous surgeries to repair his shattered jaw, as well as multiple other serious injuries. He punctuated the story by turning his head toward the ceiling, showing me the scars on the underside of his jaw.

I happily signed his physician statement.

Wearing Out My Welcome

All good things must come to an end.

As the leaves of the quaking aspen began turning yellow, Kari started to vacillate on the Bodhi Tree hosting cannabis clinics. Colleen was worried that the "riffraff of potheads" waiting for an appointment was going to erode her client base. Even though Hillari was making appointments on her cell phone, people still called the Bodhi Tree's general number—or worse, stopped in to ask questions. The clinics were a growing source of tension, with too many recurrent problems and too much suspicion. Since I had not signed a long-term lease, we mutually agreed to find another space.

Fortunately, finding another clinic space wasn't hard. After an hour on Craigslist, I found a yoga studio that had office space available that would accommodate the clinic. On my next trip to Bozeman, Hillari and I met with Suzie, a co-owner of The Alchemy yoga studio. We loved the place, although there wasn't any room for the lab. This meant another move down the road, but I'd deal with that later. The priority was now. Hillari took care of all the details. She picked out some inexpensive bamboo furniture, painted the walls, and made the space as cozy as a basement could be. By September, we moved in.

Although an unwelcome distraction, having to find another space provided an opportunity for me to reassess what I was doing in Montana. I spoke to Hillari. I needed validation that this crazy dream I was pursuing was still grounded and that I had not lost touch with reality. Much to my delight, Hillari replied that she was all in. "I think what you're doing is fabulous."

It was a blessing to hear Hillari renew her support, because hovering over the horizon was the growing stress of working with Pam in her Missoula clinic.

Pam was doing a great job marketing her River City Family Medicine (RCFM) practice into a monthly medical marijuana clinic. She placed ads in the Missoula Independent and put a lot of energy into the clinics. The response was so overwhelming that she hired a woman to manage them solely. I admired Pam's vision of making RCFM a quality and affordable health care option in Missoula.

There was no mistaking that the clinics were responsible for keeping her business afloat. Finally, in July, the money we had been accruing was split up. I wanted 60 percent of the net income (minus her clinic expenses) for showing up. Initially, she made no bones about it. I felt justified with the cut because without me, RCFM was sunk.

I ignored the growing financial tension between Pam and I because I chose to focus on the many positive things our relationship offered. The drive up from Bozeman to Missoula on I-90 was spectacular and the easiest three-hour drive imaginable. Hanging out in Missoula was a blast, with just the right mix of funk and hippie vibe with great bars and restaurants in one of the most scenic college towns in America. And most of all, I enjoyed working in her clinic; it was such a welcomed change from the grind of the ED. I worked hard, and I saw a lot of patients in a warm and welcoming environment. The patients were friendly and grateful. Many commented that they never thought they would live to see the day when marijuana would be legal for them to use.

During lunch I would play Pam's guitar. Papa John's delivered and someone from the office would bake something tasty. It was a truly excellent work environment. After clinic, we'd drive back to her place, make a nice meal, have a few beers, and pass around a joint, talking about the dream we were living. As Pam and I became better friends, she grew more open about her intentions toward me.

Well before the #MeToo era, I did the easy thing—I ignored Pam's subtle advances and flirtations, the hand pats on my trousers and her sexually suggestive comments. Playing dumb avoided a potential HR issue that I wasn't guaranteed to win. I ignored the behaviors until I couldn't.

During the September clinic, I had just driven up from Bozeman and was running a bit late. As I brought my things into the office, Pam saw that I was fumbling with my necktie.

"Here, let me help you" she said, happy to see me. Straightening my tie, she looked at me with a slanted grin, "I'm usually a lot better taking the clothes off a man like you."

I'm sure some would have embraced that suggestion and turned it into a work encounter worthy of a Penthouse forum column. But for multiple reasons, I wasn't interested in anything other than a professional relationship with Pam. I liked her a lot and truly enjoyed our working relationship. But things had gone too far, her advances were making me increasingly uncomfortable, and I asked her to stop.

The next morning while fixing breakfast, just before we were to embark for our Sunday clinic, she looked at me coldly. "I found another doctor."

It surprised me how painful those words felt. Intuitively, I knew my leaving was inevitable, as she had complained on many occasions that I cost her too much money. On a personal level, being replaced with a cheaper physician hurt my feelings. And sadly, like so many things that came to pass in Montana, it all came down to money. I had single-handedly resuscitated her clinic from the brink of bankruptcy. I was well worth the money I requested.

Pam had shown her cards. The fantasy of building a clinic with her was over. I knew that when she got desperate, she'd call me again.

Flying Standby

It was unmistakably fall.

Jacob's mother had encouraged him to sign up for peewee football. She thought that the experience would "toughen him up." I thought he was plenty tough, but after all the years of acrimony I'd learned to pick my battles. I just didn't want to see him get hurt.

During the informational meeting, the head of the league quoted a study that found the injury rate for peewee football was much less than that associated with little league. I thought about asking for the reference and reading the article myself, but I opted just to let it go, consoled by the fact that the boys playing peewee football were virtually immune to the physics that caused lasting physical damage. A fully padded fifty-pound kid can only run so fast, and most of the tackling and incidental contact seemed pretty innocuous. Relieved that I wasn't going to be subjecting my son to the horrors of traumatic brain injury, I sat back and just enjoyed the show.

I arranged my work schedule around his practices. Watching quietly on the sidelines was hallowed time. One afternoon during the first week of practice, the head coach, an acquaintance from little league, asked if I wanted to help out.

Every afternoon I took Jacob to practice. I buckled his bulky shoulder pads and helped him with his practice jersey. He looked more like the Incredible Hulk than my adorable child. And, in a final ritual of good parenting, I made sure his shoestrings were double-knotted. Then, at precisely 5:00 p.m., I'd run out onto the field with the boys to start practice. I did whatever I was asked to do and found my niche with the team.

Our first game was the second Sunday of September. I was in Montana during the workweek prior and had booked a departing Saturday morning flight. I had breakfast with Lori at the Black Cat Cafe. She kept an eye on the clock.

"Michael, what time is your flight?"

"9:38. To Minneapolis."

"Are you sure? That doesn't sound right."

"Sure, I'm sure. Here, take a look at my ticket."

Lori furrowed her brow. "I think you should look at this again."

My heart stopped. The flight departed at 9:18. I looked at the clock. "I gotta go."

I left a twenty-dollar bill on the table and waved good-bye. I had twelve minutes to get to the ticket counter and check-in.

Although it was not the chase scene from *The French Connection*, it felt like it. Traffic wasn't bad, but I still had eight miles to the airport. I raced through the rental car drop-off and made an impressive sprint to the Delta check-in counter with twenty-eight minutes to spare. Unfortunately, a new TSA rule now required a thirty-minute cutoff between departure time and assigning boarding passes. Despite my desperate pleas, I couldn't get a boarding pass.

I stepped back from the counter, shattered by the certainty that I was going to miss my flight. No amount of debate or coercion was going to change that, nor the gut-gnawing feeling about missing my son's game. I went back to the ticket counter and asked about the next flight to Albany. The agent stared into the screen and wrinkled his face in an uncomfortable array of angles.

"Looks like Tuesday morning is your best bet, sir."

"I could drive to Albany by Tuesday."

My mind raced for alternatives. "There's nothing flying out from Helena or Billings? Could you please check that? My son has his first peewee football game tomorrow. I have to get back home. I'm one of the coaches."

The young man nodded and went back to his screen.

"I'm sorry, Dr. Geci, there's a lot of outgoing traffic this time of year. The best I can do for you is to get you back to Albany on Monday morning—and that's with flying out of Helena tomorrow afternoon."

I was dizzy with disbelief. How would I explain this? How long would his mother use this against me? I wanted to sit in the middle of the road and cry. Instead, I called Jacob's mother, hoping that the game had been canceled.

"Hello?" She said in a watered-down Midlands accent.
"Hey. I missed my flight by two minutes."
"You what?"
Repeating the sentence did nothing to warm her frigidness.
"So, you're going to miss his *first* game?"
"I misread my ticket. I thought the flight was leaving at 9:38."
"You are going to have to tell him yourself."
"You think I'm happy about this?"
"I hope she was worth it!" And then the line went dead.

Having iconoclastic tendencies has its advantages when the chips are down. I've found over the years that *no* doesn't always mean *no*; persistence pays off. I put myself in crisis mode. I called the airline reservation office and told the specialist my story.

"I need to get back to New York before tomorrow morning, or I'll miss my son's first peewee football game."

"Awww…we can't let that happen. Let me see what I can find for you, sir."

After what seemed like miles of pacing in the airport parking lot, I re-booked an itinerary that would get me back to Albany by midnight. The only catch was flying standby on two fights—the first one from Bozeman to Denver, the other from Denver to O'Hare. If the flight gods were smiling, I'd catch up with my original connection from O'Hare to Albany. It was my only chance.

The flight to Denver was boarding. I clung to a fragile hope and nervously waited while the other passengers boarded. As the line dwindled, the gate agent looked up and smiled with my boarding pass to Denver.

"Last seat, sir. First-class upgrade, too. Hope you make it for your son's game."

I wanted to hug him but feared my gratitude might be mistaken as terrorist aggression, and I'd be shot by an overzealous TSA goon. I settled on a handshake. "Thank you very much."

I squeezed my pack into the remaining overhead space and took my seat. I was grateful to be on the plane. I ordered a drink and thanked God, Jesus, Allah, Yahweh, and all the other universally divine spirits for the blessing of being on the flight.

Once in Denver, I sprinted to the gate to stake out my "standby" position. The agent smiled and told me that I was number three on the list and it looked like there were at least eight open seats. Life was good. If I made the Chicago flight, I would catch the 7:05 to Albany and I'd be home by midnight.

No sweat.

I boarded the flight to Chicago. The cabin door closed, and everything was going as planned until the cabin music was interrupted.

"Ladies and gentlemen, this is the captain speaking," he calmly droned in an Alabaman twang. "Durin' our final preflight check, we just found that the aft closet lightbulb has decided to malfunction. Because safety's our first priority here at Delta, the FAA says we can't leave Denver till this little ol' lightbulb's fixed. Hopefully, it's just the bulb and nothin' electrical. The ground crew's lookin' for a replacement as we speak. This shouldn't take but a few minutes."

Famous last words.

"Bottom line, ladies an' gentlemen, we don't anticipate this little ol' bulb to be much of a problem. We got us some strong westerly tailwinds and ATC is estimatin' us arrivin' in Chicago at least fifteen minutes early. We'll keep y'all posted, folks."

A baby in the back of the plane began crying.

"Ladies an' gentlemen, this is your captain. That ol' bulb's causin' us more trouble than we thought. Maintenance says it'll be another thirty minutes 'fore we get the OK from ground control. Y'all relax and we'll keep y'all posted."

What initially promised to be an early arrival into Chicago now looked as though we might be late. With every minute that damn "little ol' lightbulb" stayed unfixed, the window for me to catch my connecting flight in Chicago got narrower.

After an eighty-four-minute maintenance departure delay, our plane finally took off. In a renewed panic, I signaled for the flight attendant and asked her to deliver a message to the captain. On a beverage napkin, I explained my plight and pleaded with him to fly faster. She read the note, smiled sympathetically, and said that the pilot could only go so fast.

"What I *can* do is get you the empty seat in first class just before we land. You can deplane as soon as we open the cabin door."

Our plane arrived at our gate at with six minutes to spare. Without the ability to teleport myself to the adjacent terminal, I was sure to miss my flight. I was bummed, but at least I had made it to Chicago and knew there would be other options to play out. The gate agent found a late flight to Syracuse. The rental car companies would be closed by the time I landed. Plan F became spending the night in Syracuse, picking up a car when they reopened, and then drive to the game.

On Sunday morning I was the first coach at the field. We lost the game, but it was an otherwise great day.

Sam

The highlight of Pam's cannabis clinic was meeting Samantha Kovak. Smartly dressed in just the right amount of urban funk, she sat across from me, telling me about the novel she was writing. Her chronic whiplash pain from a prior car accident became an afterthought, morphing into something that felt more like flirtatious teenagers. Her wiry build belied a rugged Hungarian heritage. A pearl-colored silk scarf draped under her salt-and-pepper hair that she joked was at the whim of her hairstylist. Sam was quick to laugh and wicked smart. She reminded me of Glenda, the good witch, yet spoke like an over-caffeinated Chicago reporter. I admired her edge.

At the conclusion of our appointment, she told me about an article she was writing for the *Helena Independent Record* about medical marijuana. She asked about picking my brain sometime and left me her card. The next month we met at the co-op in Bozeman. I ordered a carrot and beet juice mix with a shot of hemp oil. Sam had a coffee—black. She was interested in my idea of a testing lab and its role in the evolving medical marijuana industry.

"A lab introduces an element of quality control into a formerly black-market industry. Before analytical labs showed up, the customer was completely at the mercy of the seller," I said. "With a lab, quality control becomes quantifiable; cannabis plays by the same rules as every other medicine—or food and beverage product."

"I suppose you can test anything if you have the right instrumentation," Sam shot back. "But why do you need to know what's in the pot you smoke?"

"If you had the option, wouldn't you like to know the potency of the marijuana you're buying? Wouldn't you like to know what cannabinoids you're ingesting? Having a lab makes for an accurate way of comparing apples to apples."

"I can see the utility in this," she said, squeezing her narrow lips together. "It could be the way this plant gets taxed. If you know how much THC is in the plant, you could tax it in the same manner as alcohol. It could be the A.B.V. of marijuana."

"Alcohol by volume, absolutely."

"That's it. That's the ticket to regulating this. It's brilliantly simple."

"A lab can also clue you into the freshness of the cannabis, too," I added.

"How's that?"

"If the cannabinol (CBN) level is high, it indicates that the cannabis has undergone oxidative degradation, meaning it's either old, or the cannabis was exposed to excessive light or heat. Equally important is being able to identify some of the other useful cannabinoids, like CBD, THCV, CBG, and CBC. There are a lot of medicinal applications for some of these other cannabinoids, especially CBD. Trust me, for the medicinal market, CBD will dwarf THC."

Sam lit up like a kid at Christmas. "You gotta love you science boys."

There was a theme whenever Sam and I were together. We always had fun—especially when we hung out in her kitchen, a cozy stone-floored space that opened onto a deck overlooking the Big Blue Mountains. It was the place where we'd play music and discuss how to change the cultural image of cannabis, crafting a free-market medical marijuana bill (SB991) for the upcoming legislature. Sam and I spent endless hours discussing the politics of medical marijuana and how we could reshape the Montana program.

As the months passed, Sam and I saw each other when we could. For the last twelve year she'd worked as a lobbyist, an advocating voice for women's rights and child welfare concerns. She enjoyed the gamesmanship of being a sharp, attractive woman walking the back halls of the Montana legislature. Sam could read the political tea leaves as well as anyone. She was keenly aware of the mounting momentum of negative press coverage, and like Daubert, could see the catastrophic trajectory the industry was traveling.

Sam shared my concern that the Jason Christ MCN clinics were stirring a hornet's nest of adverse public reaction, with provocative front-page acts like Christ lighting his fabled shepherd's staff pot pipe in front of the Great Falls Police Department. The citizens had shown courage and compassion in voting to legalize medical marijuana, an initiative meant to prevent another tragedy like Robin Prosser's, not to enrich companies like the MCN. Montanans were now feeling duped.

Most providers and dispensary owners loved the MCN roadshow as the MCN traveling clinics were a great way to increase their patient rolls. According to MT-148, each new patient who signed up allowed them to grow an additional six cannabis plants under the name of that patient. It was simple math. The more patients you had, the more plants you could grow, and the more money you would make. With a green thumb, you could conceivably harvest several pounds of cannabis per plant. With top-shelf marijuana selling at upward of $3,000 to $4,000 per pound, each patient represented a gold mine to the growers. Over a year (with three indoor grows), each patient could net roughly $75,000.

Considering the money involved, it's not surprising that few openly voiced opposition to the MCN clinics. With the upcoming elections a distant fourteen months away, only a handful speculated about the next legislative session. Most were simply making hay while the sun was shining. It was a time of irrational exuberance.

The MCN clinics became the Ebola of the Montana medical marijuana industry. I felt that something needed to be done to stop this charade before it spiraled out of control. The most effective, nonlethal method of neutralizing Jason Christ was to stop his doctor. No one received a card without a doctor's signature. Physicians were the rate-limiting factor in the entire process. The solution seemed simple.

In contrast to the MCN clinics, where up to five hundred patients in a weekend could be seen, WH&H was seeing approximately twelve to twenty patients a day. Aside from the history and physical, each patient was educated on the risks of using medical marijuana. Some looked at me with askance when I mentioned the potentially harmful effects of marijuana use. Many patients perceived their bodies were being poisoned by prescription pharmaceuticals and saw marijuana as a panacea for all of their ills—in large part because cannabis is a natural product.

"Outside of love and garlic," I quipped, "most things are bad for you when used in excess." I told the same story hundreds of times.

"Chug a couple of gallons of pure mountain spring water and in a couple days you'll be dead." I explained to them the sudden shift in body salts called hyponatremia, which caused the brain to swell and herniate through the bottom of the skull, a pathological process called cerebral edema.

It was important that patients were given a modicum of balance regarding the side effects of chronic marijuana use. I reminded them of the adverse consequences of abusing marijuana: issues such as marijuana dependency, low sperm count, and decreased hormone levels of testosterone, LH and FSH.[92] Patients were informed about recent papers that suggested an increased risk of testicular cancer,[93] as well as a hypothesis that chronic marijuana use could cause a fatty liver, potentially causing cirrhosis.[94]

Female patients were warned of data that strongly suggested that prenatal exposure to marijuana could adversely affect fetal brain development.[95] Every patient needed to understand that cannabis could be a helpful adjunct to a patient's health and lifestyle routine, but there is rarely a free lunch. Marijuana was no exception.

Sam supported my decision to bring the matter of the MCN clinics to the attention of the Montana State Board of Medical Examiners. She was with me the day I dropped the letter of complaint into the blue mail bin across from the capitol. My objective was to initiate a positive change and stop the flood of negativity generated by the MCN clinics. Walking back toward Sam's house, a northerly breeze began to blow. On the horizon, thick, dark clouds were forming. Few forecast the strength of the coming storm.

Trying to be Legal

Nigel and I felt strongly that ending up in jail was not an option. We each had families and other means, besides cannabis, of earning a comfortable living. Nigel could go back to working as an industrial chemist, and I still had my life in the ED. But our respective passions for creating the lab won out, inspiring us to probe the nebulous boundary between medical marijuana and pot.

And to me, it all looked the same.

According to MT-148, there was no explicit mention of the legality of operating a marijuana testing laboratory. We were walking a blurred line between accomplishing something useful and socially responsible and engaging in something considered illegal.

My approach to staying out of jail was total transparency. I preemptively spoke with the Gallatin Country Sheriff and the head of the Montana Drug Task Force. I sent a letter to the US District Attorney in Billings, informing him about the lab. Some law enforcement officials couldn't have cared less, while others confided that criminals like heroin dealers and meth lab operators were the real fish that needed fried, not folks dabbling in cannabis.

When I spoke to an attorney in the state Attorney General's office regarding the legality of the lab, she said to, "leave a paper trail and document your attempts for clarity. It might help convince a judge that your intentions weren't criminal. I can't guarantee this will keep you out of trouble, but it can't hurt."

"That's refreshing," I sighed.

"You can blame all of this on the Controlled Substance Act."

The Controlled Substance Act? I wondered.

After a Google search, I learned that the CSA was born under the Nixon administration as a reaction to the counterculture opposition to the Vietnam War. It represented the legislative arm of the "war on drugs." The CSA is the federal policy under which manufacture, importation, possession, use, and distribution of drugs are regulated. The DEA acts as the enforcement arm under the jurisdiction of the Department of Justice, and the Food and Drug Administration (FDA) provides the regulatory bureaucracy.

The intent of the CSA is to protect the public. The FDA lists potential drugs of abuse on a scheduling system, I through V. In a nutshell, Schedule I drugs possess several identifying features: (1) high potential for abuse, (2) no currently accepted medical treatment in the United States, and (3) a lack of accepted safety for use of the drug under medical supervision. Doctors can't write prescriptions for Schedule I substances because, in theory, those substances have no medical applications.

It seemed ironic that marijuana and its dozens of constituent cannabinoids had been doomed to the dungeon of a Schedule I classification. It's the reason Montana doctors signed a physician statement for patients instead of using their prescription pad. Physicians write prescriptions to dispense Schedule II–V substances. Controlled substances such as cocaine, morphine, Percocet, Fentanyl, Xanax, and Valium are listed in descending order regarding their potential for abuse—the lower the number (e.g., Schedule II vs V), the higher the potential for abuse.

Another wrinkle of being listed as a Schedule I substance is that it creates burdensome bureaucratic restrictions, in essence, creating a de facto ban on the substance's use in US medical research and clinical trials. The Schedule I designation is why 90 percent of the scientific research on cannabis is done in Canada, Israel, Brazil, Spain, the Netherlands, and Japan. It was clear that without rescheduling marijuana, the necessary medical research needed to determine the true potential of plant-based therapies, whether they be *Cannabis sativa*, *Lophophora* (peyote), or *Psilocybin* (magic mushrooms).

Waiting for Congress to do the right thing and reschedule marijuana was a pipe dream. It would be years before that happened, and I didn't have that kind of time. I wanted my lab to be legal and beyond reproach. From the investigation I'd done, the only way to legally operate a marijuana testing lab was to have a Schedule I research lab permit. The security requirements for the permit were daunting and expensive.

Although I still didn't have a permanent spot for the lab, I figured I'd take my chances and get the ball rolling. Full of gullibility, I went online, filled out the form, and sent the DEA the application fee of $200. I was even optimistic about our chances of securing a permit—as part of my effort in trying to be legal.

In the end, applying for the Schedule I research permit was yet one more example of my utter naïveté strolling through the merry maze of the marijuana wonderland.

A Message from the Board

When I arrived back home, my answering machine held a message from Jean Branscomb, the secretary from the Montana Board of Medical Examiners. I held my breath.

"What the hell could I have done?"

I dialed her number.

Ms. Branscomb relayed that the board received my complaint and requested me to write a whitepaper regarding physician recommendations for evaluating patients for medical marijuana. She asked me to present it at their upcoming November meeting. I was encouraged that they were taking my complaint seriously and wanted my thoughts.

I called Sam. She saw the news as positive. As I began working on the paper, I was surprised by the paucity of research devoted to physician guidelines for the evaluation and management of patients using medical marijuana.

Within the confines of the Montana medical marijuana industry, news traveled in a flash. Some second-guessed my motives for going to the board. Numerous growers and dispensary owners called to wish me luck, and then ask me what I was planning to say. There was palpable tension as the date of the meeting neared.

Perhaps I should have been more mindful of pothead paranoia. I didn't understand why my motives for speaking before the board were being misconstrued as anything but honorable. My goal was to help the industry prosper in a healthy and ethical way. I envisioned an opportunity to be on the ground floor of a major economic and cultural shift regarding cannabis.

On the day of my presentation, I was as anxious as I had ever been. The drive up to Helena was cold and ominously overcast. The wind whipped occasional blasts of patchy snow across the road as I made my way north on US 287. I was scheduled to appear at three thirty; I arrived early and settled in.

There was a long, disordered line of people standing outside of the board's meeting room. The hallway was filled with slumping postures, shabby clothes that reeked of skunk, and dozens of pairs of shiny bloodshot eyes. The only people I recognized were Jason Christ and Chris Lindsey, an attorney, and partner with Montana Cannabis, who was sitting next to Daubert. The janitor brought extra folding chairs to accommodate the unusually large influx of people attending the typically deadpan monthly Medical Board meetings. I overheard a board member mutter that this was the largest public attendance of any board meeting he had ever attended.

When I was finally called into the boardroom, cold sweat began a steady drip down my armpits. I was seated in the middle of a long vinyl table, empty except for a narrow microphone on a round metal base. The board members were casually dressed and seated directly across from me.

I stole a quick look behind me. Every glazed eye focused on me.

I felt like I was the main event for an Old West gun draw.

The president of the board made a few announcements and then introduced me. It was showtime.

I spoke for about ten minutes. First, I pointed out that the American Medical Association (AMA) had just announced its support for an FDA review to consider reclassifying marijuana to a Schedule II substance. Reclassifying would allow physicians to write prescriptions for cannabis as they did other medicine.

Then I directed the board's attention to what I saw as the greatest threat facing MT-148—the traveling MCN clinics. I referenced the most recent weekend clinic held in Bozeman, where more than three hundred patients were seen at the C'mon Inn.

"Intuitively, a physician cannot appropriately evaluate hundreds of patients in a two-day period. Let's assume that if marijuana's FDA scheduling was changed to that of narcotics; then, the idea of having hundreds of patients waiting in line at a hotel conference room for the opportunity to obtain a prescription for Percocet, Lortabs, or Oxycontin, with a twelve-month window of unlimited refills, would certainly raise suspicion of potential abuse."

I stopped to sip from my water bottle, allowing the point to settle.

"If marijuana is to be used as a medicine, it should be treated as a medicine. I've read hundreds of peer-reviewed journal articles that corroborate the medical benefits of using cannabis. The therapeutic uses range from pain control and cancer therapy to suggestions of cannabinoids being used in acute coronary syndrome and stroke."

I shared my whitepaper with the board. I suggested that physicians assess patients in the same manner as they evaluate patients for hypertension or diabetes. There should be documentation that the patient has tried other therapies, and they were unsuccessful. Patients must be counseled about the contraindications of using marijuana. The physician who recommends cannabis should have a working knowledge of the ECS. Doctors should understand the pharmacology of cannabis and its interactions with other prescription drugs.

I was struck by how little the members of the board seemed to know about medical marijuana. The issue that concerned the board most was defining the traditional doctor-patient relationship. Several board members bantered back and forth, trying to gain consensus on what constituted a doctor-patient relationship. They asked for my opinion.

"It's hard to define what *is* a viable doctor-patient relationship, but what's easy is defining what *isn't* a viable doctor-patient relationship. I don't consider mass clinics held in a hotel conference room to be an example of a doctor-patient relationship." There was an audible chuckle from several of the board members.

"The board is grateful for your thoughts and suggestions, Dr. Geci. Thank you for your time."

"Is that it?"

"Yes, Dr. Geci. That's it."

The ride back to Bozeman was bittersweet. Although I was excited that my presentation had gone well, I was a little disappointed that Sam and I did not get to spend the evening together. She was one of the few people who would have understood the ordeal I'd just experienced.

The following day was my scheduled interview with the founder of Harborside Dispensary in Oakland, Steve DeAngelo. I found Mr. DeAngelo to be polite and gracious. He shared more information than I expected. When I asked him about the lab he used, he was brief. "I'm not a chemist. But I understand the value of having the cannabis subjected to some standard quality control pathways. So, I hired a team to do the work for me. Steep Hill Labs."

"Where did you get your THC standards?" I asked.

"The Netherlands."

"Did you get the DEA permit?"

DeAngelo sounded exasperated. "Of course not. Nobody gets those damn permits."

"So, how'd you get the standards into the United States?"

"We smuggled them in. It was easy."

I suppressed a nervous laugh.

I thanked Mr. DeAngelo for his generosity. As an unexpected bonus, he offered to send me a month's worth of the lab's analytical results. I came away inspired that starting a lab might turn into something big.

The Christening: MBA

I thought picking a name for the lab would be easy. I wanted a name that evoked a vivid sense of what the company represented. My inclination was to associate the name with the area's majestic local topography. Take a glance northward on any sunny day and you'd be hard-pressed not to see the Bridgers, a forty-five-mile jagged spine of mountains that frames Bozeman's northern horizon.

Big Sky Analytical Labs was my first thought.

Creative I might be, a visual artist I'm not. I needed help. Lori was quick to suggest her friend, Amy Kelly, a freelance graphic designer who worked out of her cozy North-side bungalow. Amy took my vision of a THC molecule represented as a starry constellation rising over the Bridgers and transformed it into a surreal image. It was cool, but the design gave the logo a science-fiction look—not something that suggested cannabis quality control.

I knew immediately that the design was flawed, but I wanted it to work. I persisted until Devin did what he would continue to do during his tenure as my legal representative—he gently imparted logic into the discussion. He ran a thorough web-based name check for Big Sky Analytical Labs, and although unique, he said the name was close enough to Big Sky Analytics (in Helena) to evoke consumer confusion. He suggested I change the name. I was momentarily bummed, but I was committed to honoring the advice of my business consultant.

I went back to the drawing board. The next day, on my bike, a new name appeared like a vision.

Montana Botanical Analysis

I loved it.

The Christening: MBA

Montana Botanical Analysis (MBA) had a ring to it. I was relieved when Nigel and Hillari liked it, too.

On my next trip to Bozeman I met with Amy, again. "I like the new name, Mike. Did you have a concept for it in mind?"

"I was thinking about a leaf with a molecule of CBD attached."

"Hmmm." Magically, with a series of right- and left-clicks and taps on the mouse, a sketch of the serrated outline of a cannabis leaf appeared on her screen.

"I don't like the cannabis leaf. It's too caked with prejudice."

"Sure, I can see that." Amy manipulated the design. With a click, the saw-toothed edges of the cannabis leaf were smoothed. Another swipe of the mouse, and the leaf got fatter...then it was longer. The color scheme changed. Now the leaf was a fading shade of green from bottom to top. The background colors were a horizon of blending hues of blue and yellow.

"How do you like that?"

"Wow. That's so cool," I marveled.

"What about fonts?"

"What about them?"

"What type of fonts do you want for the business cards and letterhead?"

I was still mesmerized by the design. "Oh...what are my options?"

"Last time I checked, there were about forty thousand fonts to choose from," she grinned.

My answer was easy. "What do you think?"

Within the hour, the entire concept was finished. The image popped. Then I added the tagline below Montana Botanical Analysis, "Unlocking the science of cannabinoids."

It was perfect. I loved the logo.

Amy had just given the lab a tangible identity.

I ordered business cards, letterheads, and envelopes. As the final marketing tool, we got a special deal on a three-by-six-foot heavy-duty color banner.

The only piece if the dream missing was finding a space for the lab.

Christmas in BZN

Since March, I'd been making monthly trips to Bozeman. I was still working in the emergency department and trying to carve out as much dad time as possible. As best I could, I scheduled around my son's school events, little league, peewee football, and now swim meets. But I still missed things, I still lost opportunities to spend time with my son. Routinely, I asked if I was being a good father. Was my commitment to forging a new life for myself really worth it?

I tried to answer that question with the tool that seemed to work best for me: logic. The experiment to shift my life seemed to be working. Happiness was no longer a "blue moon" occurrence. Happiness became my only barometer of whether I was indeed, on my proper path.

However, voices in my head resisted full acceptance. Guilt and fear were constant companions, dogging me at every opportune moment. I feared accusations of abandoning my son for the sake of *my* happiness. I feared being labeled as self-aggrandizing. The demons fed on my insecurities, twisting reality.

But I did my best. When I was gone, I made daily calls to my son to check on his day. Rarely would he pick up the phone, and I yearned to hear his voice. I wondered if he ever heard the messages I left on their answering machine. Seldom, my calls were returned.

Yet I persisted. What choice did I have?

Jacob is an only child. We share custody, but he lives with his mom, a twenty-minute drive away. When I was home, I'd see him almost every day, helping with homework, playing catch, shooting hoops, or grabbing dinner at one of our local hangouts.

He's the sole reason I didn't sell my house and move to Bozeman. His mother tried to be supportive of my dual-state life, but often she felt like a single parent, despite my attempts to pull my weight.

Our divorce, although amicable, leveled me. I grew up in a boundaryless environment, thinking that boundaries were merely imaginary lines between states. Subsequently, I found the demands of marriage confounding and illogical. I struggled, determined not to make the same mistake as my parents, who were married multiple times. I vowed to stay married for as long as it took to make it work, or until Jacob was out of high school. But his mother wasn't bound by the same chains of guilt as me. Divorce is never simple, especially when kids are involved. And in the dance that Jacob's mother and I did, I always believed that there was some sliver of hope for reconciliation.

Occasionally, the stars would line up, and I would feel a thaw in her bitterness; brief episodes when the woman I fell in love with would appear. I also considered the other uncomfortable option; maybe I wasn't open to her version of love and kindness. In typical male fashion, I tried to repair the damage, but few things that broken can ever be truly made whole again. A hard-boiled egg can never be viscous again.

Still, years out from our separation, I continued reaching out to her, trying to somehow make up for not being the husband that she wanted or needed. I brought her veggies from my garden, I'd cut her grass when she was away, and I brought her firewood. For her, they were hollow tokens. Too little, too late.

With Christmas approaching, I reached out to her again, an optimist holding his last match on a damp and windy day. My idea was simple. Montana had changed me, and so, perhaps it might change her, and maybe even us. Since the beginning of the year, everything in my world seemed to change. With my gloom lifted, I entertained new ideas about reuniting my family. Perhaps I could find a way to reconcile with her. So, I wrote her a letter.

Although we never talked about my note, she accepted my invitation to visit Bozeman and agreed to bring Jacob out for Christmas. I was overjoyed. Everything was looking up.

Through another friend of Lori's, I found a more permanent place to live. Roan is a middle-aged ski bum who's skied some of the best mountains in the world, selling real estate and ghostwriting to feed his ski habit. Together, he and I rented a nicely furnished two-bedroom condo five minutes from downtown. Everything was set for my family's visit, just days away.

For some odd reason, I came back to the condo for lunch after morning clinic. Roan looked frantic. "We have three hours to get out."

"Get out? What do you mean?"

Roan looked annoyed. "Our landlord got a last-minute Christmas rental on the condo."

"What about my family?"

"What about them?"

"Did you forget that they're coming for Christmas? Where are we supposed to stay?"

It was clear Roan hadn't been married and certainly didn't have kids. "I don't even fucking know where I'm staying right now. I'd suggest you get your stuff out pronto."

I loaded my car and then scrambled to find a place for us to stay. Luckily Craigslist came through for me again. I found a comfortable home on the north end of town.

Jacob and his mother flew into Billings on a brilliant sunny day. The drive back on I-80 snaked along the Yellowstone River and netted dozens of bald eagle and osprey spottings. The views of the Beartooth and Absaroka ranges to the south and the Crazy and Bridger ranges to the north were a stunning backdrop to what I was hoping might lie ahead for us as a family.

It was a memorable trip. Jacob and his mom loved the house, they were surprised that I could find something so nice. We skied Bridger several days and every evening we dined at one of the many terrific restaurants in town.

On the drive to the airport, Jacob's mother was moved by her first visit to the American West. The raw beauty had exceeded her expectations. At the airport, I bid them good-bye. I'd be flying back the next day.

"I had a nice time," she said softly.

"I'm really glad you guys came out."

"It's a lovely place, but it's even further from my family." Her parents had moved to Spain years ago to a large British ex-pat community.

Reconciliation was never discussed. And that was OK. The trip proved to be my final attempt to bring the three of us together again as a cohesive unit. It was time that I accepted that letting go and moving on wasn't the worst thing you can do.

Rumblings

Like stocks, relationships can't continue in an upward trajectory forever, and so it was with Hillari. Initially, I ignored the complaints from patients and providers about unreturned clinic appointment phone calls. I sent her notes and spoke with her about it, hoping that would fix the problem.

Aside from her essential administrative role, Hillari was a confidant. She understood me at a time when I barely understood myself. For a time, our lives were enmeshed in a non-romantic dance that only we could translate. When important events were happening, she was the first person I called. But our relationship was mostly a one-way street. I needed her way more than she needed me, and it was rare that I ever saw her outside of the clinic.

When I wasn't seeing patients or on my bike, I would often hang out with Anthony Gallo, grilling on his deck and talking about cannabis. He was a gracious host and he offered me a room at his house until I could get alternative housing worked out. During our visits, I got an inside view of how he operated. He was as greedy and power-hungry as anyone I'd met in the marijuana business; he was just considerably subtler about it. Anthony bragged about keeping his competition awash in misinformation so he could maneuver an advantage. In the back of my mind, I wondered if our friendship was a form of his manipulation. I was a huge target. I signed physician statements, and Gallo needed a doctor to sign up his patients.

Aside from Nigel and Hillari, Anthony was the first person I told about the lab. Once he understood the concept, he embraced the idea enthusiastically.

"I'll be your first customer, dude. I'm getting all my shit tested through your lab, buddy. Then everybody will know how badass my shit really is," he winked.

It meant a lot that he wanted to be the first one in line for the lab.

Gallo loved to brag. He was quick to tell me the number of patients he had and how big his operation had grown. When he hit patient number three hundred, he came over and showed me his business binder filled with patient cards. Anthony was a control freak and hated to be outdone by anybody, including me. I never felt threatened by Gallo, but I know others who were. Maybe because I had something that he desperately wanted—a college degree. He chose to grow pot rather than go to college. Anthony loved money, but he respected intellect with an equal fervor. Hanging out with me gave him something he couldn't give himself—intelligence by association.

Then one evening, out of the blue, Anthony called me. He was baked, and after the obligatory pleasantries, he got right to the point.

"Listen, buddy—I decided I don't need my medicine tested. Patients don't really care about numbers; they just want to feel better, and that's what I do. I make patients feel better."

His words stung, and it felt personal. "But you told me you wanted to be the first provider to have his medicine tested. You said you wanted to be on the cutting edge of this industry."

"Things change, buddy. You know that. You're a doctor."

I said good-bye and made a mental note. As much as I liked Anthony, he was just like the other pot hustlers I'd met. I called Hillari to vent.

Despite Anthony's fickleness, he was always a good source of gossip. One afternoon he invited me over for supper. After smoking his third joint in twenty minutes, he turned to me, his eyes shimmering like iridescent saucers.

"Yo, Doc Mike, I got the scoop on your girlfriend."

I ignored his jab.

"Did she tell you that a bunch of us went out last week?"

There was no reason to engage in his baiting. I wasn't interested in a conflict with someone who was stoned.

Anthony persisted. "And I know why your pretty little receptionist ain't calling your patients back!"

"How do you know?" I smirked, disappointed that I'd caved.

"Your boy here has big ears. They hear everything."

"We're working on problem. I get that it's not perfect."

"Perfect? Dude, my gals at the dispensary tell me they leave a dozen messages a day on your message machine. Lots of times the voicemail is full for days. No telling how many folks just give up."

"I know. If talked to her about it."

Anthony hunched toward me. "Ask her about Richie, dude. See what she says."

Richie was an iconic local underground grower who'd been crafting his trade for decades. He was rumored to have one of the biggest grows in the state. Gallo was frozen in smiling anticipation, awaiting my reaction. Maybe this was some fucked up stoner game he was playing, but his words felt sharper, deeper.

I's had enough. "Listen, dude, thanks for supper. I have clinic in the morning. I gotta go."

"Don't forget to ask her. I'm dying to hear what she says."

The next day, Hillari wasn't surprised about what Anthony had told me. She acknowledged joining the Christmas party celebration but was quick to point out that nothing inappropriate had happened.

Then she told me about leaving for Costa Rica.

For the past eight months, Hillari had been my third eye, but now she was taking a job teaching massage therapy somewhere in the Costa Rican jungle. Hillari said she'd talked to a friend of hers, a red-headed glassblower named Dana, to take over her job. She assured me that there would be a seamless transition.

Seamlessness is relative.

The final month of 2009 was hectic. Nigel and I were still looking for a space for the lab. I'd paid Arno to help Nigel set up the lab and he also agreed to give a lecture at MSU on the chemistry of cannabinoids. I was also hosting a public presentation on medical marijuana at the Emerson Theater, with Arno as the featured speaker.

Not unexpectedly, Pam called. I figured it was just a matter of time before she asked me to help her out again with her clinic.

"I thought you'd found another doctor?"

"We didn't get along so well. I'd rather put up with you."

"I'm not surprised."

"C'mon, Michael. I miss working with you. We got along so well. Why don't you think about it?"

I voiced my concerns about reopening our professional relationship. Without hesitation, Pam agreed to my terms. There was no telling how long this would last; it could be a one-time gig, or maybe she'd had a real change of heart.

Only time would tell.

The MMGA

Every agricultural crop has an organization of farmers and people who are vested in promoting and protecting the crop's economic and political welfare, and cannabis is no exception. The Montana Medical Growers Association (MMGA) was the group of cannabis growers that formed after Obama took office.

The group was loosely led by Jim Gingery, a real estate salesman, and native Ohioan, and Mark Sigler, a silver-haired Floridian dental supply salesman. Sigler was leasing an abandoned veterinarian office on the outskirts of Bozeman and was converting it into a dispensary and a large indoor grow facility.

As part of my marketing plan, I reached out to Gingery and Sigler and invited them to dinner. I shared my vision for the lab and hoped they'd become customers.

"If you call it a medicine, you need to treat it like a medicine," I said.

"How much is it going to cost?" Sigler grunted.

"We're working on the numbers now. Like all things new and innovative, the cost will come down the more people use the service."

"How often will the products need to be tested?" Gingery asked.

"If the plants are grown from seed, every generation because the genetics and therefore the cannabinoid concentrations will also change—sometimes dramatically."

Sigler followed up. "What about clones, Doc?"

"Good question," I admitted. "I think it depends on the grow. Some people do a good job keeping their growing conditions consistent; others, not so much. Without consistent conditions, the concentration of cannabinoids, even from clones, can vary."

The officers of the MMGA weren't nearly as savvy as Daubert and Sam. I brought up the public relations problems being generated by the MCN clinics. Sadly, Sigler wasn't critical of the operation because he had a booth at their clinics. He was making thousands of dollars from the marijuana he sold to patients he recruited at the traveling MCN roadshows.

I moved onto a different topic, floating the idea of the MMGA and MBA cosponsoring an educational conference with Arno speaking as the headline event. I was confident that an alliance with the MMGA would yield benefits for MBA. My gut screamed that we would face a tough political battle in the 2011 legislative session and now was the time to begin gathering the troops. There was a lot at stake. A partnership between MBA and the MMGA seemed like a good fit.

The dinner went as well as could be hoped. I wasn't sure if I'd convinced them of the necessity of cannabis quality control, but at least I planted a seed. They liked the idea of the educational conference, especially if I was paying for Arno's trip. As a bonus, I accepted their invitation to join the MMGA, as part of their advisory group.

By the end of 2009, Montanans were expressing grave concerns about the unfettered growth of the medical marijuana industry. Cities, towns, and municipalities were overwhelmed by the torrent of growth. Since no regulatory ordinances were in place, dispensaries were opening up everywhere. I could see the writing on the wall if the industry didn't undertake some sort of self-regulation.

A perfect storm requires numerous variables had to align, and the political squall brewing over medical marijuana was no exception. The economic fallout from the Great Recession of 2008 took longer to reach places like Bozeman, but eventually, the pain of the housing bubble collapse found its way to the Big Sky state. New housing starts stalled, and construction jobs were scarce. As the slowdown accelerated, the economic incentive to partake in the marijuana gold rush was irresistible. Vacant office space was leased to medical marijuana dispensaries, and empty warehouses were being converted into sizable indoor marijuana grows. For commercial real estate market, marijuana was a godsend.

On other fronts, the HPLC would be arriving any day. Nigel was boning up on his cannabinoid chemistry, and in a few weeks, Arno would be in town.

All we needed now was a permanent space so we could move the lab out of Nigel's garage.

Birthing the Lab

Hiring Arno to apprentice Nigel on the HPLC was priceless. In order to turn my dream of opening a lab that made a positive impact on the medical cannabis industry into a reality, the lab needed to be scrupulous, it needed to command respect and earn the trust of its customers. Taking shortcuts made no sense.

Convincing Arno to help me was the embodiment of fulfilling my dream. Besides being one of the leading experts on cannabis analysis, he was also the chief scientist at Bedrocan, the sole producer of Dutch medical marijuana. Plus, there wasn't a better person on the planet to teach Nigel the subtleties of cannabinoid analysis.

My relationship with Arno was much personal as it was business. I admired marveled at his Spock-like way of looking at the world, especially his perspective on cannabis. Arno had detached himself from the excitement and hype surrounding cannabis; to him, it was simply a plant, albeit a very special one.

Cannabinoid analysis is tricky.

Under Nigel's direction, I bought a reconditioned Agilent 1100 HPLC—at the time, a state-of-the-art machine. An HPLC is a powerful analytical tool, able to separate, purify, and identify molecules based on the chemical polarity (a function of the molecule's native electrical charge), the size, and the pH of the molecule. Additionally, the molecular separation is also affected by the properties of HPLC column itself; nuanced factors such as the solvent, pressure, and the physical size and electrical charge of the beads within the column. As the sample flows through, large, highly charged substances move through the chromatography column at a slower rate than smaller non-charged molecules.

The art of the HPLC is understanding the sample to be analyzed and providing the appropriate milieu for the separation of the molecules and compounds of interest. As the various substances within a sample are separated by the HPLC column, their chemical signatures are recognized by the detector, which records their identity as a curve on a graph. The identity of the substance is based upon the time it takes for the substance to be recognized by the detector, called the retention time. The retention time of the sample and the standard should match.

The HPLC allowed Nigel to accurately measure the cannabinoid content of medical cannabis. Finally, there was a way to treat cannabis like other medicine. The lab could now provide the dosing information for any cannabis preparation. Testing CIPs, like brownies or tinctures, allowed patients to know the amount of THC found in the product so patients could reliably dose themselves based on their symptoms. Knowing the dose made obsolete the blind guessing and risking either underdosing or, most worrisome, overdosing themselves with THC.

The information from the HPLC would be applied to dried floss (trimmed bud) as well. Growers could test their harvests and have empirical results to gauge their growing techniques. Growers could assess their breeding program success, too; testing permitted growers a reliable method to search for new strains with varying cannabinoid concentrations.

Although I knew that the economic cost of entry into the cannabis testing market was high and there was a significant intellectual capital obstacle to entering the market, I was obsessed that someone else would capture the testing market in Montana. Devin assuaged my anxiety.

"Competition in the marketplace is a good thing. It validates your business model," said Devin confidently.

Daubert promised to post the press release about the opening of the lab in the December PFU newsletter. To my chagrin, the MBA press release was overshadowed by an announcement of another cannabis testing lab opening in Missoula, Cannabinalysis. I felt Daubert had undercut me. Considering the collegial relationship I'd cultivated with Daubert, I asked for an explanation. To his credit, Daubert offered an apology. It was another lesson that working in the cannabis world was not for the thin-skinned.

Cannabanalysis was the brainchild of Beth Thorner. She earned a biology degree from SUNY College of Environmental Forestry and had spent the last twenty years doing quality control work for a nutritional supplement company in Missoula. Like many others, she saw the promise of the cannabis boom. Her ad in the PFU newsletter suggested that cannabinoid analysis, as well as testing for pesticides and molds in cannabis was quick, simple, and cheap.

Remember, in 2010, there were no cannabis testing requirements by the state. In a perfect world, all cannabis would be tested for toxins such as pesticides, as well as molds and heavy metals, which would be expensive. Providing safe cannabis to patients was MBA's priority since growers were under no state supervision regarding how they grew and processed their marijuana.

Treating cannabis like a medicine meant identifying and quantifying the cannabinoid content, as well as any contaminants, or toxins in the cannabis sold to patients. Only a lab could undertake appropriate quality control testing.

Nigel told me a story that highlights the importance of quality control. An employee from a local grower told Nigel about an accident at their facility. While flushing the irrigation system for their crop of nearly mature marijuana, someone had accidentally dropped a large mercury thermometer into the water holding tank. The thermometer broke, and hundreds of silver droplets of mercury disappeared through the irrigation tubing and into the perlite medium where the plants were rooted. The employee told the owner that he was sorry for ruining the large crop of succulent female plants.

"What do you mean you ruined the crop? The plants look fine to me," he said.

"We can't sell this as medicine; it's been contaminated with mercury. These plants will suck up mercury like a dry sponge."

"You're looking at half a million dollars worth of primo bud, and you want me to trash it all because you spilled a little mercury in the water? You're crazy. Nobody's going to know."

The employee was correct. Cannabis is one of many plants that the Environmental Protection Agency (EPA) uses to re-seed chemically spoiled Superfund sites. The plants chelate the contaminants, cleaning up heavy metals and organic solvents from contaminated soil. The process is called phytoremediation.[96]

I cringed thinking how many patients used the mercury-contaminated cannabis, and how many other such stories remained untold. Birthing the lab was the only way to make medical marijuana safe.

Full Spectrum Labs

Full Spectrum Labs (FSL) was the first analytical lab in Colorado devoted to medical marijuana. The lab was founded by Bob Winnicki, a graduate from the University of Michigan with a degree in Molecular and Cellular Biology. He was a fourth-year student who dropped out of the University of Colorado School of Medicine to start his cannabis testing empire.

As impressed as I was with his cannabis vision, I always wondered why anyone would drop out of med school with just months to go.

FSL advertised that it could test cannabis from all the existing medical marijuana states. At the time, Cannabanalysis and FSL had drop-down tabs to each other's websites. Apparently, samples collected in Montana were sent to FSL. It seemed like a pretty gutsy move since any shipment of cannabis across state lines is a felony offense. FSL had also enlisted another start-up lab, MontanaBioTech rumored to be running out of a basement.

The knowledge that other labs had just sprouted up and were rumored to be sending their samples to Colorado bothered me. I was trying to play by the rules because spending time in prison on account of cannabis wasn't an option. Six weeks passed and I hadn't heard a peep regarding my DEA research lab permit. My patience was fading, knowing that a competitor lab in Colorado was illegally attempting to secure the entire US market for medical cannabis testing.

After pondering my options, I called the DEA.

The first person I contacted was DEA Import/Export Unit Chief Dan Gillan. Mr. Gillan was helpful and polite, directing me to the supervisor of the Rocky Mountain Division, Lynne Powers, in the Salt Lake City office.

Ms. Powers sounded like a northeast corridor transplant, aside from her accent, her answers were terse and vague. Her responses left me with the impression that she couldn't have cared less about my research lab permit.

"Is there some sort of time frame I can count on?"

"Doctor, you'll just have to wait. These types of things take time."

Having accomplished so much in such a short time I wasn't going to let a wound-too-tight bureaucrat obstruct me. After a couple of more weeks, I called the Salt Lake City office again. This time I spoke with an amiable young agent who told me that Agent Powers wasn't in the office. I told him my story about starting MBA and my impatience awaiting a DEA research lab license.

"Unfortunately, sir, I've only worked here for two years, so everything has got to go through the proper chain of command. We're a little understaffed at the moment, which isn't an excuse, but it helps explain the wait. You'll have to await word from Agent Wingert when she returns back to the office. I can connect you to her voicemail."

"That would be great." I left another message and sent her an email.

After two weeks without a response, my patience was gone. I had spent more than $40,000 on the lab so far. I was playing by the rules and getting nowhere. The competition was usurping federal law, taking local market share from MBA. Something needed to be done.

Since the Salt Lake City office wasn't being responsive, I called the DEA's Denver office, hoping for some sort of response.

The Grand Illusion

After New Year's, the pace picked up appreciably; it seemed like a million things were demanding my attention. The HPLC had finally arrived and had been set up in its temporary residence at Nigel's home. Hillari had promised she'd have Dana trained for the January clinic. Arno was arriving in a few days. And the final preparations for the MBA/MMGA-sponsored medical marijuana expo were far from complete.

My stress level felt like a busy day in the ED, except this stress didn't end at the completion of my 12-hour shift. Fortunately, the day before Arno's arrival, Bridger Bowl got ten inches of fresh powder. Skiing had a way of shifting my perspective, and since I couldn't ride my bike, making fresh tracks through the trees was a welcomed consolation and stress reliever. It was a bluebird day, and the snow was treating me good when I received a text from Anthony Gallo about speaking at the MMGA meeting that afternoon.

"Be at Sigler's shop by two."

Reluctantly, I cut my day short to attend the meeting. I thought it would be an opportunity to market MBA to the group meeting at Mark Sigler's dispensary, Montana Caregivers. I arrived just after 2:00 p.m. Gallo said the meeting wouldn't start until 5:00.

"You cost me two hours of powder, dude." I hissed.

Gallo looked puzzled. "It snowed?" He wasn't a skier. His idea of exercise was playing *Call of Duty* and counting his money.

Gallo, Sigler, and the rest of the dispensary staff went into the break room office and began lighting up.

"Give me a shout when the meeting starts. I'll be down the hallway." I excused myself, sitting in one of the empty offices. I found a banged-up Ovation six-string that was leaning against one of the walls. Playing music is a reliable means for me to re-center.

When the meeting finally began, I only recognized a couple of members who'd come to WH&H to get their medical card. The rest of over two dozen men were strangers. Panning across the room, I thought of the bar scene from *Star Wars*. Suddenly, I understood the disbelief that Luke Skywalker must have felt when he entered Chalums's Cantina on the planet of Tatooine to meet Hans Solo and Chewbacca in search of a ship to take them to Alderaan.

Understanding the concept of the bell curve, I expected the MMGA group would be diverse, but never so radically skewed to the bizarre end of the curve. One man showed up dressed in full camo, hat-to-boots, with a matching mountain-man beard; some looked disheveled and unwashed, a few appeared to have had some sort of genetic syndrome that predisposed them to a troll-like appearance. But the guy who most caught my attention was a young, heavily tattooed grower who had the molecular structure of THC etched into his neck. It was hard not to stare.

My curiosity got the best of me. "Is that the structure of THC?"

"Good eye. Well, it's supposed to be. As you can tell, they put the hydroxyl group in the wrong position," he said with a shrug.

"I see that."

If this represents the backbone of the MMGA, MT-148 is in a lot of trouble, I thought.

The president of the MMGA gave me a brief introduction, and then I spoke to the group about the lab. I thought the presentation went well, but their reaction was muted.

While I was at the meeting, Nigel was picking Arno up at the airport. I planned to meet them for an informal dinner at Jamie Stumble's house, Mike Singer's business partner. Mike's dispensary, Sensible Alternatives, had just opened a few months prior. Lori came her longtime friend Annie, who I hired expressly to cater the event.

While we waited for the finishing touches of the meal, Jamie gave us a tour. At the top of the stairs was a room with a brightly lit array of LED grow lights hanging in a corner. "This is my temporary grow room, and these are my new seedlings," he said with the pride of a new father. "I bought the seeds in this tray from a store in Holland," Jamie said excitedly to Arno.

Arno bent down, carefully inspecting the tray of cannabis seedlings. "These are very nice, Jamie."

"Did you get all of your seeds from Holland?" I asked.

"No, I got them from a couple of different places," Jamie said. "A got a bunch from the Vancouver Seed Bank and a few from Bulldog Seeds in Amsterdam. And then I found a bunch of really interesting medicinal strains from Seed Supreme in the UK. There were so many kinds. It was so hard not to get a little bit of everything."

"How many strains did you get?" Nigel queried matter-of-factly.

Jamie turned to me and grinned. "Forty-two."

"Seriously?" I quipped.

Jamie nodded with a blush, and we all laughed.

"I could have easily spent five grand on seeds had my wife not said, 'Enough!' When the seeds got delivered, it was better than Christmas. I can't wait to see what these plants turn out like."

I appreciated Jamie's enthusiasm. I love plants, too. My dad was a gardener. I planted my first solo garden when I was twelve.

"How do you keep track of which strains are which?" Arno asked.

"I was an accounting major in college, so I really groove on keeping meticulous records." Jamie proceeded to show us his germination notebook.

Arno looked at me and smiled. "This is quite impressive, Jamie."

Jamie is the last guy you'd pick out of a crowd as a marijuana grower. He's clean-cut, bathes regularly, and consistently articulates his points without endless ramblings. Jamie seemed to have found his niche. "The more strains, the better, is what I've read. Patients like variety; they get bored of smoking the same strain. We're growing traditional strains like Sour Diesel, White Widow, AK47, G13, and Northern Lights. But we're also growing some really underground stuff like Headband, Eight Ball, Afghan Cow, and Bubba Kush. It's pretty exciting."

Nigel affirmed his enthusiasm with a repetition of crisps nods. He tried not to act professorial, but his confident demeanor suspended any notion that he wasn't knowledgeable; he wasn't your typical scientist. "Wow. That's pretty cool."

Annie called us for dinner. We enjoyed a terrific meal and a few bottles of wine. It was an unusual gathering of committed cannabis activists.

The next day, Arno and I hiked up the "M," at the entrance of Bridger Canyon. The temperature was mild for January, and we lucked out on another bluebird day. We talked about my son, medicinal plants, and Arno's first trip to Thailand. I knew that Arno was selective about who he let into his private circle, and I was grateful for his trust in me. Having spent the last eight months working in the cannabis field, I was amazed that he was still so affable.

After the hike, I took Arno back to Jamie's to freshen up before our community presentation at the Emerson. I hadn't personally communicated with anyone in the MMGA since we agreed to host the event cooperatively—that was Dana's job. I trusted that they would honor our agreements.

The MMGA did all the marketing of the event, which was titled "The Medical Marijuana Educational Series." They sponsored a series of free public lectures and workshops earlier in the day. Additionally, the event offered an exhibition area for vendors of products and services supporting the medical marijuana community.

I met Nigel and Arno at the Emerson. As we entered the building, I noticed the promotional posters hanging. The MMGA logo was prominently displayed at the top, while at the bottom of the poster, and half the size were the logos of MBA and WH&H.

"Fuckers," I whispered.

My naïveté was exposed once more. I trusted the MMGA because I wanted them to trust me. I wanted recognition for my pivotal role in bringing Arno to Bozeman. If it weren't for my efforts, this event would never have happened. I was angry and felt deceived. But by now, I shouldn't have been surprised. The MMGA was promoting their agenda. It was another lesson that integrity in the cannabis industry is defined differently. I was beginning to understand the concept of the grand illusion.

I complained to Nigel and Arno about the posters.

"Big deal, Mike. Look with your own eyes at what you have done," Arno admonished.

Nigel was quick to follow. "Yeah, Mike. It's no biggie. Just let it go. It's not worth it."

I appreciated their support. Regardless, it was not the time to let petty anger get in the way of Arno's presentation and the announcement of MBA's opening. I was thrilled that the event had filled the theater with cannabis-friendly folks from around the community.

At 7:00 p.m., the president of the MMGA went to the podium and introduced me. I discussed "The Therapeutic Aspects of Medical Marijuana." Then, I had the honor of introducing Arno. His presentation, "The Future of Medical Marijuana," was terrific. The reception afterward was also well attended. Numerous admirers flocked to talk with Arno. They treated him like a rock star. It was entertaining to watch my Dutch friend navigate the crowd of glazy-eyed admirers.

Afterward, the three of us went to our favorite watering hole, Montana Ale Works, to have a few pints, shoot pool, and talk about Arno's upcoming chemistry lecture the next day at MSU.

All or Nothing

Nigel and I had been working on fostering a relationship with the MSU chemistry department since his arrival in Bozeman. The department had expensive machines engineered to unlock the secrets of molecules and chemical reactions that we could never afford.

One of the most powerful machines were spectrometers—*Star Trek*-like devices that allow chemists to peer into the invisible world of molecules, shedding insights into how they bond and interact with other molecules. Spectrometers are the Rosetta Stone of the chemistry world, opening up our knowledge of both natural and synthetic compounds. Without these analytical devices, the world as we know it would not exist. Not only are these instruments expensive (some costing upwards of a million dollars), many of them, like a magnetic resonance spectrophotometer, are large and require a restricted space for operation. The chemistry department had all the toys a chemist could want—and lots of them.

A month before, a meeting took place between me, Nigel, and Dr. David Singel, chairman of the MSU chemistry department. Dr. Singel is a silver-haired academic whose research centered around the biological activity of nitric oxide, an important biological reactant. Singel quietly listened to our pitch for a cooperative arrangement with the department and MBA. He found our ideas impressive, but he wasn't about to offer us anything concrete; he didn't become chairman of the department without understanding the chain of command and the concept of political liabilities. Singel wasn't going to make a potentially career-ending decision to help a couple of newbie medical marijuana researchers.

I'd hoped to garner an agreement that Nigel would have unfettered access to the resources of the chemistry department, but what we did get was Dr. Singel giving us a lecture hall for Arno's presentation. Despite the dissolved fantasy that Dr. Singel would embrace our idea of turning the department into a national center for medical marijuana research, I was grateful for the support we got.

Unquestionably, Dr. Singel was a gracious host. Aside from giving us an arena for Arno's lecture, he invited us to lunch at the faculty dining room. The faculty were fascinated with MBA's agenda. Several of the professors, including Dr. Singel, confided that they'd done postdoctoral fellowships at Leiden University. They schmoozed Arno with their stories of Holland and by speaking in broken Dutch.

To accommodate the overflow of both academics and laymen in Arno's topic, "The Chemistry of Medical Cannabinoids," the lecture was moved to the larger Byster Auditorium. Dr. Singel graciously introduced Arno. And Arno didn't disappoint.

During the Q&A session, an MSU undergrad asked. "What would I have to do to have a legitimate cannabis testing laboratory?"

Arno looked at me and smiled. "Maybe my friend, Dr. Geci, owner of Montana Botanical Analysis, who is responsible for sponsoring this lecture, would be better to answer that question?"

I was caught off-balance by Arno's deflection. "I think the most important thing about establishing a reputable cannabis testing facility is having qualified people running the lab. Real scientists, with real degrees. Don't you agree, Dr. Hazekamp?"

Arno nodded. "Yes, indeed. Cannabis research needs to be done with the same respect to academic integrity as any other discipline. And maybe even more so because of all the political controversy that surrounds the plant."

After the lecture, Nigel, Arno, and I toured the department's facilities. At the conclusion of the trip, Dr. Singel held a private meeting with us. He was impressed with our work and wished there could be a way of fostering a partnership, but the politics were too dodgy. Regardless, the three of us walked out of Gaines Hall elated.

We piled into my beat-up Subaru and headed to Ale Works.

The next day, I received an email from a reporter at the *Bozeman Chronicle* asking me for an interview about the lab. A lengthy piece about the lab appeared in the *Chronicle* a few weeks later: "Taking the Mystery Out of Marijuana."[97]

The disappointment of the MMGA partnership paled in comparison to the momentum I felt with MBA's introduction to MSU. Nigel and I were a team of highly credible professionals on the cusp of opening the door to changing how the country perceived a beneficial plant that had been maligned for so long.

Arno taught Nigel his protocols for cannabinoid analysis. The pair tinkered with the HPLC in the spare room next to Nigel's garage. The symbolism of a garage start-up wasn't lost on me. I wondered if the likes of Jobs and Woznick, and Bill Hewlett and David Packard had felt a similar excitement as Nigel and I. Arno had become our friend and colleague. I was grateful that he had given us a chance to prove our commitment to sound cannabis science.

After dropping Arno off at the airport, I read the PFU newsletter that had just been posted. The lead article was a wrap-up of the medical marijuana expo held at the Emerson. Nowhere was MBA or WH&H credited for cosponsoring the event, or for bringing Arno to Montana. Incensed by the omission, I sent Daubert an email detailing my disappointment. I didn't hold back my frustrations, suggesting that "egos prevail over principle and honor," and asked for an addendum placed in the next newsletter.

Daubert again sent a lengthy apology. He said that he'd post an addendum, giving the lab the recognition that it was due. The incident bolstered my suspicions of trusting anyone in the cannabis industry. I was beginning to feel a little paranoid.

Back in New York, I told Devin that Anthony Gallo had given Nigel a new iPad. Nigel was slow to disclose where he'd gotten the device.

Devin frowned. "It's a little concerning that Nigel is the critical piece of the MBA operation. Do you think he would break ranks with you and work for someone else?"

After nearly a year into this journey, I was past the point of no return. There was no going back or changing the crew now. "I trust Nigel like a brother. If we can't do MBA together as a team, considering all that we've overcome and accomplished, I'd just as soon close the lab and go back to the emergency department."

"You remember the story of Cain and Abel?" Devin asked.

If that was our fate, then so be it. But until then, I was unconditionally committed to the path that had gotten he and I to this point. It was all or nothing.

Into the Darkness

Nearly a year had passed since immersing myself into the world of medical marijuana. One observation was apparent: the image of the plant was blurred—the myths surrounding cannabis cast long shadows and seemed to flourish in the darkness.

The lab was created to beam the light of knowledge and transparency onto the plant, adopting its rightful place as a beneficial medicinal offering. Initially, the concept of testing cannabis as part of a quality control regimen was lost on many growers. While some saw the benefit, most thought it was a waste of time and money.

"Patients are going to buy my product whether it's tested or not" was the most common response I heard. I knew it would be an uphill battle. I needed a marketing strategy.

Having attended lots of drug rep lunches in medical school, I took a page out of big pharma's marketing book. Nigel and I wined and dined prospective clients, educating them on how MBA could make their businesses more profitable. It didn't take long for the strategy to start paying dividends.

One brisk November evening, I agreed to have dinner with a grower who was opening a dispensary in Bozeman. He asked me to meet him at a nondescript Mexican joint at the back end of a strip mall on North Seventh Street. I walked into the dimly lit venue with the sounds of a Mexican horn section playing in the background. In the rear of the restaurant, a man raised his hand.

Dan Phinney contacted me after the PFU announcement of the lab opening. He wanted to meet for dinner and get more information. Dan is a California native and was the spitting image of Patrick Simmons, the long-haired lead guitar player for the Doobie Brothers. Phinney came to Montana for the express purpose of growing pot. His wife, Maxine, could have easily been mistaken as his daughter. Street smart and ambitious, she was also conspicuously pregnant with their first child.

"It's my second chance to get things right, Doc." Phinney smiled as Maxine snuggled against him. Over dinner he interrogated me about the lab. He gauged my interest in sharing the new high-end suite he had just leased.

I liked Phinney and Maxine, but I was crystal clear. "I'll be happy to look at the space, but the lab is independent, and the clinic will be open to anyone—not just patients who use you as their caregiver."

Phinney clasped his hands. "Doc, if that's what you want, that's what you'll get. I was going to split space as a grow and a dispensary, but then I heard about your lab." His idea was to subsidize my space so he could have direct access to the lab and a doctor.

"When people see what a cool place we have, they won't wanna go nowhere else. C'mon, Doc, let's go take a look."

The pair got into their black Hummer and led the way. I knew I was in for a treat when they pulled into the gated basement parking lot of the Snowload Building on Eighth and Main. It was a luxury office space, down the street from MSU. On the elevator to the top floor, Phinney detailed his vision for the space. When the door opened, I was overcome by the smell of pot.

Aside from the smell, the place was nothing short of palatial. The cabinets and shelves were teak while the floors were a yellow bamboo under vaulted ceilings. The walls were painted in spring shades of green and yellow and lined with expansive windows. A huge balcony faced Eighth Avenue toward the university. The east balcony looked toward downtown and the Gallatin Range. The north balcony had a hot tub and overlooked the Bridgers. The months-long search for a space for the lab and the clinic seemed to be over.

I felt a flush of gratitude, immediately followed by an odd feeling that this seemed too good to be true.

Full of surprises, Phinney took me into his "medicine" room. He had a selection of marijuana varieties that dwarfed even Gallo's offerings. I'd never seen so many different types of marijuana in one place, not even in Amsterdam. Phinney read my mind. "Thirty-eight strains, Doc. Count 'em."

Phinney excused himself and returned wheeling around in a bulky, antique electric wheelchair. A tattered leather cowboy hat framed his sun-bleached face; his long gray-streaked locks silhouetted a boyish smile that rippled across his lips. He reminded me of a kid in a bumper car.

"How'd ya like to get ya one of these, Doc?"

"I'll pass for now."

"I bet your son would like one of these, Doc! What'ya think? You'd a liked one of these when you was his age, wouldn't ya, Doc?"

Maybe it was the reference to my son, or my childhood, or maybe the way he said "Doc." Whatever it was, Phinney pushed a button.

"I don't like being called Doc."

He laughed. "Why the fuck not?"

"Could you please call me Mike, Michael, or Dr. Mike?"

Phinney turned his body and angled his head. "What the hell's wrong with me calling you 'Doc'?"

"I find it patronizing."

Phinney pulled up next to me in his twelve-volt Electrocart and took a quick hit off a blunt he'd had on the armrest of the wheelchair. His coal-black eyes sized me up as he blew out the smoke and patted me on the knee. "You're OK, Doc. Let's get down to business."

Maxine tossed out random building specs as we toured the space. I envisioned a place for the clinic and the best spot for the lab. I was so excited I could have wet myself. I couldn't wait to tell Nigel.

"This place is so cool. It seems perfect. The only thing missing is a guitar."

The space oozed sophistication. It was nicer than any house I'd ever lived in. "And the landlord knows what you are planning on doing, and they're cool with it all?"

"Yep. And we even talked to the boys downstairs at Merrill Lynch. They even asked me about investing some money in our operation."

"Seriously? This is an absolutely sweet spot for the lab and the clinic, but the dispensary is the sketchy bit. It's the one thing that's causing me any negative reaction. I just need to think about it."

"I understand. We weren't expecting you to sign a lease this evening, Doc. We're just thrilled that you like it so much."

The ghosts of Pete Jones and JC sat on my shoulders like smirking demons. Phinney's space was tempting—it was lovely and professional-looking. The stakes of my decision were sky high, economically, professionally, and personally. This was no time to be impetuous. There would be no deal until I had filtered Phinney through my confidantes—Nigel, and then Sam, followed by Jerry Taylor. Although everybody loved him, the consensus was that having Phinney as a business partner would be a calculated risk.

One afternoon we were looking at security systems when Phinney mentioned that he was a born-again Christian. I nearly pissed myself laughing.

Phinney's affect flattened. To brand the insult deeper into my soul, he took out his pocket New Testament and turned to 1 Corinthians 13:4-8. He momentarily glared at me and cleared his throat.

"Love is patient, love is kind. It does not envy, it does not boast, it is not proud. It does not dishonor others, it is not self-seeking, it is not easily angered, it keeps no records of wrongs. Love does not delight in evil but rejoices with the truth. It always protects, always trusts, always hopes, always perseveres. Love never fails." Then he stopped, looked at me square in the eye, and smiled. "This is my favorite verse of scripture, Doc. It's the one that turned the light on in my soul."

"Wow. I'm sorry I laughed, but surely you know why?"

"Doc, I'm not a two-year-old."

I liked Phinney. I felt a kinship toward him similar to that of a wayward yet charming older brother. But he wasn't my brother; he was a guy offering me a business space that I desperately needed. The business community was scared to death of the medical marijuana boom. Building owners were afraid that anything associated with marijuana would poison the shopping experience of local patrons. Picture *The Walking Dead*, stoned.

Nigel and I looked at dozens of commercial spaces throughout the Gallatin Valley. Once we mentioned the word "marijuana," everyone said no—our respective MD/Ph.D. combination meant nothing. My concern with Phinney was the appearance that we were in cahoots together. I was adamant not to let that happen.

Before Christmas, Phinney and I were meeting with a group of smartly dressed professionals about a security system that would pass a DEA lab inspection. Hours were spent mulling over

Nigel's detailed drawings of the lab. I sketched out the medical office space, while Phinney drew out the dispensary. I was glad that he also embraced my idea of a community cannabis health co-op, agreeing that the dispensary would donate 10 percent of sales back to the co-op. It felt like everything was coming together.

It was a wondrously giddy time. Hanging out with Phinney and Maxine was fun. She brought a balance to his eccentricities. He treated me like a long-lost son, dolling out his pearls of wisdom of life, parenthood, and healing from failed marriages. I soaked up every morsel of advice.

The afternoon before flying back to New York, I stopped by to wish everyone a Merry Christmas. Phinney, Maxine, and her older cousin, Junior, were sitting on the couch, watching TV. The ceiling was layered with thick smoke. Junior sat slumped into a blob of cushions. He munched methodically at the half-empty bowl of popcorn anchored in his lap. Junior slid his aviator glasses back up his nose and waved.

Phinney jumped off the couch and gave me a big hug. "Doctor Mike!"

"Merry Christmas." I gave Maxine a bottle of wine with a note attached: *Wine, like marijuana, shouldn't be consumed until after the baby is born.*

"I'm so glad you came by before you fly back to New York." I'd never seen Phinney so excited. "Now you sit down, Doc, cuz I got something I know you're *really* gonna like."

Feeling a bit awkward, I complied.

"Close your eyes, Michael," Maxine whispered.

"Now, how 'bout that, Doc?"

I was speechless. Staring me straight in the eye was another Alice-in-Wonderland moment. Before me was an expensive leather guitar case, with *Logan Guitars* emblazoned on the top. I'd heard of the company but had never seen one of their guitars—until now.

Surely this wasn't a gift?

Suddenly, I felt an appreciable imbalance—a deep visceral discomfort. I'd never received a gift like this from anyone in my entire life. I was reluctant to open the case.

Maxine sensed my hesitation. "Michael, let me help you open it."

What appeared from the plush cushioned case was an arch-top guitar with a bright glossy burgundy finish. The tuners were gold-plated, the fretboard was Mother of Pearl inlay, and the pickguard was weathered tortoise shell. The guitar must have cost at least $10,000.

"I don't know what to say. Are you giving me this guitar?"

"I told you I can't play a lick," Phinney said flatly, reaching for a joint. "It's our gift to you. For all you are doing for us."

"Take it out and play it, Michael," Maxine suggested.

I picked up the guitar. It was perfectly balanced. The fretboard was thin, with a supple neck, and when I plucked the first chords, I wondered if I'd ever played a guitar that sounded as delicate.

As I readied to leave, Phinney insisted that I take the guitar. "It's yours, partner."

That evening I had dinner with Allie, one of the women who also rented space at The Alchemy. I told her about the guitar.

"Sounds like a bribe to me."

"Really?"

"Think about it, dude. It seems pretty obvious to me."

A bribe? Why would he do that? He seems like such a nice guy...plus he's a Christian.

Sharing a space with Phinney was not without considerable risk. Our physical proximity threatened to alienate the lab and the clinic with others. Although I hadn't done a formal background check, I felt comfortable with his vibe. But what if Allie was right about the guitar? It was starting to feel creepy.

The next day during my layover in Minneapolis, Phinney called me. "Hey, Doc, you got a minute?"

"Anything for my wheelchair-bound friend."

"You'd better sit down."

"What's up?"

"We just got evicted from the Snowload Building."

It took a moment for me to process. "You're joking, right?"

"This ain't no joke, Doc."

"What happened?"

"The motherfuckers at Merrill Lynch complained. They said it wasn't them but a decision from corporate."

"Holy cow...I'm sorry to hear about that."

"Me too, Doc. Listen, we'll get something worked out. Have a good time with your boy. Call me when you're back in town."

"No worries. Take care."

Into the Darkness

Then, prior to boarding my plane, I received a call from the DEA field office in Billings requesting me to withdraw my application for the Schedule I research lab permit. Agent Jester promised me that the DEA would refund my application fee. And now, without a lab space, there was no need for an inspection.

I was now back to the drawing board.

It was a Sunday afternoon, a few weeks later when I returned to Bozeman. I stopped by to help Phinney move his stuff out of the Snowload Building. The last thing to be loaded was the Electrocart.

Then my phone rang.

"Hi, Michael. I'm downstairs." Hillari had returned.

Like a Spielberg film, the light caught Hillari at the apex of the open stairwell. With her Costa Rican tan, she was glowing. I'm not sure I'd ever seen anyone as beautiful. We gave each other a big hug.

"I'm so glad you're back, Hill. I missed you."

We Got Peaks!

In baseball terms, having Arno come to Bozeman was a grand slam. Arno helped Nigel work out the kinks of the HPLC cannabinoid protocols. Hosting Arno's lectures was also instrumental. Although a majority of the growers didn't understand a lick of chemistry, the fact that MBA was associated with a cannabis scientist from the Netherlands was huge. Growers from across the state began calling the lab for additional information.

Being at the forefront of an emerging industry has it's drawbacks. Pioneering a wilderness or a technology is fraught with uncertainties, will the path you're taking be the most efficient, the most sustainable, the most popular, the most successful. And so it was with MBA; how would our idea of cannabis testing would play out in the marketplace?

After some consideration, Nigel thought a statistically reliable sample would require less than two grams of dried flos (the proper term for the harvested bud) per pound of cannabis. An MBA cannabinoid certificate required that each independent strain would be tested using two grams of flos or CIP, such as a tincture or butter.

I was concerned that growers and dispensary owners just wanted numbers they could put next to their product; for most of them, testing was just a marketing gimmick. At that time, no one seemed interested in any cannabinoid other than THC.

Anthony Gallo was quick to validate my concerns. "The higher the THC number, the better the weed," he spouted off repeatedly.

In the recreational market, if you were looking for marijuana that would alter your reality and get you the most stoned, the higher the percentage of THC, the greater the potency. And marijuana entrepreneurs knew that the higher the percentage of THC, the more they could charge. They knew that patients were willing to pay big bucks for top-shelf (high THC potency) marijuana. In 2010, few people had even heard of cannabinoids like CBD, THVC, CBC, or CBG, let alone appreciate their therapeutic benefits. From my perspective, the Montana system was all about selling pot, not medicine. This was something I was determined to change.

MBA testing offered an empiric way to take the guesswork out of deciding which strain to use, allowing patients to compare apples to apples and help educate and protect patients when purchasing their medicine. On January 13, 2010, MBA ran its first cannabis samples.

"We got peaks!" Nigel wrote me. MBA was now operational. It was an exciting moment for both of us.

Less than a year after finishing his doctorate, Nigel was living his dream, fully immersed in the contemporary world of cannabis chemistry. He was genius; interacting with the motley crew of marijuana growers and dispensary owners curious about what MBA could do for their businesses. Although Nigel's staccato and frenetic expressions belie the furious spinning of his academically oriented brain, he was a chameleon when it came to meeting folks on their level. Whatever the situation, Nigel made you think he was just one of the guys—which was one of the skills that made him so valuable.

Nigel loved sitting with clients and methodically explaining the results of their cannabis analysis. Clients' eyes lit up seeing the quantitative peaks that represented the cannabinoids in the cannabis they'd grown and hear Nigel explain the data. Showing a client their cannabis chromatographic peaks was like showing an expectant mother her baby on ultrasound. Testing gave growers and patients alike a means to assess the potency and cannabinoid composition of the product. The expression "good bud" took on a new meaning. Many dispensaries framed their MBA certificate over their product display tables.

With Devin's help, I scaled the volume of our testing to provide a better value. Devin also suggested that each client sign a master services agreement (MSA), so clients knew exactly what testing services they were getting for their money.

Word spread fast.

Clients learned that the value of testing exceeded mere THC potency. Cannabis with a high percentage of CBN (a degradation product of both THC and CBD) indicated that the flos had been degraded and was not fresh. Cannabis testing was an industry game-changer. Dispensary owners no longer had to take a grower's word about the relative freshness of the product; if the CBN percentage was elevated, the cannabis was not recently harvested. The likely interpretation was that you were being sold old cannabis. The lab provided a means to objectify the data. The numbers didn't lie.

Without the HPLC, there was no way of knowing if the cannabis contained other medicinal cannabinoids like CBD and THCV. These blockbuster molecules couldn't be detected by smoking, unlike THC-rich strains. MBA testing also included spot checks for mold and mites, suggested growing conditions that were less than hygienic. Growers could use the cannabinoid testing to tweak their grow protocols and quantify if changes in their growing techniques yielded significantly higher cannabinoid content.

MBA changed the marketplace. One of the more interesting observations was how MBA precipitated a THC arms race. Numbers became an extension of their botanical ego. The first strain to break 20 percent THC was hailed as a great achievement. MBA testing demonstrated that with meticulous growing conditions and thoroughbred genetics, cannabis in Montana soon broke the 26 percent THC barrier. The MBA cannabis certificate became a badge of honor, certifying that they had the most potent marijuana in town.

It wasn't long before MBA's impact hit the CIP market. These products spanned the limits of processor creativity in the form of lip balms, skin creams and salves, and all edible products, like carbonated beverages, tinctures, butter, oils, candies, and baked goods of every variety. And it was in the CIP market where I thought testing had the most impact on patient safety.

Searching for a Home

For the next four months, MBA operated out of Nigel's spare eight-by-ten room. After the disappointing loss of the Snowload Building we continued to check out dozens of potential spaces. Nothing was working out.

Reluctantly, I enlisted the help of a commercial real estate specialist. I settled on Dennis Hardin, an ex-Marine and lifetime resident of Gallatin County who'd been in the local commercial real estate market for nearly thirty years.

The first place he showed us was the west section of a large duplex that he owned; the east part housed his office. Mr. Hardin was curious about what kind of business Nigel and I were operating.

"I'm a physician looking for a space for a small medical office and a laboratory."

Mr. Hardin seemed impressed.

The place had plenty of space for a reception and waiting area, as well as a series of private rooms where I could see patients and have my office. There was also a separate area upstairs that was large enough for the lab, a conference room, as well as an office for Nigel. After touring the entire space, we looked at each other and smiled.

Mr. Hardin sensed a deal and invited us back to his office. Hardin is a rather wide man whose suspenders strained as he leaned back in his heavily padded leather office chair. He's a matter-of-fact, Bible-quoting, unabashed Montanan Republican. When we were all seated, Mr. Harden delicately pressed his fingertips together. "So, Doctor, just what is it that you are going to do in this laboratory of yours?"

"Uhmmm…" I looked at Nigel, and he gave me a tacit nod.

"We really like your space, Mr. Hardin," I said gingerly.

"That's terrific, but if we are going to do business together, I would like you to call me Dennis," he said, thumping his right hand on his tidy oak desk.

"OK. And you can call me, Mike...Dennis."

"Alright then, Michael, since you are going to be right next to my office, I think it's important that I know what type of laboratory you are planning on putting there. Nothing criminal I assume," he said with a hearty chuckle.

"Well...it's nothing illegal."

Hardin's cheeks turned ruddy as he leaned forward. "So, Michael, what's the mystery?"

"Do you have an open mind, Dennis?"

"Michael, I've sold more than $100 million dollars of real estate in this valley. I have worked with thousands of clients. I think if I was a closed-minded individual, my success would have been greatly compromised."

"What do you think of medical marijuana?" I asked sheepishly.

Dennis looked at me with a perplexed glare. "I think it's nothing more than an excuse for legalization, personally."

"Can I explain something to you?"

For the next thirty minutes, I detailed the journey of how I became interested in medical marijuana. "We want to bring an element of quality control to this industry. Our goal is to make medical marijuana in Montana as safe to use as any other medicine you would buy at your local pharmacy."

Dennis listened, poker-faced.

"That's why I hired Nigel. He's got his doctorate in chemistry. I'm staking my reputation as a physician on this. Cannabis could help a lot of people if it's used properly, and that's what we want to do—eliminate the fear and the prejudice about this plant. It has the potential to help a lot of people. It would probably help the knee pain you were telling me about earlier."

"Well I'll be," Dennis said shaking his head slowly, his chins swaying as he contemplated his next words.

I looked at Nigel expectedly. "So, when can we move in?"

Dennis measured his words carefully. "Michael, I like you. I really do. I like your partner Nigel, too. I think that what you're trying to do is admirable. But I'm a teetotaler and a church deacon. I'm proud to say that I have never, in all my years, taken so much as a sip of alcohol. My biggest indiscretion is having a Coca-Cola on Christmas. I'm not a fan of marijuana, but you've convinced me that it might not be as much of a problem as I once thought. I want to help you and Nigel find a place for your clinic and laboratory," Dennis pulled nervously on his already taut suspenders, "but not next to my office. I would be happy to have your clinic here, but I don't want to be associated with marijuana—medical or not. I think it would be bad for business."

"Really?" I said with the best puppy-dog eyes I could muster.

"Michael, I'm afraid so."

Our meeting with Mr. Hardin simply validated what we'd already discovered: the business community was not eager to embrace the cannabis culture—medical or otherwise. On one level, I can't say I blamed them. Nearly every day there were media stories about the MCN clinics, about dispensaries being robbed, and about fire bombings of dispensaries. The fear of God had been placed into the minds of Montana citizens and business owners. Dennis Harden was no exception.

Unraveling

Hillari and I kept in contact while she was away. I kept her abreast of how the clinic had unraveled since she'd been gone. I asked her to consider coming back and working until I could find someone to replace Dana. There was no telling how many patients I'd lost because of Dana's incompetence. Patient phone calls went unreturned. She was consistently late for clinic and wasn't able to carry out simple instructions like assembling a patient chart. I tolerated the situation because I had no alternative for my January clinic. I spoke with her several times about her responsibilities until one day she just up and went to Aspen, taking the office cell phone with her. The clinic sat paralyzed until I paid her to FedEx the phone back.

On top of the business stresses, there was family stress, too. While I was away, I called my son every evening, mostly leaving messages on the answering machine. I was never sure he heard them. I sent him emails through his mother's account—again, hoping that my notes would reach their intended target. I appreciated the pitfalls of long-distance parenting.

When I was home, I went to all of Jacob's after-school events, including his basketball games. Basketball was something that brought us together, and we enjoyed watching college hoops. For spring break, we planned a trip to the second and third rounds of the NCAA basketball tournament in Cleveland, beginning our March Madness tradition.

Little league was just around the corner. I had coached the year before, but my monthly trips to Bozeman hindered my ability to spend the time with the kids that they deserved. It was stressful trying to plan which games and practices I could attend. It was unfair to the other coach and the kids.

"I hope you're not planning on coaching this year, Michael," Jacob's mother said with a weighty hint of frustration. Although I didn't appreciate her intrusion, I knew she was right. If I was going to keep the Montana enterprise going, I needed to be more realistic. I loved coaching Jacob's little league teams, but I had to make a choice. I felt that once the lab got off the ground, I would be able to kick back and spend more time with my son.

But it didn't quite turn out that way.

During the elementary school open house, Jacob took part in the school's traditional fourth-grade assignment: describe yourself to the class through a poster. I meandered down the hallway, curious what his friends had produced. Each poster was loaded with identifying items that students colored, penciled, highlighted, or cut and pasted. The kids disclosed their future career plans, names of pets, favorite sports or teams, favorite food or drink, and invariably, a family photo. I eased my way down the family-packed corridor, marveling at each child's depiction of themselves and their world.

At the end of the hallway, near the overhead exit sign, was Jacob's poster. My eyes veered straight for the family photo in the center of the poster. Suddenly, I felt like I was suffocating. Under the pencil-sketched title of "My Family" was a photo that I'd seen on their refrigerator. It was a jolly shot of Jacob, his mom, Casper the cat, and Barney, the remaining canine from our pack. It was a lovely photo.

I found the exit and drove back to my empty farmhouse. I pondered what I'd done to push my son away.

My life was unraveling.

Jackpot

As the winter gave way to spring, the collection of plates that I had been spinning continued to grow. Nigel's wife had been patient, but as one month turned into four, her insistence that we find another space became a regular topic of discussion between Nigel and me.

Mr. Hardin offered us the lower level of the Anderson Building, a six thousand square foot space just off East Main Street. It was an older building with the entire ground floor available. It was another of Mr. Hardin's properties, but it was a much bigger space than we needed. Mr. Hardin was selling me on the idea that it was a perfect space for the clinic and the lab, with plenty of space to sublet out to other practitioners.

The space had potential, but it didn't feel right. Aside from the ten-year lease, which was frightening, it was expensive. During our walk-through, the space was gutted, and to renovate the facility into anything that resembled a modern alternative health complex would cost a fortune. I wasn't willing to spend time trying to lease out the unused space. The stress of looking for a space was beginning to gnaw at me, and Dennis's daily inquiries about the property felt like I was being pushed over a ledge. Devin stalled Dennis several times with lease issues, but time was ticking. Something had to give, and I was feeling pressure to succumb to Dennis's proposal.

And then a miracle happened.

Phinney called. Maxine had found the perfect spot. He asked me to meet him at the Bozeman Medical Arts Building. The property had been the original hospital during the early days of Bozeman and was just three blocks from the heart of Main Street.

The building was a well-known landmark, and it had plenty of parking.

Nigel met me before Phinney and Maxine arrived.

"Could be a cool place," I suggested.

"Sure, seems that way, but we just have to take a look and see what it looks like inside."

"We've been down this road before."

"For sure. But it sure would be nice if this was it."

Phinney pulled up in his Hummer, and we went inside to meet the office manager.

"So how'd you find this place?" I asked.

Phinney pointed affectionately toward Maxine. "Ask her. I think it's the Cheyenne blood that gives her special tracking powers."

Nigel chimed in. "So, how'd you find this place, Maxine? We've been looking for months, even with two real estate agents helping us!"

Maxine just smiled. "I have my ways."

The building manager, Mike Tweeters, was stretched out in his chair, feet crossed on the edge of a cluttered desk intently staring at his smartphone. He was an unimposing fellow who was happy to show us the space. We shook hands and followed him to the southwest end of the building.

"The space just opened up, so it's a little messy. The Red Cross had been leasing the space for years and just moved into their new place last week."

"I can't wait to see what it looks like," I said.

We walked to the end of the corridor, past a few large metal sculptures, and a couple of physician offices. At the end of the hallway was a white metal door with a sign: Suite 105. Tweeney unlocked the door.

"What's the total square footage?" Phinney asked.

"I think it's right at 1,480."

"Ought to be big enough for all of us," Phinney grinned, tugging on his braided goatee.

"And I assume Maxine told you that we want to open a medical marijuana testing laboratory in the space, along with my clinic?"

"You bet. It's the first thing she mentioned."

Despite the expected debris scattered about, the space was big. Aside from the roomy foyer, there were two rooms in the back, one with a small bathroom that I envisioned for the lab, and a room across the hallway that would make the perfect office space. I envisioned the receptions area as an evening yoga studio, and one of the spare rooms could be a space for an alternative practitioner, like a massage therapist or acupuncturist.

Nigel and I walked around like a couple of newlyweds looking at our dream home. I was doubly excited because, for the first time in my life, I would have my own office. The room was the corner unit of the building and had multiple full-sized windows that looked onto Willson Avenue; it even had a private entrance.

"All the utilities are included, and there will be a tenant allotment for painting and flooring. I'll check with the specifics for this space," Tweeters said. "And there's a non-compete clause in the lease, so if you wanted to open a dispensary, you would have exclusive rights."

Phinney gauged my reaction. "I'm sensing from the smile that seems to be stuck on your face that you like the spot?"

"It's way better than I could have imagined."

Mike was eager to rent the space. "We can get it all worked out the way you want. We'll draw up the details in the lease and get it done."

Devin taught me how little I knew about business. He warned me not to sign anything until I had spoken with him first. "I really like it, but I need to speak to my attorney about the lease." I turned to Tweeters and asked him if I could have till the end of the week to work out the details.

"That's no problem," Tweeters said softly. "We haven't even had time to clean the space out yet, so it'll be at least a week until we even list it. Just give me a call or have your attorney call me if you guys have any questions."

A few days later, I met with Devin, and we talked about the Medical Arts Building. Devin wasted no time in assessing the situation. "I think that MBA should be the sole tenant of the Medical Arts space."

"Why's that?"

"Well, personal liability protection for one. You don't want MBA to come crashing down on you personally—not that it would, mind you," Devin inserted quickly. "This is just the nature of business, especially a business with as much hocus-pocus as the marijuana industry. The government could come in tomorrow and end this whole thing. We've got to make sure that you're personally insulated from as much of that liability as possible."

But Devin wasn't finished. He objectified what I tended to emotionalize. "Even though I know you think Dan is a good guy, and he most probably is, we're not *really* sure why Mr. Phinney lost his space in the Snowload Building, are we?"

"No, we're not sure, exactly."

"I'm just not comfortable allowing you to enter an agreement with him if he's in charge. Since MBA is an LLC, it will shield you from personal liability should any untoward legal issue confront you. WH&H and Montana Medicine (Phinney's company) will need to sublet their space from MBA. I can have those papers drafted by the end of the week."

I called Nigel and told him about the lease.

"How do you think Phinney is going to take it?"

"Hopefully, he will see the logic in it. If he trusts me the way I trusted him, I think it'll be OK."

"I hope you're right."

The conversation with Phinney went without a hitch. He understood my position and agreed for me to lease the space under Montana Botanical Analysis LLC. We were taking a bit of a gamble allowing part of the space to be used as a dispensary. Nigel had mixed feelings as well. Neither of us wanted to compromise our reputation by our appearance of enmeshment with Phinney. I felt stuck between a rock and a hard place. I was enormously grateful that Maxine had found this location and thought I owed Phinney an opportunity to prove that his dispensary could operate professionally.

It seemed worth the risk.

The upside was our facility would be the first facility in the entire country to have a medical facility, a lab, and a dispensary under one roof. Suite 105 represented a chance to set up the cannabis health co-op—something Jerry Taylor and I had contemplated the previous summer. I told Phinney that other growers, aligned with our vision, could sell their products out of the dispensary space, as well.

"Doc, you drive a mighty hard bargain."

"Everything has got to be above board. And most importantly, all the cannabis has to go through the lab for testing before it gets sold. No exceptions. It's non-negotiable."

"Understood, Doc."

We drew up plans on how we wanted the space reconfigured. Having been a housing construction manager in California,

Phinney said he'd take care of all the construction details.

Suite 105 was going to be a sweet place.

Once the lease was signed, Devin sent Phinney a sublease agreement. The next day, the remodeling began. When I called Mr. Hardin with the news, he wasn't happy. Since the Willson space hadn't yet been listed in the MLA, he wasn't going to get a commission for being our agent. Mr. Hardin wasted no time telling me that I was under contract to have his agency find a commercial space for MBA and presented me an invoice for his services. He made no bones about holding my feet to the fire on a contractual technicality.

I felt blessed our search was over. I felt like I'd just hit the jackpot.

I wrote Dennis a check and dropped it in the mailbox.

Road Trip

A patient told me about an organization called Patients Out of Time that advocated for patient access to medical marijuana. The organization was having their biennial meeting in Providence, Rhode Island, and it seemed like an excellent opportunity to see the national face of the medical marijuana movement.

I asked Sam if she wanted to go.

Patients Out of Time was a spin-off of an earlier organization founded by Robert C. Randall. He was granted permission to use cannabis as part of the compassionate Investigational New Drug (IND) program for the treatment of his glaucoma in 1976.[98] Randall's case marked the first time since the removal of cannabis from the US Pharmacopeia in 1942 that a patient was legally permitted to use the plant.

Randall and his team of attorneys from the prestigious Washington, DC, law firm Steptoe & Johnson used a series of unique criminal and civil legal proceedings that ultimately procured the medication that saved his eyesight. He gained notoriety as "America's only legal pot smoker" and became the undisputed "father of the medical marijuana movement."

In 1981 Mr. Randall and his wife founded Alliance for Cannabis Therapeutics (ACT), the nation's first nonprofit organization dedicated to the issue of cannabis therapeutics. The organization's most significant accomplishment was catalyzing the first federal legislation seeking to remove prohibitions against marijuana's medical use.[99] At one point the ACT had 110 cosponsors in the US House of Representatives, but politics prevented the bill from having a congressional hearing or coming up for a vote.

In 1988, again, with the help of Steptoe & Johnson, the Randall's became the lead party in the court-ordered hearings before the DEA's chief administrative law judge on rescheduling marijuana. The judge ruled in their favor, but the DEA administrator ignored his judge and kept marijuana locked in Schedule I status.[100]

By 1995 Robert Randall was diagnosed with AIDS and forced to retire from his cannabis re-scheduling efforts. At about the same time, Al Byrne and Mary Lynn Mathre began Patients Out of Time, established a 501(c)(3) nonprofit organization focused solely on the education of medical professionals and the general public about the therapeutic value of cannabis.

After reviewing the Patients Out of Time conference syllabus, I registered. I was happy that Sam had decided to meet me there, too. I was curious if there would be any other labs represented in Rhode Island. As a precaution, I registered the "Botanical Analysis" domain name for the other thirteen legal states, wary that someone might want to use the name "California Botanical Analysis." Plus, I was entertaining the idea that we could open labs in other states. It was time for a road trip.

Providence is just a four-hour drive from my New York home, so I drove down and picked Sam up at the airport. Once at the hotel, we went to our respective rooms and met at the evening reception. Sam and I split up to scope out the crowd. I spotted Mr. DeAngelo, the owner of Harborside Dispensary in Oakland. I introduced myself and thanked him for granting me a telephone interview. We chatted until we were interrupted by a group of DeAngelo admirers.

The next day I headed for the conference lectures while Sam got into her investigative reporter mode. During the first break, I viewed the various cannabis product booths. I stopped at a booth staffed by a pudgy, well-groomed man in a gray polyester suit. He was alone, selling his book, *My Medicine: How I Convinced the U.S. Government to Provide My Marijuana and Helped Launch a National Movement.*[101]

Rosenfeld explained to me his tribulations in gaining access to the marijuana compassionate IND program that had been pioneered by Robert C. Randall. Mr. Rosenfeld is a middle-aged Florida stockbroker who has a rare and painful disease, multiple congenital cartilaginous exostoses, causing bony tumors throughout the body. What Rosenfeld discovered, quite by accident, was that smoking marijuana not only relieved the pain of the growing tumors but also acted to shut off the tumor growth.

Irv (as his supporters affectionately call him) eventually was included in the Federal Medical Marijuana Program. Seventeen patients were ultimately admitted into this program before it abruptly ended in 1992. Irv told me patients are shipped cannabis grown for "research" purposes at the National Institute of Drug Abuse (NIDA) marijuana farm at the University of Mississippi. I told Irv that I had started an analytical lab in Montana.

Rosenfeld brightened and said he would be in Montana later in the year. "Would you guys be willing to test my cannabis? I think its crap, but it does the trick."

"Send me a copy of your IND paperwork, and MBA would be happy to do it. You'll be our most famous client." I took his card and told him I'd be touch.

After lunch, I started talking with a Bay Area woman who was looking to open a dispensary with an on-site testing lab. Diana Chu is a nutritional therapist and yoga instructor. She struck me as an incredibly bright and passionate patient advocate. When I told her my story, she asked if I would be willing to speak at a medical marijuana conference near her home in Garberville, in the heart of California's famous Emerald Triangle. The triangle is the region of Northern California, namely Humboldt, Mendocino, and Trinity counties, that became legendary in the 1960s as the largest producer of marijuana in the United States. The marijuana grown there took on a mythical status for its quality. I took her card, too.

After the final day's lecture, I met Sam. "So, what'd ya think?"

"I think the conference is pretty cool. I talked to the guy who wrote a book about getting cannabis from the government. Irv Rosenberg or something..."

"Rosen-feld," Sam promptly corrected.

"Yeah, that's the one."

"I talked to him, too. Did you know about the IND program through the NIDA?"

"Not before today," I said.

"Me neither. I thought he was making it up, but I checked it out. It's all legit. They had seventeen patients in their program before the feds shut it down. Everyone else in the program, like Irv, got grandfathered in. Did he show you his pot canisters?"

"They're pretty cool. I asked him if he had an extra one. 'Sure, for a $300 donation,' he told me," I said, rolling my eyes.

"He said he'd give me one if I had dinner with him," Sam smirked.

"Nice. And I met a cool woman from California who wants to open a dispensary with a lab. She wants us to come out and speak at a local grower's conference in Humboldt County. She seems to think we represent a sane view of the world of cannabis."

Sam burst out laughing. "You and me representing a sane view on anything; that alone is pretty funny."

Then she told me about another person she'd met. "You should meet Jeff. He's a super-smart ex-hacker who grows weed in North Carolina. I told him about your lab, and he's really interested in talking to you."

Just before dinner, me, Sam, Jeff, and Diana met at the bar. Jeff suggested that we go to dinner and discuss the future of cannabis. He made a reservation at the elegant Bouchard Inn and offered to drive us in his black Cadillac. Once we were all buckled in, he asked if we wanted to try some of his bud he'd brought up from North Carolina.

Without hesitation, Sam chirped, "Sure."

Diana was quick to follow. "Thanks, Jeff. I'd be up for that."

"Dr. Mike?" Jeff asked.

"What do you have?"

Jeff beamed. "This, my good friend, is some of the finest Sour Diesel grown in the South. I can attest to its superior qualities."

After two hits, I reclined in the leather seat and asked what I thought was a germane question. "Is there anyone else who can't feel their arms or legs at the moment?"

There was dead silence until Sam burst out laughing. "I'm not sure if I can answer that question, because I can't feel anything. My entire body is numb."

Jeff chortled. "I dun warned y'all. I grow some sweet ass marijuana. Mike, you'll get to feelin' yourself back to normal in a while. You just lay there and relax while I drive us all to this fancy restaurant."

The sudden body high didn't last long, and my full neurological function returned by the time we got to the restaurant.

Jeff ordered a bottle of wine. Diana invited us to a toast.

"To new friends who want to change the world of cannabis." We clinked glasses, believing that we were indeed at the forefront of a historic transformation.

The next day, word of the lab spread. I gave out dozens of business cards and brochures. At the lunch lecture, I sat next to Fred Gardener, editor of the cannabis magazine *O'Shaughnessy's*.

He was one of the founders of Project CBD, an organization that advocated for patient access to cannabis strains rich in cannabidiol. It was refreshing to meet someone who understood the therapeutic applications of CBD.

During Arno's week in Bozeman, I learned about the subtleties of cannabinoid testing. It was relatively easy to tease out many of the major cannabinoids found in cannabis, but CBD was different. CBD's retention coefficient, which is the area under the curve when the substance is detected by the HPLC's detector, is very similar to another cannabinoid, cannabichromene (CBC). Without using proper CBD protocols, it was difficult to accurately determine whether the area under the curve was solely represented by CBD, CBC, or a combination of the two. Having observed the lack of attention to detail in the cannabis community, I suspected that most of the CBD numbers that Fred shared were overstated.

I discussed the issue with Fred. He listened quietly, uncomfortably tugging at his thick salt-and-pepper mustache. At the same time, I cautioned him that the testing information he was gathering on CBD and publishing in his newsletter might not be accurate. Fred seemed unfazed.

A little later, I learned that *High Times* magazine was hosting a Medical Cannabis Cup in the Bay Area. They planned to have a group of expert "tasters" gauging the quality of the buzz from each strain. I objected to the competition because it made a mockery of the very concept of using marijuana as medicine. I'd seen marijuana help many Montanans over the past year and took offense at organizations that jeopardized patient access to cannabis by their lamebrain marketing schemes. The idea of a Medical Cannabis Cup really bothered me. I sent a letter objecting to the competition to the contest organizers, to which I received no response.

On the final day of the conference, I was asked by someone if I'd be willing to take some of his marijuana samples he'd brought back to Montana so I could have Nigel run them on the HPLC.

"Sorry, I can't do it. I have too much to lose if I get caught."

His body twisted in disappointment. "How are you going to get caught? You're a fucking doctor. Who's going to find less than a gram of cannabis on you?"

"Sorry."

Upon my return from Rhode Island, I received numerous emails from people I had met at the conference. Numerous folks had written to get more information about starting labs in their particular state. The trip was a huge success.

As promised, Diana called and said that she was making plans for Sam and me to travel to California. She was an inspired woman on a mission, and I felt grateful that my ideas had resonated with her.

A Mouse Trap

The medical marijuana industry in Montana accelerated into hyper-growth mode after the official release of the Ogden memo on October 19, 2009.[102] The memo stated that compliant individuals in states with medical marijuana programs would be free of the legal scrutiny from the Department of Justice and the DEA.

Many cannabis advocates believed this memo represented the beginning of the end of federal involvement regarding state medical marijuana programs. Many saw the memo as a godsend. I witnessed numerous patients openly weep when talking about the perceived changes in federal marijuana policy.

Despite the Ogden memo, there was plenty of confusion regarding what the State of Montana regarded as legal under MT-148. The law was full of nebulous language and loopholes. Tom Daubert, the principal architect of MT-148, had tried to amend the legal confusion in prior legislative sessions, without success. MT-148 worked fine for a thousand patients statewide, but it couldn't accommodate the enormous scale of growth experienced in 2009.

Many growers and dispensary owners pleaded with local and state law enforcement for clarity of regulatory interpretation. Rarely were there any definitive explanations given for such issues as the number of plants you could grow at a single facility or whether you could swap or purchase marijuana from one caregiver (or dispensary) to another. Ironically, MBA's existence hinged on an implied legal premise that MT-148 allowed a "middleman" to provide cannabis to patients.

The response of most law enforcement agencies was simple and completely irrational. "We don't know what the law means. But if you break the law, you'll be arrested."

I witnessed cannabis industry proponents (e.g., growers, caregivers, and dispensary owners) plead with law enforcement, often asking them point-blank questions regarding their business plans, desperately trying to work within the framework of the law. They rarely received clarity that their business model was safe from prosecution.

"Try it and see" was the response many received from law enforcement. It was an extremely frustrating issue for everyone involved. Reform of MT-148 was desperately needed in the upcoming legislative session, but that wouldn't happen for another year because it's one of only three other states in the country where the legislature meets every *other* year. Lawmakers in Helena adjourned on April 30, 2009 and wouldn't return to address the growing marijuana problem until January 3, 2011. In the meantime, Montana was in the midst of an epidemic of cannabis fever.

In the spirit of American entrepreneurship, dispensaries were sprouting up all over the state, from cities like Billings and Bozeman to small towns in the middle of nowhere, like Wolf Creek and Miles City. The sudden explosion of the medical marijuana industry caught everyone by surprise. As long as medical marijuana was "out of sight and out of mind," there had been little adverse fallout to MT-148. But now that marijuana was everywhere, Montanans were becoming increasingly uneasy about what had happened to their compassionate citizen initiative.

Political panic ensued. Medical marijuana in Montana had become a mousetrap.

The city of Great Falls held a public hearing on February 2, 2010, on a proposed "emergency" ordinance. The proposal temporarily banned an unknown number of currently operating caregivers and dispensaries for up to three months, during which time the city would develop a proposed permanent ordinance to regulate the growing and dispensing of medical marijuana.[103] Cities and towns across the state imposed temporary and sometimes permanent bans on marijuana dispensaries.[104]

This anti-marijuana blowback was something that I had feared since I attended my first MCN clinic. As the summer of 2010 approached, next came the mandate that became the catalyzing event in the perfect storm that ultimately destroyed MT-148: Obama Care.

Obama ran on a platform of sweeping change from the policies under the Bush administration. The Affordable Care Act

(ACA), better known as Obama Care, was intended to be his legacy legislation. The ACA was sold to the public as health care reform designed to provide comprehensive medical care to the over forty-seven million Americans who had no health insurance coverage. Opposition to the ACA was bitter and divisive, often running along party lines. An unintended consequence of the ACA was the rise of the Tea Party.

The Tea Party marketed itself as a libertarian political fringe party, a sensible alternative to the stale and antiquated politics of the Republican and the Democratic parties. The Tea Party offered a third-party alternative to disenfranchised voters of all political ideologies, and its appeal gained significant political momentum during the midterm elections of 2010. My first inkling of the Tea Party movement was positive, until I realized what the party really represented.

There were few states in the country where the Tea Party was more successful in gaining a foothold than Montana. The Tea Party consolidated their power in the Big Sky state, focusing on the red-hot issue dominating all bandwidths of the media, as well as barbershop talk around the state.

The rallying cry for Montanan Tea Party supporters was repealing medical marijuana.

Battle Preparations

Sam and I spent countless hours pondering the fate of MT-148. Everything depended on the outcome of the 2010 midterm elections.

For the past dozen years, Sam had been a fixture at the capitol, lobbying for noble causes. She'd developed numerous connections that gave her access directly into the governor's office, as well as a friendly ear as far east as Pennsylvania Avenue. When I first met Sam, she thought that the lobbying phase of her life might be over.

"I'm focusing on my new love—being a writer."

Having an overabundance of talent was not something that Sam lacked. But like me, she too had been infected with the cannabis virus. Despite the novel she was working on, Sam kept close tabs on the snowballing medical marijuana machine, recognizing that we were in the midst of a gigantic percolating social revolution.

Sam's kitchen was our sanctuary to discuss the cannabis-crazed world evolving before us. Here we discussed how we could guide it to a safe place of free markets and good intentions; here is where Sam and I realized that we could mold the medical marijuana industry into something viable, sustainable, and good for the citizenry. And it was in her kitchen that Sam told me she'd decided to enter into political battle again, this time not for uninsured babies and children, nor the homeless and unemployed women, but for my lab and me. Our agenda was to save the cannabis world using only logic and science as weapons.

Rhode Island opened Sam's eyes. The experience demonstrated the momentum medical marijuana had accrued and just how big it could become. Viscerally, she sensed the enormous economic and social implications of more reasonable and realistic policies regarding cannabis. She felt the passion and couldn't ignore the once-in-a-lifetime opportunity that hovered before us.

Since the spring of 2009, medical marijuana had become the most polarizing topic in the state. MT-148 had been a tremendous opening-round win in the fight for patient access to medical cannabis. Perhaps we were delusional, but Sam and I believed we could help formulate a medical marijuana reform bill that would be an example for the rest of the nation.

As a first step, Sam suggested we send a letter to House member Diane Sands, a two-term Democratic member of the Montana House of Representatives from Missoula and its first openly gay legislator. She was perceived as a progressive, and we hoped that medical marijuana would be added to that list. The need for medical marijuana reform was so great that a special interim committee, the Sand's Committee, was formed during the summer of 2010.

The complexities of hammering out a medical marijuana reform bill would take a serious amount of time and energy. The bipartisan committee would hold hearings, listening to testimony from citizens and law enforcement. The Sands committee was a clear reflection of the priority that medical marijuana reform had become. The idea was to have a reform bill crafted that would pass both the House and the Senate by the time the Legislature reconvened in January and then be signed into law by the governor.

"How much will it cost to start helping us?" I asked Sam.

"I need a thousand bucks. I'll write a letter to Diane Sands' committee."

I nearly choked. "A thousand dollars. For a letter?"

"I guess you don't get how expensive this is going to be, do you?"

"I guess not."

I didn't want to sound cheap, but I was burning through money at an impressive (and alarming) rate. I'd just spent $30k on the HPLC. The renovation to the Medical Arts Building was already at the $40k mark, and it was still weeks away from completion—and thousands of dollars over budget.

After a brief negotiation, we agreed on $750 for the letter. I was reluctant to tell Nigel the cost of the letter, as he'd agreed to work for a meager $20/hour until the lab was profitable.

A few days later, I was meeting with Mike Singer when Sam called.

"Listen, we need to chat," she said flatly. "If I'm going to do this thing for you, I need a retainer. This is damn expensive work, and I can't work for free."

"I understand that, but I'm also trying to keep a start-up business afloat. How many companies hire a lobbyist within their first year?"

"I told you that this was going to cost you some green. It just seems like you want me to work for you for free."

"What do you mean *free*? I just sent you a check for the letter."

"It was discounted because I like you. Listen, if you can't pay, you can't play. It's as simple as that," Sam said tersely.

Her tone was off. I was talking to someone I didn't recognize. I wasn't sure what to say next, so I thought I'd just try being honest.

"You know…I'm feeling as though you're taking advantage of me."

"What? You're fucking kidding, right?"

"No…I'm serious. I've been straight up with you about everything."

"Listen, this is just a bad idea. You need to fucking get a grip on reality." And then she hung up.

I was stunned. I needed a reality check, so I called Nigel.

Among his many gifts, Nigel's a great listener. He nods at all the right times and seems to say the right things even when there isn't anything right to say. "Don't let it bother you too much, Mike. I think this is a Sam issue. It's not the first time we've seen this behavior from her."

I waited for a reply from the Sands Committee, but one never came.

Broken Promises

Nigel was anxious about having the lab free of construction noise and clutter. He'd finally moved the delicate HPLC into the newly renovated lab space, but the rest of Suite 105 was still in full renovation. He complained of the distractions, unable concentrate on his delicate analytical chemistry with a constant clattering of hammers, the chop saw's shrillness, and the steady accumulation of sawdust.

Of course, Phinney had plenty of excuses for why the renovation was weeks behind schedule. Despite his charm and my endearment toward him, I was getting impatient.

Phinney had invited me out to his home a couple of times. Nearly an hour outside of Bozeman, it was a cluster of odd-sized buildings and half-mended fences strewn amid assorted abandoned vehicles that hadn't moved in decades.

The most memorable visit was the tour of his marijuana operation. He had two greenhouses dedicated to growing cannabis, a smaller one where he kept his clones and starter plants, and the one where he grew out his mature female marijuana plants to maturity. The structure was an eighteen-foot-tall enclosure that he'd erected with steel beams that were wrapped in thick, translucent plastic. My jaw dropped when I saw their size, dozens of giant plants, defoliated skeletons bending at the apex of the greenhouse roof.

"Holy cow..."

"Crazy isn't it, Doc? I needed a damn chainsaw to cut some of 'em."

I marveled at the scene. "There's still so much pot left on some of these plants."

"Well, let me assure you that we did the best we could do. What else can you do, Doc? We got five, six pounds off some of these."

"That's just unreal."

"For sure, Doc. God has blessed me in many ways, my friend."

After the greenhouse tour, we went inside his trailer home. Phinney was the poster child of what I'd imagined a Californian cowboy. Instead of riding a horse, he drove his Hummer. Rather than washing down the trail dust with whiskey, he smoked pot and ate hash brownies at a rate that would have sedated a platoon of Marines. Often I was amazed that he could cogently finish a sentence, let alone maintain consciousness. Phinney was as charming as he was funny and laughed at my jokes, appreciating the edge to my wit. We talked about politics, spirituality, and family. He understood the depth of my feelings about Jacob and how much I missed him. I hoped that our friendship would continue to blossom, but considering that it was cannabis that brought us together, sadly, I had my doubts. I was afraid of broken promises.

Still, within my world, plates continued to spin.

After the HR disaster with Dana, Hillari agreed to help me until I could find another replacement. Once we moved into Suite 105, the job description changed. Now the receptionist for WH&H also needed to manage MBA. Nigel joked that it would be ideal if we could hire someone to help in the lab, too. We were looking to make the lab as efficient as possible, so having a Ph.D. running cannabis samples all day was not the best way to utilize Nigel's other considerable talents, like consulting.

After Nigel and I had sifted through dozens of Craigslist applications, we found Erin. A sturdy redhead that proved to be as smart as she is tough, Erin had the swag of the Abby character on CSI (without all the tattoos and goth overtones). She was the idea candidate, finishing her master's thesis in plant sciences at MSU, Erin possessed an impressive knowledge of analytical instrumentation, and understood plant genetics. She was spunky and funky and was honest to a fault. If the lab grew as I anticipated, Nigel would need someone he could trust. We hired her with the understanding that she would split her time between WH&H and MBA. We were stoked to have her become part of our team.

Erin effortlessly waded through the chaos, overseeing construction deliveries, scheduling the next month's clinic, and learning Nigel's cannabinoid protocols for the HPLC. In a week she ran the businesses as though she'd been doing it for years. At times she seemed more driven than Nigel or I combined.

Work on Phinney's dispensary had yet to begin, so, when Erin told me about Phinney selling untested cannabis from the cabinet-sized safe he was keeping in our space, I became alarmed. It felt like Phinney was baiting me with broken promises. Nigel independently corroborated Erin's reports. I spoke to Devin. The problem needed to be addressed immediately.

I called Phinney.

"Doctor Mike, what can I do for you?"

"How's it going, Dan?"

"Oh, you know…it's going. How 'bout you? How's life in New York? How's your son?"

"Things are good. He's playing little league. He's a star."

"So I've heard, my man. What's on your mind, Doc?"

"You remember the agreement we signed when you subleased the space from MBA?"

"I don't have that particular piece of paper in front of me at this very moment, but I do recall what you are talking about."

"You recall that all the cannabis sold from Suite 105 must be tested by MBA prior to leaving the premises?"

"I have a vague recollection of that, indeed," Phinney slurred.

"I've been hearing multiple reports that you're selling untested cannabis out of the safe."

Phinney's tone abruptly changed. "You have been hearing reports? From who? Erin and Nigel? Or do you have other spies, too?"

"I'm not sure if it really matters. Is it true?"

In the background, I could hear a lighter firing up.

"Well Doc…I ain't gunna lie to ya. Junior's been taking medicine from the safe to pay some of the bills. You're only back once a month, and we need cash to cover costs while we're finishing up your pretty new office."

"If you need money, Erin can take you to the bank. We had a deal. I put a lot on the line by going in on this dispensary with you. It's supposed to be squeaky clean."

"Listen Doc, calm down. Let me talk to Junior. I'll get it all straightened out."

"Maybe you don't understand," I said. "This is not negotiable. All the cannabis within Suite 105 needs to be tested. There's no exceptions."

"Listen, Doc, I'll take care of it. Go play that new guitar of yours and write me a song."

Going to California

As promised, Diana booked our plane tickets. She'd pick us up on Friday afternoon. Our trip to California was upon us.

I called Sam a few days after she'd hung up on me and apologized for suggesting that I was being manipulated. She wished she hadn't gotten so angry and said everything was good.

Before Sam and I left for the airport, we drove to the outskirts of Helena for a house call. Harold was a sixty-nine-year-old lifelong Montanan fighting for his life. For the past six months, he had been fighting a losing battle with Stage IV pancreatic cancer until he read that cannabis could help. Too frail to travel, the former railroad engineer was a wisp of his former self.

His wife invited us into their home. We sat in the meager living room, scattered with dozens of framed family pictures. Harold confided that he'd been eating pot brownies for several weeks and wanted me to sign his physician statement so he could be legal. Although I respected his ethos, I found it incredulous that a person with a terminal illness cared about the legality of their cannabis use.

I talked to Harold about several research papers that suggested cannabis might be helpful for his disease.

"I know it's helping me, Doc," he said with a hopeful smile.

His wife of forty-nine years sat next to him on the faded sofa. "Tell the doctor how much weight you've gained, Harold."

A weak grin cracked across his lips. "I gained eight pounds since I started this, Doc. I finally have an appetite. I can play with my grandson now and go for walks around the neighborhood with my wife. After I beat this, I'm going to write a book about how marijuana helped me."

"That's terrific. I'd love to read it." It wasn't for me to sprinkle reality onto his hopefulness. His cancer had metastasized to multiple organs. The median survival is less than five months.

I reviewed his medical records, filled out the paperwork, and explained the application process to Harold and his wife. He took my hand and held it warmly. "Thank you, Doc, for helping me with this. God bless you."

I contained a swell of emotion. "It's my pleasure, sir. Good luck and keep me posted."

Unfortunately, I never heard from Harold again.

Back in the car, Sam turned to me. "That was a really moving experience. Thanks for taking me along."

"I'm glad you came along. So many people think this whole medical marijuana thing is just a farce. You spend some time with folks like Harold, and you begin to get a different spin on things."

Sam turned on the radio and Led Zeppelin's "Going to California" was playing. We looked at each other and laughed. As Sam and I boarded our plane to Oakland, the song danced through my head.

What started as a crazy idea, MBA was now taking me to the epicenter of the most famous marijuana production center in the country: Humboldt County. Diana had lobbied to get Sam and me onto a local Humboldt cannabis forum presented by the Civil Liberties Monitoring Project (CLMP) and set to be broadcast live on KMUD radio.

Diana was waiting with heartfelt hugs as we cleared the security corridor at the Oakland airport. We gathered our bags and drove across the Bay into San Mateo, where she had an phenomenal second home with a postcard view of Sausalito Bay.

"I'm so honored that you guys have come out here."

I was overcome with humility. "You're honored? I'm still pinching myself that you asked us."

"I'd like to second that," Sam chimed in.

"Michael, what you've started is going to change everything. I feel so blessed that we met in Rhode Island. It feels as though the universe is opening up and taking us on an incredible journey of healing for many, many people."

"Awhhh. Diana, you're so sweet," Sam said.

"I mean it. I'm so excited to share you two with my friends and my community up in Humboldt. The place has been so isolated from the rest of world. They see only what they want to see and rarely go outside the county. The changes that are sweeping across the country are going to have an impact on all of us. Soon this place is not going to be the only place in the country to grow premium cannabis. We have a huge marketing advantage that we can leverage because the reputation of this area is legendary."

Diana took us on a tour of the dispensaries in the northern Bay Area, including the building where she was hoping to put her dispensary and lab. The facilities were all clean and professional; no lingering stoners aimlessly passing the time in a drum circle or playing hacky sack. Nothing was frightening about it.

The next morning, after I biked around the steep hills of San Mateo, we loaded up the car and picked up a friend of Diana's. It was the perfect day to be driving up to the Emerald Triangle. On most days, a six-hour car ride wasn't something to cherish, but I was on a road trip with three beautiful and raging smart women. A joint was passed at appropriate intervals. I marveled at my good fortune.

Driving up Highway 101, a tingling surge of excitement coursed through me as we crossed the South Fork of the Eel River and the highway sign read *Humboldt County*. I'd arrived at the marijuana Mecca.

Dianna's partner Benny greeted us as we pulled into the gravel driveway. Dressed in a tie-dyed shirt, gardening shorts, and flip-flops, his laid-back Californian demeanor belied his scrutinizing vibe. He was wary of strangers, having descended from a long line of local marijuana growers. Caution was a pretext for survival. The Emerald Triangle was a clan community. Everyone knew someone who was a grower. Most were involved in something illegal, and they protected each other's flank as if it were their own. It reminded me of Appalachia, without the drawling accents and the sound of banjos in the background. Here, top-shelf marijuana was a west coast substitute for moonshine.

I liked Benny immediately. He was smart and full of mesmerizing stories. "Want me to show you my garden?"

Sam and I looked at each other. "We never thought you'd ask."

Their Humboldt mountain home sat high on the western edge of the Coastal Range. In the distance, you could see the sparkling glint of the Pacific. Benny's garden consisted of several house-sized plots of land. Within each concrete block perimeter were dozens of chest-sized aromatic plants swaying in the gentle coastal breeze.

"These look amazing, Benny," Sam said, carefully wafting the aroma. "Mmmm. They smell incredible."

"They're happy plants. I can promise you that."

"Why do you have them inside this foundation?" I asked.

"It makes it easier to dep them."

Benny was someone I would have liked to have impressed with my knowledge of cannabis chemistry, but today I was the student. "Uhmmm . . . what's a dep?"

"Oh right. A dep is all about light deprivation. It's how we induce the flowering cycle around here. When the plants are where we want them size-wise, we unroll this tarp over the top to induce the dark cycle," Benny said, pointing out the neatly rolled six-millimeter black tarp at the north end of the concrete block enclosure.

Sam's eyes panned the enclosure. "Wow. That's pretty cool."

"We call it depping. It's how we can get multiple grows done in a year. That's why the town sort of empties out around six. They all gotta check their dep," Benny grinned.

"Wow. Just one more thing my mother never taught me," I joked.

"It's why the pot here is so nice. We can get the crop in before the rainy season starts. No mold issues like they have on the East Coast."

I scanned the horticultural expanse before me. There were dozens of bags of organic soil from Canada next to stacks of ten-gallon plastic grow pots. A wooden palate held a few bags of highly prized Peruvian guano, as well as a couple bags of vermiculite.

I patted Benny on the back. "So, this is how you grow the best pot in the world?"

Benny shrugged off the compliment. "We do the best we can. Diana has some friends who take this to a whole other level. We call them the canna-goddesses. They put the seeds they're going to germinate that season under their tongue, hold hands in a circle, and chant under the light of a full moon. They claim it makes their bud more spiritual."

"Those are my kind of goddesses," quipped Sam.

"They're all over out here. Let's go back and I'll show you the house."

When it was time to try some of Benny's herb, we used a vaporizer. Although I was well aware of what a vaporizer was, I had never used one. They had a German-designed Volcano, the Mercedes-Benz of vaporizers, complete with a digital thermometer for precise temperature regulation.

The idea of a vaporizer was simple. The device was engineered to take advantage of the difference between the vapor pressure of the cannabinoids contained in the trichomes and the combustion temperature of the cannabis leaf. With the Volcano, you dialed up the heat to the desired temperature, hit the start button, and waited for the plastic exhaust bag to fill. If done correctly, the bag slowly filled without smoke, only with the invisible evaporating cannabinoids from the heated trichomes. Once the bag was full, you removed it from the device, and inhaled the vaporized cannabinoids. There is no harshness as you might expect with smoking—only the faint aftertaste of the terpenes.

Arno had done a lot of the preliminary research for perfecting the Volcano as a technical consultant to Storz-Bickel, the vaporizer's manufacturing company. He'd told me that the Volcano was so efficient in vaporizing the cannabinoids from flos that there was no detectable change in cannabinoid strength from the first bag through the fourth bag, with a single sample of flos. It made sense since the cannabis wasn't combusted after a single use like with smoking.

I tried vaping for the first time. The buzz was different. I felt a little silly but not feel incapacitated, like with Jeff's Sour Diesel.

After a bit, we drove into town, stopping at Benny and Diana's favorite restaurant. They led us to the outside terrace that had a canopy of grapevines shading the patio. We sat at the back and ordered drinks, and while we waited, Benny produced a beautifully rolled joint, fired it up, and passed it around. I looked at him aghast.

"Dude, no worries. You're in the triangle."

And so I was. Who was going to say anything here?

The CLMP forum was the next day. We got to the Veteran's Memorial Hall around six o'clock and mingled as the crowd began to gather. I was a little nervous lecturing to people who'd been growing marijuana all their life. These folks grew pot as a generational way of life; it's how they provided for their families. They weren't growing as some Holy Mission to provide medicine for people who were sick. They didn't care who bought it, as long as they paid with hard currency, cash or gold.

The panelist began to assemble just before 6:30. After a brief, the moderator turned the microphone over to Sam. She spoke for 30 minutes about the politics of cannabis, defining the conflicts between the economics of cannabis and the politics of the plant. She was a tough act to follow.

I looked out into the packed room. People squeezed into the hallway, looking on with interest. I thanked Diana for the invitation and then veering into an explanation of how cannabis affected the body by discussing the ECS. I touched on the evolving role of medical marijuana in therapeutic medicine, listing several conditions where cannabis had been effective. Finally, I made the case of why medical marijuana should be subjected to the same quality control as any other medicine.

"You need to have a foundational basis for calling cannabis a medicine. If you don't know what's in your medicine, how do you dose it? Although it may happen in California, it's highly unlikely that most doctors are going to tell a patient, 'Take two hits and call me in the morning.'" A few chuckles came from the crowd.

"For decades the underground marijuana industry has been breeding cannabis for the highest THC content possible. But patients deserve to know what's in their medicine. A lot of them don't want to get high. They just want to get better. Without testing, how do patients sort out what type of cannabis is best for their condition? Most doctors don't know anything about medical marijuana. So, who does grandma ask? The kid behind the dispensary counter?"

I sipped from my water bottle. Sam returned a confident smile.

"Having cannabis tested gives you important information regarding the cannabinoids you ingest. Cannabis testing can also detect if the cannabis has been sprayed with pesticides or has been contaminated with mold. For patients with a compromised immune system, like those getting chemotherapy, smoking mold-contaminated cannabis has resulted in fatalities."

I looked around the room. The crowd was attentive.

Perhaps they've never heard these things?

"Testing evens the playing field for everyone involved in the cannabis industry. We no longer have to rely on a handshake when a grower tells you that their bud is the best in the county." A rumble of laughter filtered through the room.

"Not only does testing tell you the major cannabinoids found in the particular strain of cannabis, but it can also suggest its age. Analytical chemistry provides an accurate method: look at the cannabinol or CBN content. CBN is the end degradation product from both CBD and THC: the higher the CBN, the older the cannabis. It's like rings on a tree; the numbers don't lie."

A low mumbling came from the audience.

"How many of you know if your cannabis contains the anti-seizure compound THCV? Are any of you growing strains high in CBD? Does anyone out there have a strain that contains the anti-hypertensive cannabinoid, CBG?"

You could have heard a pin dropped.

"Montana Botanical Analysis is working with Diana in bringing a lab to the new collective she is planning. We hope to bring a new era of quality control to the entire cannabis industry, both recreational and medicinal. With the testing that our lab can provide, we hope to enhance the already impressive marketing advantage of cannabis grown in Humboldt County. Thank you very much."

Amidst the clapping, Diana and Sam gave me a "thumbs-up."

After an extended question-and-answer session, we moved to the concession area. I grabbed a beer and talked with several concerned growers. They worried about the crops' price stability in light of the explosion of cannabis being produced from warehouse-sized indoor grows in the Bay area.

"We found that using same-strain clones, indoor-grown cannabis is 8 to 12 percent more potent than outdoor-grown cannabis."

Sam played devil's advocate. "Does that mean indoor is better?"

"Good question. Better is relative. With outdoor-grown cannabis, the plants are exposed to a full spectrum of natural sunlight and moonlight, the way nature had intended. Indoor grows use the limited light spectrum from HPS (high-pressure sodium) and mercury halide bulbs. And then there's the whole debate of soil-grown cannabis versus cannabis grown hydroponically and using artificial chemicals and fertilizers."

I took a sip from my beer. "To me, it's important how the plants are grown. The soil and microbial interactions at the root are really important. Plants take up nutrients better when there is a balance of good organic matter and the right bacteria living around the roots. And think about an indoor grow; the rooms are airtight and completely automated to attain the perfect temperature and humidity. Then they juice the plants with artificial liquid nutrients so they get the buds as big and fat as they can get. They're like plants on steroids. And then throw in a little CO_2..."

"What difference does that make? Folks want potency," said a guy with frizzy white hair; he reminded me of Jim from *Taxi*.

"Maybe in the recreational world, but not necessarily in the medical world. A lot of folks don't want to be stoned. They just want relief. I don't know about you, but *Train Wreck* and *Mind Bend* are strain names that don't sound overly medicinal, do they?"

Everyone at the table laughed.

Diana had been waiting for her chance to speak. "And we shouldn't ignore the biggest elephant in the room: the carbon footprint of indoor grows." She held everyone's eyes for just a moment, then made her point. "Do you realize that 40 percent of all greenhouse gas emissions come from electricity production?"

More than a few eyebrows raised.

"Indoor cannabis grows across the country consume about 1 percent of the total electricity in the entire country," she emphasized. "It costs more than $6 billion a year in energy use. That's enough electricity to power about two million homes."

Diana was spot on. An indoor grow consumes electricity at a staggering rate. Electricity is used for everything: powering a room full of 1,000-watt grow-light ballasts and running fans and ventilation systems. A room full of 1,000-watt grow lights generates a lot of heat, and because grow rooms are kept at a constant temperature, extensive heating and air-conditioning systems are necessary. Finally, you need electricity to power the pumps necessary for automated watering systems, as well as the security cameras and sensors for protecting the grow from unwanted intruders. All this electricity just to grow high-potency pot in tightly controlled, perfect conditions that could never be replicated in nature. In the context of climate change, the carbon footprint of the cannabis industry is egregious.

Off-grid indoor "guerilla" production of marijuana is even uglier. Guerrilla grows are run by drug cartels and are located in remote areas of national forests. The grows are powered by diesel-powered electrical generators that require about seventy gallons of diesel fuel per plant harvested. Less-efficient gas-powered generators burn twice the fuel. And then there's the secondary ecological impact. Off-grid growing sounds sustainable, but with guerilla grows, the diesel and gas-powered generators are prone to oil spills and foul the surroundings with engine exhaust. Watershed contamination in the Coastal Mountains along the Emerald Triangle has reached the point of pushing the native California Salmon to the brink of extinction.

Diana referenced Liz Davidson, who produced and hosted the KMUD sponsored series *The Cannabis Chronicles*.[105] The three-part series dealt with a whole slew of issues related to the growing of cannabis in light of the changes taking place across the country as marijuana laws are relaxed and public tolerance grows.

On the flight back, I asked Sam, "What was the most impressive thing about the trip?"

"Man, how can you fucking pick one?"

"I know. This industry is so ripe; you can almost feel it popping out of its pod. The grows, the attitudes, the vibe, the acceptance, and the fear. It was all so intense."

Sam agreed. "Yeah, I know. Can you imagine if we had Diana helping us in Montana?"

"That would be amazing, although I think we have a pretty good team already."

Sam forced a nervous laugh. "Maybe."

Where's My Car?

It was a treat to debrief Nigel and Erin about the California trip. It seemed all too good to be true.

"This is fantastic, Mike," Nigel grinned, excitedly tugging on his scruffy beard. "I find this all so hard to believe."

Erin fist-bumped me. "Wow, Mike, this is awesome."

I looked to Nigel. "How long would it take for you to put a lab together in California?"

"Three weeks, max. No question I could get them up and running in under three weeks. Yep. More likely in two, but three for sure."

"Make sure that Erin is fluent with the protocols. If you have to go to California, she needs to be able to run the lab while you're away."

"No prob, Mike. Erin is so far ahead of anyone else I've ever worked with without a doctorate. She'll be ready by the end of the month. No doubt. Right, Erin?"

"I could never let down my favorite analytical chemist," she smiled.

"Good. We'll need to be ready when the time comes." I shared my next idea. "I think we should host a weekend retreat. Arno is going to be in the country in July. I think Diana would come, as well as Dr. Michelle Sexton, the doctor from Seattle. Maybe we'll nail down a lab in Washington, too."

Before leaving for California, I received a call from Dr. Michelle Sexton from the University of Washington, who was interested in discussing my laboratory.

With a dulled Texas accent, Michelle talked about her interest in medical cannabis and her immunology research focusing on the ECS. A naturopathic physician who trained at Bastyr

University, she sounded knowledgeable in analytical techniques. We'd hoped we could meet up in Berkeley during my California trip, but our schedules conflicted.

Nigel seemed challenged to get his head around how fast things were moving. "This is just unreal, Mike. We're really making this thing happen. Holy cow; it's so cool."

A bit later, I got a call from Lori. I tried to meet up with her on every visit and take her to dinner. It was my way of showing gratitude to the woman who had opened the door for me to come to Montana.

"Hey, Pot Doc. Wanna rent my Airstream while I'm staying with my sister? You can water my plants and weed the garden."

"Don't call me Pot Doc."

"Why not? Isn't that what you do?"

"Gimmie a break. You helped me with my first clinic. You know I run a reputable operation."

"Michael, don't be so sensitive. Let's talk about it over dinner."

But I was sensitive about it. I was more than merely a pot doc.

At dinner, Lori said she was going back to Seattle, where her older sister was having yet another round of experimental chemotherapy for recurrent breast cancer. The cancer was something she'd been battling for the past decade.

I told her about an offer I'd put on a house.

"Good God, Michael, why do you keep wanting to buy a house here?" She scolded. "Don't you get that they could shut all this down in a heartbeat?"

Lori was right. But this Montana journey had saved my life. I didn't want to go back to the way things had been. "I could still see patients in the clinic."

"And if they shut it all down, do you really think there would be any patients left to see? And you could just forget about the lab, too." Her assessment stung, but it was hard to argue with her.

Lori's Airstream turned out to be the perfect summer pad while I looked for more permanent housing. And being just two blocks from downtown, it was perfect.

As a favor to a patient, Erin and I agreed to a clinic in Billings. I was assured that the clinic space wasn't a dispensary. But when we arrived, the building was clearly a dispensary. Aside from the distinctive smell, there were numerous glass display units filled with like pipes, bongs, hookahs, and other pot paraphernalia. The manager showed us where we could set up to evaluate patients.

As I waited for the first patient to finish the WH&H patient intake form, I moseyed to the dispensary window. I admired the wall of MBA certificates that identified the various cannabis strains with their respective cannabinoid potency. Then something caught my eye. The date on the document read April 5, 2010. Today was August 26; the cannabis that MBA tested for this dispensary had sold months ago, but the dispensary owners continued to market subsequent untested product as MBA-tested cannabis. They sold it as "premium" marijuana.

"There's no end to the corners these folks will cut."

Fortunately, the solution would be easy: expiration dates on all our labels and certificates.

From my experience, most growers and dispensary owners didn't care about the integrity of the analytical numbers; they just wanted a number. Nigel said that more than once he had been offered money to fudge the numbers. Our clientele was keenly aware that the higher the THC content, the more they could charge. I was confident that some of these guys would sell their grandmother for dog food if they could get a decent price for her.

Erin sat at a makeshift table and ran the reception area; every twenty-eight minutes there was a knock on the door. By the end of the day, I had seen fourteen patients but only wrote physician statements for eleven of them. Three patients who complained of chronic pain had no medical records. I clearly stipulated that medical records were necessary. When we went to settle up, the dispensary manager handed me a check for $2,200.

"Erin, how many patients did we see?"

"Fourteen."

"That's fourteen times two hundred dollars a patient, which is what I believe we agreed upon. That's twenty-eight hundred dollars."

"But, Doctor, you only gave certificates to eleven of those patients."

"The agreement was two hundred per patient. Period. I made it crystal clear that patients needed medical records for chronic pain. No records, no signature. That's pretty simple. If they can produce the records, I'll happily sign their physician statement and mail it to them. If not, then they can go somewhere else."

Where's My Car?

The manager returned and handed me another check. Then we left.

"That was great the way she tried to snake us out of our money, wasn't it?" Erin laughed.

"We'll never go back there."

Interstate 90 shadows the gentle oscillations of the Yellowstone River, just a few hours downstream from its origin in Yellowstone National Park. The straw-colored landscape greens up around its wide banks, a narrow oasis of greenery canopied by tall cottonwoods, with bald eagles and ospreys perched atop the branches of the thick trunked canopy.

The ride back was full of captivating stories. I told her about my whitewater trip on the Alsek River.

"Eleven days on the river, with a helicopter portage through Turnback Canyon." The Alsek is a class VI river that National Geographic rated as the best extreme wilderness expedition on the planet.

"I flew over that river. Turnback Canyon has never been run by a raft; instant death in those cataracts," Erin inserted, nonchalantly.

"What?"

"Actually, I flew over it a bunch of times. The entire summer of 2006, uhmm…seventy-eight times to be exact," she giggled.

I was speechless.

"I was a bush pilot in Alaska a few summers ago."

"Holy cow."

As we pulled into Bozeman, I dropped Erin off. I was a little sad that Erin wasn't likely to stay with us much longer. Her mind was craving a Ph.D. program, not a biotech cannabis start-up. I went back to the Airstream and prepared for Thursday's Music on Main Street.

The next morning, I was off to look at a room for rent on the other side of Bozeman. To my surprise, my car wasn't where I parked it.

What the heck?

I walked around the block again. I'd misplaced my keys numerous times, but never an entire vehicle. After a bit more looking, the reality of the situation began to settle in. *Why would anyone steal my car in Bozeman?* It was a 1986 Subaru Impreza with 312k miles. Who would want it?

Finally, when I could no longer deny that my car was not going to reappear spontaneously, I called the police. A stern-sounding officer questioned me. "How much did you have to drink last night, sir?"

"I beg your pardon?"

"Sir, it was Music on Main Street last night. A lot of folks—"

"Officer, I wasn't drinking, and I know that my car is missing. What do I need to do next?"

"Was it locked, sir?"

There was a long pause. "Was what locked?"

The officer remained patient. "Sir, was your vehicle locked?"

"Does it matter?"

"It's for our FBI crime statistics."

"No. I never lock my car door. It's Bozeman."

"Sir. I can assure you that people steal things in Bozeman just as frequently as they do in most places."

"I guess I know that now. It's sort of a downer to know that car theft has reached us out here."

"Some call it progress," he said, deadpan. "Sir, did you have your keys in the vehicle?"

"Does it sound so obvious?"

"It's just the next logical question, sir. If you are too enamored with the vibe of not locking your vehicle, may I suggest at least taking your keys out of the ignition?"

"Absolutely, Officer. Thanks for the advice."

The officer took my information over the phone and told me to call my insurance company next. "Don't get too concerned about it yet, sir. Most stolen vehicles turn up. Please lock your vehicle. Don't be so trusting. You don't need to be asking for trouble, sir."

After I called the insurance company, I called the bank with my story. Jenn, the bank manager who'd help me set up my business accounts, laughed. "I'll take care of it, Michael. You'll just need to come in and sign a few papers."

"What's so funny?"

"I had my car stolen a couple of years ago, too. I'll tell you the story when you get here."

Mike Singer was the next person I called.

"Dude, who the fuck would steal *your* car?"

"If I knew who took my car, I'd tell the police."

"Dude, that's fucked up. Why do you think somebody would take your car?"

"I don't know. Maybe because it was unlocked and the keys were in the ignition?"

Mike strained not to laugh. "Dude, no shit. You *really* did that?"

"Why would I make something like that up at a time like this?"

"Dude, get this. Same fucking thing happened to me. Three years ago, right after I moved here."

"That's cool. Did you find it?"

"Oh yeah. One of my buddies found it the next day."

"Nice. Please keep your eyes peeled for my car."

"No worries, dude."

About four hours later, I was getting dressed for a bike ride up Hyline Canyon when Singer called. "Dude, I think I found your car."

"Seriously?"

"Fucking right, dude. It's right here. Window's open and your new sleeping bag's still in the back."

"Where are you? I'll bike over."

For the next day or so, I spoke with eight or nine people who had their cars stolen. All but one got them back.

Later that day I called Michelle and invited her to the MBA retreat I'd discussed with Nigel and Erin. I dubbed it *The Summit*. I sent an email to Roan, Arno, Sam, and Diana, asking them to commit to the dates.

Plant 2 Product Program

It was not uncommon to hear marijuana-related horror stories.

Among the medical marijuana crowd, rumors were rampant. People loved talking about somebody else's dirty grow, gossiping about an operation shut down due to spider mites or aphids, and occasionally you'd hear about someone going to the ER because they ate too many brownies. I was concerned about my patients having access to safe cannabis. And Sam helped me see that waiting for regulations to take shape might take years.

Knowing this, I developed the Plant 2 Product program (P2P). It was a marketing program designed to offer patients access to tested medical cannabis. The plan was to have the larger dispensaries buy into the concept, and the smaller ones would eventually follow. Once patients knew that MBA-tested cannabis products existed, they would gravitate toward those products. Recheads (slang for recreational potheads) didn't care where they got their cannabis, but patients did.

The P2PP was marketed to dispensaries as a way of demonstrating their commitment that they carried the highest quality medicine, symbolizing their commitment to patient safety. Tested cannabis products that were accurately labeled and dosed would decrease the dispensary's potential liability risk of THC toxicity—a hazard not uncommon with patients using CIPs. Patients would know the THC potency of the cannabis products and therefore dose themselves accordingly, rather than just guessing or taking the word of a dispensary worker.

Ultimately, the best sales pitch to enroll dispensaries in the P2P was the one that I hoped would most resonate with everyone in the industry: increased cannabis sales. This idea wasn't based merely on a hunch; I surveyed patients. Would they prefer tested cannabis over medical marijuana that was simply sold as is, fresh out of the ziplock baggie? Patients overwhelmingly preferred MBA-tested cannabis products.

I understood that most dispensary owners didn't care about the cannabinoid content of the marijuana they were selling (other than THC); nor did they necessarily care if the bud was contaminated with mold, sprayed with pesticides, or exposed to heavy metals. What mattered most was selling more product. If we could get a few growers and dispensaries into the P2P program and label all the products they sold, patients would begin looking for our logo, serving as a Good Housekeeping Seal of Approval for medical marijuana.

And that's exactly what happened.

The Rev

One of the most exciting events during my tenure in Montana was when MBA signed its first long-term testing contract with one of the biggest dispensaries in the state. Clancy, otherwise known as "the Rev," had pin-balled his way through the drug culture, finding a home selling medical marijuana under the auspices of the Roger Christie's THC ministry: the Hawaiian Cannabis Ministry. Christie believed that the cultivation and consumption of the cannabis sacrament is a gift from God and therefore protected as freedom of religion under the First Amendment of the Constitution. The Rev even went to Hawaii to meet Mr. Christie. He was formally anointed as a minster and had a fancy certificate to prove it.

Nigel thought the Rev was walking a fine line with his First Amendment argument. "It's pretty shady if you ask me, Mike. But who knows? It seems to be the norm that people do strange things out here with cannabis." We later learned that before his ordination, the Rev had navigated his way out of some sticky legal issues with cocaine possession and distribution charges.

Nigel and I were excited that the Rev was having all of his cannabis products tested and labeled by MBA. It was an enormous shot in the arm to have our first contract signed by such an influential dispensary. The Rev was happy with the business arrangement as well; his sales rose 40 percent after signing the testing agreement. Word of the deal went viral across the state. It was just a matter of time until others followed suit.

Although not the only cannabis testing lab in the state, Nigel and I felt we'd set the standard. Our prejudice against the other labs was based on hard data as much as instinct. Nigel showed no limits to his creative investigative skills. His relationships with so many growers allowed him to secure cannabis samples that the other labs had run; he obtained their results and then tested those same samples on the MBA machine.

"They're off by well over 60 percent on the THC alone. And none of them even report out any CBN." His Lennon-like glasses dipped down his nose, and he looked out over them nervously. "Their technique certainly doesn't impress me, Mike."

Nigel laid out the lab book and showed me the HPLC peaks and the calculations. It was amusing to hear him empirically dismember the other labs with his recalculations. "From what I see here, there could be several possibilities for why their numbers are so far off."

I was grateful Nigel was on my team.

"I couldn't wait to show you this stuff, Mike," he said excitedly. As a professional chemist, he resented the sloppiness of their work.

Integrity was the focal point of MBA. Despite my confidence in MBA's ability to operate at a consistently high professional standard, we welcomed an independent agency that would monitor and certify quality control on the cannabis labs. We approached the state regarding implementing independent quality control checks on testing labs. We advocated for an independent state bureau to regulate the labs, not unlike how the states regulate gasoline pump dispersion by an agency focused on standards and measures.

Nigel had lunch with the director of the state forensics lab. The bureaucrat was interested in the idea but asked Nigel, "Who's going to pay to have an independent cannabis testing service?"

Quality control of the state's medical marijuana program clearly wasn't a priority. The state wasn't interested in how MBA (or any of the other labs) was testing cannabis. It was another example of Nigel and I having to forge this path of cannabis quality control alone.

Wall Street & the Sketchheads

Dr. Michelle Sexton and I weren't able to meet up when I was in California, but we kept in regular contact. We'd become not only colleagues brought together by this misunderstood plant but also friends. Since starting my canna-venture, I'd met several people that I'd grown to really like; folks who'd validated my reasons for taking this Montana gamble—folks like Mike Singer, Tom Daubert, Sam, and the person I trusted the most, Nigel. I felt I had woven a tight-knit tribe in Big Sky country, friends who connected me to the pulse of the medical marijuana community across the country.

Yet, once again, I was soon proven wrong.

One afternoon, Michelle sent me a link to an article. Considering my cannabis network, I was surprised that I hadn't heard about a critical collaborative agreement that had just been announced. Cannabis Science Inc., a pioneering biotech company specializing in the development of pharmaceutical cannabis products, had just signed a partnership agreement with Montana Pain Management (MPM), a dispensary/grow operation based in Missoula and purportedly run by Rick Rosio.

The article reported on Montana governor Brian Schweitzer's tour of the MPM facility, commenting positively on the Cannabis Science partnership. In the article, Rosio saluted Governor Schweitzer for his concern for veterans with PTSD, a major focus for MPM and Cannabis Science.[106]

My first encounter with Mr. Rosio was during the first clinic I hosted with Pam in Missoula. Although I appreciated his purported mission for being in the cannabis industry—helping veterans and other less fortunate souls secure cannabis—my gut suggested I keep my interactions with him at a minimum.

An important lesson I learned as an emergency medicine resident was that if something smells fishy, it probably is. This MPM/Cannabis Sciences deal smelled like the inside of a StarKist factory.

Why had this deal garnered the attention of Governor Schweitzer? I called Sam. "Schweitzer's got a nephew that's a grower. Maybe Rosio buys some of his weed from that guy. Who knows? What I do know, though, is that Schweitzer is as big an opportunist as you'll find. He's not the Bernie Sanders type."

I was confused. "Is this bad news for us?"

"Nah," Sam said, dismissively. "It's not good or bad. It just means that this action will have no bearing on how things turn out for us next year. Schweitzer will do the thing that's most politically expedient for him at the moment a decision has to be made. Never bet against that."

Later, I asked Anthony Gallo about the deal, and he laughed. "Rosio's just another sketchhead."

"Uhmmm...what's a *sketchhead*?"

Gallo rolled his eyes. "Dude, you know a lot about a lot of things, but you don't know the street. Allow me to shed some badly needed light in that dark corner for you. A sketchhead is just what it sounds like—a sketchy, sly dog that you'd better keep your eyes on, cuz if you don't, he'll make you wish you had. Got it?"

"Yeah, I got it. Thanks."

In a couple of weeks, the next press release regarding the MPM and Cannabis Sciences Inc. appeared. Anthony was spot on. It's only a matter of time before a sketchhead reveals its true colors. I wasn't surprised to read about Cannabis Science taking legal action against MPM.

Dr. Robert Melamede, Ph.D., Cannabis Science Inc., President and CEO said in an email on July 23, 2010, "We are extremely disappointed that the actions taken by Mr. Rosio to deliberately breach a non-disclosure/non-circumvention agreement by contacting and conducting business with a scientific advisor of the Company, Dr. Arturo Morales. This blatant breach not only damages the reputations of Mr. Rosio, MPM, and Dr. Arturo Morales by circumventing binding legal agreements, but it also demonstrates a lack of moral and ethical character in addition to not acting in good faith."[107]

This was the landscape I was working to transform. There was a definite pattern emerging—the medical marijuana industry was littered with sketchheads. Although I wasn't a psychiatrist, working in the ED, I'd seen plenty of psych patients. Psychological disorders are characterized by the psychiatry community and referenced in a book called the DSM-5 (Diagnostic and Statistical Manual of Mental Disorders). It's a 991-page manual that categorizes mental illness on a multi-axial scale of I–V.

Before the DSM-5, paranoid, avoidant, schizotypal, antisocial, borderline, narcissistic, and obsessive-compulsion personality disorders were called Axis II disorders. These disorders are usually lifelong problems that first arise in childhood and are accompanied by considerable social stigma because they are endured by people who often fail to adapt well to society. A high percentage of the people I'd met in the medical marijuana industry suffered from some form of personality disorder. From my perspective, those individuals who weren't sketchheads were like manna from heaven.

The medical literature suggested a reason for such a high incidence of sketchheads within the cannabis industry: many individuals who use cannabis do so to self-medicate, easing the daily pain of living.[108] This pain is both covert and overt—physical, emotional, and psychological. I recalled Pete Jones confiding to me about the torment he carried from living with an abusive and alcoholic father. I saw a lot of self-medication.

It became increasingly clear that many of those advocating for practical reform for MT-148 would be their own worst enemies. This minority of harmless, yet unkempt, oppositional–deviant, hobo-looking individuals were framed by the marijuana opposition as the core of the medical marijuana movement—not the hidden fringe that only emerged from their reclusive lifestyle to publicly advocate for reasonable cannabis access.

Summer was right around the corner, and the renovation of Suite 105 was still incomplete. I was getting billed for work that had been backbilled and paid from the previous month. Phinney was avoiding my calls and lost the passion he'd initially brought to our venture. And the elephant in the room was that Phinney was still selling marijuana in clear violation of our lease agreement.

Devin said, "He's got to go."

"I know. He keeps giving me lame stories and excuses. If I hadn't liked him so much, this wouldn't' be so hard."

"Then it would likely not have been an issue," Devin admonished.

He advised me to find an attorney in Bozeman and have Phinney evicted. I chose Art Wittich, a high-profile litigation attorney, who would win a Tea Party Senate seat in the upcoming 2010 November elections.

Phinney was served his eviction papers for failure to pay his rent on time. It was unfortunate the relationship ended the way it did. It was yet another example that reality is often distorted within the cloud of marijuana smoke.

Mike Singer was a godsend and finished the remaining renovations.

Getting Chunged

The weekend of the Summit had finally arrived.

I picked Michelle up at the airport. Nigel brought Arno back to his house from the bus station. Sam was driving down from Helena with Diana, who had flown in from Oakland the day before. We were all meeting at Nigel's for a barbecue on Friday evening.

Nigel grilled elk steaks that Roan had brought from an earlier hunt. Roan said he was carrying the elk's front and rear flanks out of the Crazies when he tripped, and somehow the Weatherby Mark V accidentally discharged just inches from his face. "It scared the shit out of me," Roan blushed. Everyone laughed.

It was great seeing everybody having a good time. The conversation was robust: postulation of wormholes, Kundalini yoga poses, and the unavoidable exchange of smartphone pictures of kids (and grandkids). Anthony Gallo brought gifts for everyone from his new dispensary—a sample bag of his Popular Provider line of cannabis products. And he brought the pot.

Since our meeting during my inaugural clinic back in May 2009, Anthony had made a lot of money selling marijuana. His success nicely dovetailed with his preference to live big, buying fancy cars, expensive clothes, and avant-garde art. Yet despite his financial ascendency, Anthony felt the need to compensate for the thing that money couldn't buy—knowledge. Even without a college degree, he recognized the value of the lab and became an ad hoc student of chemistry. It wasn't uncommon for Anthony to call Nigel several times a day. When MBA started to post the "Strain of the Month" in its monthly newsletter, Anthony wanted to be number one—to grow the most potent marijuana in the state.

As the elk was cooking, Anthony edged toward me and pulled a gold cigarette box from the inside pocket of his tan Fioravanti jacket. His Cheshire cat grin belied his motive.

"Dr. Mike, how's it going, buddy?" He said, shaking my hand, before turning toward Michelle, who was sitting beside me. "Is this your beautiful doctor colleague from Washington?"

Michelle politely acknowledged the compliment. Anthony cleared his throat and leaned toward me. "I got the record again, buddy. I hit 24 percent on my new strain. It's killer."

"Nice! What's it called?"

Anthony rolled his eyes. "Dude, you're not going to believe me. They call this strain Connie Chung," he snickered, obviously stoned. "Dude why would you name a killer strain of weed after an Asian TV reporter?" he said, smacking his waxed scalp. "I don't get it."

"And Nigel tested this?" I asked.

"Absolutely."

"And it broke 24 percent?" I said incredulously.

"You know it, brother. Don't take my word for it; ask your lackey chemist."

Nigel looked over and nodded. "It's really remarkable how potent this strain is, Mike, considering the range of cannabis that comes through the lab. I didn't believe the numbers the first three times I ran the sample. Then I had Erin run a sample and her results were within 1.8 percent of mine. That's pretty damn good."

"Let's light it up." Anthony suggested, sparking up the joint and passing it around.

Michelle was talking to me about her grandkids when I started to feel weird.

"Hey Michelle, what'd you think of that pot?"

"What's wrong, Gecko, you didn't like it?"

Michelle called me Gecko because it was easier to pronounce than Geci, plus Gecko's were her favorite reptile. I gestured for her to move closer. "I don't think I'm feeling too good right now."

"Gecko, are you alright?" She noticed my paleness and reached for my pulse.

Suddenly, I felt my heart racing and broke out into a cold sweat. I thought I might pass out. I looked up at Michelle's turquoise eyes.

"I'm really not feeling so good." Time became a blur. People were asking questions. I wasn't able to speak.

Michelle had been a midwife for twenty years before she went to Bastyr University to become a naturopathic doctor. She put her arm around me, gently leading me to the edge of the patio where she guided me to lie on my back "There you go, Gecko. You're going to be OK as soon as your brain gets some more blood."

Soon, I was feeling better. My heart rate slowed, and I felt a reassuring sense of reality settling over me. The music was familiar, and I recognized the faces standing over me.

Michelle laid a cold rag on my forehead. "Welcome back, Gecko. How are you feeling?"

"Way better, now." I looked up at the circle of friends. "What the hell happened, Mike?" Roan laughed.

Anthony snickered. "I think you just got whacked by the MBA Strain of the Month, dude."

Michelle grinned. "You just got an ole fashioned plant whoopin', Gecko."

I sat up. Anthony and Arno came over to check on me.

Arno gave a modest look of disapproval. "Michael, cannabis can be very powerful if you're not used to it."

Anthony was less subtle. "Dude, you got Chunged."

The Summit

The group assembled Saturday morning in the Medical Arts conference room. Erin took care of all the administrative details like paper and pens, and coffee and donuts.

Over the past year, I'd read a lot of business articles dealing with workforce creativity and productivity. I wanted MBA to operate in a Google-like atmosphere, to be a fun, creative workplace, where everyone loved their job and saw purpose in their work.

The goal of the Summit was to discuss the expansion of MBA. At that moment, there were analytical cannabis labs in three states: Montana, California, and Colorado. My goal was to have labs in every state where medical cannabis was legal, and then when the recreational market opened up, the labs would test the recreational product as well. I even had a dream one night that Nigel and I were on the cover of *Newsweek* with the caption "The Kings of Cannabis." The dream became a reminder that the lines between delusion and reality were frequently blurred.

After introductions, I asked each person to offer their vision of MBA and encouraged them to think outside of the box. "I want everyone to be honest and kind," I urged the group. "Everyone here has an opportunity to change the way that cannabis is perceived by this reefer madness, brainwashed culture."

Looking around the room, I was deeply grateful for those seated around me. Seated across from me was Arno. He offered to head the MBA science advisory board. His affiliation with the lab gave MBA impeccable credentials. I was elated by his proposal.

Michelle brought her considerable talents as a physician, researcher, and chemist to the Summit. She was well connected with key politicians in the Washington legislature, hinting that the state was destined to go recreational soon. I envisioned her help in securing another MBA satellite lab, Washington Botanical Analysis.

Sam was our strategic genius. She brought a real-world political perspective to our group of geeks and idealists who thought the truth would set us free. Sam reaffirmed her commitment to lobby on behalf of MBA.

Diana had flown from California to attend. I was impressed with her vision and her unparalleled ability to get stuff done. Having her as an advocate validated the course I was taking the lab.

Erin was the youngest member of the group—an organizational juggernaut and an all-purpose prodigy. I knew that she wouldn't be part of MBA for the long term, but while she remained with us, she set a standard for others who followed her. She infused the room with a refreshing Generation X energy.

I invited Roan, my ex-roommate, to give a layman's perspective about MBA. He brought considerable experience with writing grants and business proposals. He'd written the business plan for MBA, and I thought his business experience could be an asset.

Aside from me, Nigel was the focus of the group. His task was to manage and operate the lab in Bozeman, as well as any satellite labs we might open in other states. At the outset of our relationship, Nigel accepted the challenge of guiding MBA to become the premier analytical cannabis laboratory in the country.

For the next two days we met, concluding Sunday afternoon with a picnic at Hyalite reservoir. Although everyone contributed to the Summit's success, the star was Arno. He understood the importance of quality control testing if medical marijuana was ever to be wholly embraced by the American medical establishment. His analytical experience in the field was unmatched.

Unbeknown to me, the Summit was the peak of the wave that MBA would ride. It was a time of commitment and cooperation toward creating a sustainable business in the fledgling medical marijuana industry.

It was the calm before the storm.

Freefall

My life seemed like an endless game of spinning plates. Running the lab and the clinic was an enormous undertaking on top of my parental and home obligations; all of which was made even more daunting by my monthly travels between Montana and New York. The longer those plates spun, the higher the probability of an adverse gravity event. Before the summer of 2010, many of the plates seemed headed toward the floor. Money was tight and I felt like I was perpetually traveling at warp eight.

Summer vacation was an opportunity to reconnect with my son. I had spoken to Jerry Taylor about staying at their house for a few days and letting the kids hang out while he and I talked about life and changing adult health care.

Jacob and I caught a morning flight into Bozeman for the start of the annual Sweet Pea Festival. Once there, we met up with Hillari and Kia. For the duration of the weekend, we tie-dyed T-shirts, listened to an array of musical artists, and ate a lot of ice cream.

Monday, after breakfast, I asked Jacob what he'd like to do next.

"I want to learn chemistry, Dad. Could I talk to Nigel?"

"Really?"

He nodded with enthusiasm.

I was delighted that my dude wanted to go down to the lab. "Let me call Nigel."

"Wow. That's pretty impressive, Mike," Nigel chuckled. "I hope my kids like it. Tell him I'll give him a lecture over lunch. Bring us some burritos from La Perria. We'll have a blast. He'll know more about general chemistry than any fourth grader I know."

When the lesson was over, he thanked Nigel and shook his hand. "Let's go, Dad!"

We headed to Helena to see Jerry and his family. A devout Latter-Day Saint convert, he and his wife have always been gracious hosts. We spent the next several days camping, fishing, and canoeing on the Missouri River, before Jacob and I began the second leg of our trip.

I'd spent a lot of time in Grand Teton National Park during several cross-country road trips before finishing med school. I wanted to take Jacob to the campground that bordered the Gros Ventre River, just outside of the park. Back then, I'd run the river in my kayak—a torrent of foaming, bubbling whitewater that sharply wound its way around steep banks lined with birch and cottonwood.

Now, the river was calm and shallow as my boy and I walked along the pebble-strewn riverbank, skipping stones and catching toads. As the sun dipped below the ridge line, the solar-powered headlamp he wore looked like a glowing third eye. "Follow me, Dad."

And I did, but not with the full attention that he deserved. Even within the wildness of the Tetons, I couldn't free myself from obsessing about the lab and the marijuana maze I'd lost myself in. Instead being fully focused and devoted to my son, I still carved out time to call Nigel, the Bozeman city attorney, Sam, Daubert, and a filmmaker who was doing a documentary about Montana medical marijuana. My obsessive neurosis convinced me that if I checked out for too long, I'd miss out on something important.

What I'd forgotten in the thirty years since I'd last been to Wyoming is how long it takes to get anywhere. We left the Tetons and headed for Thermopolis, enduring countless hours in the sweltering un-air-conditioned car. A few hours before dark, we arrived, stopping at the Wyoming Dinosaur Center, a place famous for its Green River fossil collection that included the first Archaeopteryx fossil unearthed. We could have easily spent the entire day there, but we had just an hour.

I'd also promised Jacob that we would stop at the Star Plunge water park, a thermal hot spring. The place had an early 1950s Las Vegas neon look, but we cared little for the outer aesthetic. It was a beautiful, warm summer day, so we changed clothes and hit the pool.

There was a twenty-foot diving board that challenged the kahunas of everyone who dared to climb up. Jacob convinced me to go first. He waited until my head popped out of the deep pool of water before he leapt in. After a number of descents Jacob was ready for the next challenge.

"Dad, let's go do the water slide!"

The forty-two-foot spiral water slide was at the far end of the pool. The sun-faded fiberglass tube sharply descended four stories until it straightened and dropped out of sight. Here, the slide dumped the participant, freefall, into the darkness of an awaiting pool of warm mineral water. We marched up the wide concrete stairs as screams echoed out of the cylindrical chamber.

"It sounds scary, doesn't it, Dad?"

"It always sounds worse than it really is, Bud," I said tentatively.

When we reached the top, several veteran sliders were standing in line, merrily shivering and dripping. I could tell that Jacob's enthusiasm was vacillating. I turned to the skinny Hispanic kid standing in front of me.

"Is it pretty fun?"

The kid's teeth were chattering so much all he could do was nod. When it was his turn, he eagerly crawled into the tube, shouted something in Spanish, and disappeared down the water slide.

Suddenly Jacob's face tightened. "I'm not going." No amount of convincing or cajoling or guilt was going to change his mind.

"Listen Bud, you walk back down, and I'll meet you at the bottom. I'll tell you what it's like. It'll be fun."

So down the slide I went, my body stiffened, becoming an aerodynamic missile. I was whipped around the slide, corkscrewing with increasing velocity toward the bottom. The light through the first part of the tube was bright, until the section where the pipe entered the building and straightened. Then everything went black. I was in free fall.

Without warning, the nanosecond of zero-gravity yielded, plunging me into the warm resistance of the pool water. When I came up for air, Jacob stood above me, smiling.

"How was it, Dad?"

"Pretty amazing, Bud. You need to try it. It's pretty scary the first time."

"OK. You stay here and watch me come out. OK, Dad?"

And I did.

After a couple of hours of pool fun, hunger prevailed. After supper, we set out to find a place to camp. Years of running rivers taught me the finer points of finding free campsites. We found an isolated spot on a knoll to pitch the tent on land managed by the Bureau of Land Management.

The next morning, we drove to the Bighorn Mountains, just west of Sheridan. I had spent a lot of time in the Bighorns when I was Jacob's age and wanted to share this special place with him. We took a hike to the Medicine Wheel, an ancient Native American ruin. Jacob insisted that I carry him on my shoulders the entire three-mile hike. I didn't mind, though, knowing that the days of lugging him around like that were numbered.

After spending a final night in a tepee in Cody, we drove back to Bozeman. We took the Beartooth Scenic Highway, winding through the spectacular mountains of the Shoshone, Custer, and Gallatin National Forests. The drive back was bittersweet; our vacation together was coming to a close.

Soon I would be back in the shark-infested waters of the marijuana world. I was beginning to wonder if I'd made a colossal mistake.

A Listing Ship

What did the Affordable Care Act (aka Obama Care) have in common with Montana's medical marijuana program? At first glance, one might think nothing, but that would be inaccurate. After President Obama signed the Affordable Care Act into law, there was a political backlash not seen in this country for decades. Rumors of hospital "death committees" raged fear into an already vulnerable right-wing base. Sensing a change in the political winds, the Tea Party used Obama Care as a primary tactic to gain a foothold of power in the 2010 midterm elections.

Nowhere did the Tea Party gain as much political influence as Montana. The state is full of fiercely independent souls who are as hardheaded about politics as they are ranch-tested tough. Obama's presidency precipitated a steady public relations nightmare for the invigorated medical marijuana industry. There was certainly an element of right-wing media bias designed to make the nascent medical marijuana industry look as unscrupulous as possible. Still, the potheads did little to dispel the images presented to the public.

If the endless drum of negative press coverage of the caravan of MCN clinics wasn't bad enough, in April 2010, things got worse. On April 17, police in Kalispell, responding to an anonymous tip, found the body of Wesley Collins dumped in the woods south of town. According to police, Collins had been beaten to death, most likely during a botched robbery at his apartment five days prior. Collins was a medical marijuana patient, and three small marijuana plants he was cultivating for his medical use were stolen. The local media dubbed Collins's death a "medical marijuana murder."[109]

In May, there was a series of fire bombings involving several medical marijuana dispensaries in Billings.[110] The night of the second arson attack, droves of concerned citizens–both for and against medical marijuana–flooded City Hall, necessitating the use of ancillary conference rooms to hold the overflow of citizens for a meeting that would drag on until nearly 2:00 a.m. The Billings City Council condemned the acts of violence and additionally voted to approve a six-month moratorium on any new medical marijuana businesses.[111] Billings wasn't the first city to react with a moratorium.

Despite an overwhelming show of support from caregivers, patients (and their families), and other members of the community, the Kalispell City Council imposed a city-wide ban on medical marijuana businesses.[112] Moratoriums and restrictions ranging in both severity and duration were implemented in several Montana municipalities, including Cascade, Whitefish, Deer Lodge, Belgrade, Manhattan, and Bozeman.

The Billings-based group Safe Communities Safe Kids (SCSK) formed to halt the flood of marijuana-related businesses in the state's largest city.[113] Co-founders Cherrie Brady and Susan Smith took the momentum gained from the Billings City Council six-month moratorium and began waging a statewide battle to revive marijuana prohibition. SCSK was supported by the Montana Family Foundation, a right-wing Christian group with ties to Focus on the Family and the Alliance Defense Fund. SCSK then led a ballot initiative to repeal MT-148. Despite garnering fifteen thousand signatures in a single week, their repeal initiative failed, nonetheless, they provided a glimpse of the anti-marijuana sentiment that was fomenting across the state.

Dave Lewis (not to be mistaken for Sen. Dave Lewis, R-Helena), treasurer and spokesperson for SCSK, talked about Montana turning into "Gomorrah" due to the growth of the medical marijuana industry. Anti-marijuana sentiment was echoed by several influential legislators, such as Sen. David Essmann (R-Billings), Rep. Mike Milburn (R-Great Falls), and Rep. David Howard (R-Park City), who called medical marijuana "a scourge."[114] A repeal bill banning all medical marijuana was rumored to be in the works.

Sam and I talked about the growing opposition to MT-148. How to stem the negativity? I thought we should be waging our own media campaign and hatched the idea of a public informational meeting to balance the flood of corrosive public relations blunders the new industry had been absorbing since the start of the MCN clinics in April of 2009. I dubbed it the Cannabis Forum, renting the Helen Theater in Bozeman's Emerson Cultural Building and, together with a small group of MBA clients, assembled a panel of guest speakers that might have a mediating impact on the surging anti-marijuana sentiment.

The panel was composed of Barb Trego, a longtime medical marijuana patient; Tom Daubert; Dr. Spencer Ward, a pain management specialist who'd recently published a paper on the efficacy of cannabis in weaning patients off of prescription narcotics; Nigel; and me.

To my dismay, attendance was scant. It was an omen. A glimpse into the electorate's appetite for medical marijuana. Over the past eighteen months Montanans had been saturated with the issue. Many reasonable and compassionate Montanan citizens who had first voted for MT-148 now felt duped by the gimmicks of folks like JC and the MCN clinics, as well as the unregulated explosion of a heretofore illegal plant now being called a medicine for the masses.

The Cannabis Forum consisted of Barb Trego, a former sheriff's deputy, spoke first about her path to medical marijuana. A short, solid woman, she described how a back injury and subsequent degenerative disc disease had disabled her. Before discovering medical marijuana, her only option to treat her chronic back pain was taking prescription narcotics multiple times a day. "If I took all the pills the doctors had prescribed for me, I never would have gotten out of bed. I lost two inches in height and was paralyzed for six months. Doctors told me I would never walk again. Then a friend suggested that I try medical marijuana."

After she tried marijuana, Barb exclaimed, "I couldn't believe I didn't hurt. It was the most amazing day of my life." Barb is the poster child for medical marijuana—a conservative skeptic who has never smoked because her mother died of emphysema. She informed the crowd that she ingested marijuana as an edible or using a vaporizer.

Tom Daubert was his usual impressive self. He spoke of his crusade to "warn the medical marijuana community that too much boisterous, opportunistic, exploitive, and culturally inappropriate and greedy behavior surrounding medical marijuana would risk inciting a political backlash that would jeopardize survival of the law and of patient's rights." He noted that the chaos was not what he had envisioned when he helped draft the original legislation.

"The backlash has taken on a life of its own. We will be facing, for the first time, organized citizen opposition that truly feels that marijuana is evil. These are folks that feel that a patient using marijuana on their block is simply too disruptive to their sense of morality."

Daubert outlined the threats that were looming in the distance. "This entire law is about civil liberties. It speaks to core Montana values of liberty and self-reliance; of the right to use a natural plant in the privacy of your own home, to produce it, and take some personal control over your manner of health care. The bills micromanage and practice medicine from the legislative floor rather than from the privacy of your doctor's office."

Tom summed up a political battle with widespread ramifications. "As discouraging as current events have seemed over the past six months or so on this issue, there are lots of reasons for optimism. This battle is one we can win, but it will take a lot of organized, focused, and mature participation by patients and caregivers. Keep in mind that the reason we face the political backlash is because of gross immaturity and a lack of sophistication and dignity on the part of some. We all have to live up to this ideal if we want to hope to combat the forces that we face right now."

It was a sobering thought.

Dr. K. Allen Ward spoke next. A neurophysiologist from Great Falls, he was tall and pale. Ward sported thick black glasses resting below a Liberace-style silver bouffant. He had come to understand cannabis during his years as a consultant in a chemical dependency center. He hunched over the microphone, speaking in a nasal drone.

Dr. Ward conferred his recent study, comparing cannabis and opiate use. "More than fifty million prescriptions are written for opiates in the United States. The most widely prescribed drug in America is hydrocodone with Tylenol. One of the biggest problems with chronic pain is that more than 80 percent of providers who prescribe opiates have no formal training in chronic pain management."

Setting aside his notes, Dr. Ward continued, "In 2010, nearly 3,000 kids under the age of 18 died from prescription opiate overdoses. There were 299 confirmed prescription opiate deaths in Montana in 2009, down from 321 the year before. How many cannabis overdose deaths have I seen in Montana over the last 10 years?" he asked, looking out into the empty seats. "None. Misuse and imprudent behavior, yes, but not a fatal overdose."

After thanking Dr. Ward, I segued into some data that I wanted to share about chronic pain. I discussed a recent study noting that more than 80 percent of women treated for chronic pain issues had experienced sexual or physical abuse as a child or adolescent. "Pain is way more complex than most of us understand."

I reviewed the basic science of medical marijuana, including the ECS, to provide an insight into the complexity of how cannabis worked in the body. I touched on the irony of cannabis being a Schedule I substance, considering the little-publicized FDA Investigational New Drug program using medical marijuana, and gave an overview of the clinical applications of using cannabis as medicine. I pitched having all cannabis tested so patients could understand the potency of the medicine they were using.

My concluding remarks were aimed at the intrusion of an uninformed government into the doctor-patient relationship. "Forty percent of prescription drugs prescribed by physicians are done so in an off-label manner. This is a perfectly acceptable practice unless you want to recommend cannabis for one of your patients. If your patient doesn't have one of the qualifying conditions as mandated by the state, you are not permitted to sign their physician statement. I find it interesting that none of the legislators in Helena have a medical degree in order to base their legislative action."

Nigel concluded. He reminded of the importance of analytical chemistry in sifting out the subtle difference in the cannabinoid content of the plethora of cannabis varieties.

"THC isn't made on the cannabis leaf at all. All the cannabinoids on the cannabis plant are synthesized on the plant in the acidic form. So, THC is actually found in the form of THCA (tetrahydrocannabinolic acid). In order to activate the THCA, the product is heated, and THC is the byproduct." Nigel illustrated how UV light and long exposure to atmospheric oxygen would also precipitate this decarboxylation reaction.

Nigel explained the early days of MBA; the tests on the cannabis tinctures brought into the lab. "Two-thirds of the tinctures had no appreciable evidence of cannabinoids, yet the tinctures were being sold to patients as cannabis medicine."

Nigel made his way through the array of slides. "The chemistry of cannabis isn't simple, but it is predictable and well-studied. And the cool thing is that it all takes place on the sticky trichomes of the flowering female leaves."

The organic genesis of cannabis begins with a cannabinoid that few have ever heard of—cannabigerolic acid (CBGA). From there, an organic synthesis takes place that converts CBGA into one of three cannabinoids—namely THCA, CBDA, or CBCA. Nigel emphasized the complexity of chemistry, that the science provides "an accurate way of telling if the cannabis you are buying is fresh or part of last year's harvest. CBN and delta-8 THC are the two most commonly occurring breakdown products on the trichome. They're not found in any appreciable amounts in freshly harvested cannabis."

Nigel talked about the data generated by MBA. "Not surprisingly, the most common cannabinoids are THC, CBG, and their respective acidic counterparts. We've seen CBC, CBN, and occasionally THCV. But unfortunately, the compound that we'd really like to see is CBD; it's just not there...at least we've not seen a strain yet in Montana. And quite frankly, the reason we're not seeing CBD is because cannabis growers over the decades have bred cannabis to be as potent in THC content as possible." He showed a slide that summarized the more than three hundred compounds, other than cannabinoids, that are found in cannabis. "It just goes to prove that there is a lot more chemistry going on in the cannabis plant than THC."

During the question-and-answer session, Nigel concluded with a plug why cannabis analysis is critical. "Edibles are consistently over-dosed or under-dosed. And that's because there is a narrow window of opportunity between heating the preparation up enough to precipitate the decarboxylation reaction, but not so high a temperature or cooking time that you degrade all the cannabinoids to CBN. It's a tricky process. We can accurately dose edibles for patients. Batch verification would make things safer for everyone. It would give everyone peace of mind."

MT-148 was a listing ship in turbulent waters and with a dismal forecast. The very existence of the law was in serious trouble, but few in the medical marijuana community appreciated this. I did my best to wake up the troops. I hoped the election results weren't as gruesome as the polling predictions.

Just before election day, I'd felt a brief glimmer of hope. I received an email from the president of the organization, inviting me to be a founding member of the board. A new national cannabis lobbying effort had started in Washington, DC, called the National Cannabis Industry Association (NCIA). I was flattered and called to get more information. I hoped this new national organization might somehow help us in our upcoming political battle.

After exchanging a few pleasantries, he informed me that my seat on the board would cost a mere $5,000.

Incredulous, I asked, "So, everyone on the board pays $5,000?"

"That's the way it works, Dr. Geci."

The flattery was short-lived. I declined the offer.

A Strain Called Misty

Serendipity is a common theme in history. Michael Pollan's, *The Botany of Desire* is a series of essays regarding four plants that helped shape human destiny. Not surprisingly, cannabis is one of the plants explored, although my favorite story from the book is the origin of the Red Delicious apple. Year after year, a farmer in Iowa mowed the same volunteer apple squatting in the middle of a field row. One year, the farmer transplanted the hardy little tree. And the rest is history.

If Pollan had talked to me, I would have shared my own version of cannabis serendipity: the discovery of the first Montana strain to contain significant amounts of cannabidiol (CBD). As unbelievable as it may sound today, in 2010, few people knew anything about CBD, the powerful medicinal cannabinoid; now it's found in everything, from massage oil to pet food.

Nigel and I talked to growers about CBD, educating them that this non-psychoactive cannabinoid could completely transform the medical marijuana industry. Although skeptical at first, our efforts to encourage a CBD-rich strain of cannabis set off another botanical race—this one promising to be an even more lucrative market.

During the daily course of my clinic, patients asked where to purchase their medical marijuana. WH&H kept an updated list of dispensaries having their cannabis products tested by MBA. My recommendations to patients was an additional incentive for dispensaries to have their cannabis tested. If I knew a dispensary was selling a CBD strain that the lab had tested, I told patients.

While most of our customers were ignorant about what MBA did with cannabis, all of them were eager to have Nigel explain the results and the implications. People in the industry were starting to understand that there was more to growing medical marijuana than getting people high. For many, developing a rare strain with an unusual cannabinoid composition was a fascinating proposition. There were rumors from Colorado of a strain called Charlotte's Web, said to be rich in CBD, and reported to have induced dramatic decreases in seizures in children.[115]

Although rumors were rampant in the cannabis world, the reports about CBD and the Charlotte's Web strain were substantiated by what I'd read about the drug Sativex, a plant-based compound made by GW Pharmaceuticals. Sativex is an extract from a strain of cannabis with a 50:50 mix of CBD and THC. It's effective in decreasing the spasticity in multiple sclerosis and in chronic pain management.[116] I hoped the lab could find a blockbuster strain.

Data that Mr. DeAngelo shared from his Harborside Dispensary supported MBA's findings that strains containing high concentrations of CBD were rare. There's no way of knowing if a strain contains CBD without having it tested. Smoking a joint containing CBD won't get you high or alter your sensorium in the way a THC-rich joint would. Alternatively, due to the "entourage effect,"[117] the phenomenon where CBD mitigates the euphoric effects of THC, highly psychoactive strains of THC-rich cannabis produce little or no CBD.

Our efforts finally paid off. As the story goes, a grower had been cultivating a few dozen cannabis plants from a handful of seeds he'd inherited from an old-timer. Most of the seeds grew into recognizable cannabis plants: verdant green and bushy with long branches of skunky colas. But one of the plants failed to mirror its robust siblings; the plant was short and scrawny, with narrow pale leaves. The guy called it his "retarded plant."

As harvest neared, he felt bad about pulling the outlier plant, so he gave it to an herbalist friend who happened to be one of MBA's earliest clients. The herbalist took the plant and nurtured it to harvest, then brought a sample in for Nigel to analyze.

Later that day, Nigel called. "Hey, Mike, you're never going to believe this."

"What's going on?"

Nigel sounded out of breath. "I tested the first strain of cannabis that had a significant CBD content today."

"Really?"

"Absolutely. I reran the sample three times to be sure I wasn't manufacturing an errant peak. Sure enough, it's there all right. It's pretty exciting."

I was really curious. "What's the name of the strain?"

"Misty. I think it's kinda cool."

I shared the excitement. I'd read dozens of studies suggesting the healing anti-inflammatory power of CBD. And now we had it. Within a few weeks, we'd found another strain that had a 50:50 ratio of CBD: THC, similar to the Sativex strain.

It was an intoxicating time in the lab.

Now that Nigel was comfortable with cannabinoid analysis, we were eager to explore a research and development strategy for MBA. One of the physical properties that make cannabinoids so fascinating is how fat-soluble they are. No matter how hard folks thought they needed to shake their glycerin tinctures, oil and water just don't mix. Finding an efficient way of getting cannabinoids into a water-based solution opened a gold mine of clinical applications using water-based nasal sprays and eye drops.

Although cannabinoids are important and the most recognizable phytochemicals in cannabis, they are not solely responsible for the entirety of the plant's medicinal potential. Other organic compounds called terpenes and sesquiterpenes are also found in the plant. These aromatic compounds are volatile essential oils; they evaporate to our olfactory nerve and are responsible for the distinctive aromas of cannabis.[118] Some cannabis aficionados claim they can sniff the difference between strains. Perhaps so, but the only way of empirically discerning volatile oils is with a gas chromatograph (GC).

Another untapped market was plant genetics.

Cannabis has been grown for millennium, but highly potent THC-dominant marijuana strains have been commercially bred for roughly fifty years. I suspect that there are a few legend growers who have been meticulous in keeping records of their marijuana breeding. A good breeder keeps records. For example, the breeder takes note of the Northern Lights strain crossed with the Purple Kush strain, recording the results of the journey from seed to harvest. Good record-keeping takes the guesswork out of marijuana breeding, although the downside to keeping records is twofold: it takes time, and most importantly, it leaves a discriminating paper trail that most growers in the pre-legalization era found unnerving. And law enforcement loves good record keepers.

My experience with cannabis growers left me with a demonstrative lack of confidence that these folks kept anything remotely resembling good records, nor were they particularly meticulous in their growing techniques. I think a majority of the marijuana strain names are gimmicks; seeds got mixed up, records weren't kept, and growers called their marijuana whatever the market wanted to buy.

That being said, I've always wanted to be a fly on the wall at a strain-naming party.

Suspicion of strain names and getting "clean" genetics was rampant among growers. Many clients were interested in MBA confirming the genetics of their marijuana. I often heard people like Anthony Gallo asking, "Is this *really* a pure White Widow? Or is it a cross? And if so, what'd they cross it with?"

Whether it's an heirloom Afghani Northern Lights cannabis strain or a Red Delicious apple, the only way to accurately determine the genetics of any plant or animal is to sequence the genome using polymerase chain reaction (PCR). This technology is available and affordable now, but in 2010, the commercial utilization of DNA sequencing through PCR sequencing wasn't economically feasible; Nigel could only report upon phenotypic variation of the cannabinoid content.

The MMGA Does It Again

Daubert took the Cannabis Forum political roadshow to Billings for an election fundraiser in collaboration with the MMGA. I wasn't able to attend, so Nigel represented the lab. My first instinct was to avoid anything associated with the MMGA, but with the 2010 midterm election just weeks away, the stakes were much bigger (and more important) than my ego.

Although I'd hoped for the best, I knew that things were going south when Nigel began complaining, blasting numerous MMGA members and organizers of the Billings Cannabis Forum. One guy who particularly caught his ire got tagged, "a jackass."

Due to the gravity of our dire political situation, I was hopeful that petty differences could be overlooked; and everyone with a stake in the industry would work together. Reality revealed my fantasy. With rare exceptions, the pro-cannabis crowd didn't comprehend the determination of the opposition. For the repealists, it was simple: repeal or bust.

The keynote speaker of the Forum was cannabis activist and author Irv Rosenfeld. I'd heard that Irv was going to auction his Montana medical marijuana card off at the fundraiser. The grower with the highest bid would have the distinction of being Irv's Montana cannabis supplier. Buying cannabis in Montana would supplement the medical cannabis that was being shipped to him every month from the federal government's farm in Mississippi. Technically it was legal, but I viewed the auction as a cute PR type stunt that had no business being part of the fundraiser.

Although Irv Rosenfeld is not a high-profile pro-cannabis celebrity like Snoop Dogg or Woody Harrelson, he was the best they had. His struggle to use medical marijuana legally has made him an icon among the pro-cannabis activists. To many in the cannabis movement, Irv is considered sacred; he'd fought the US government and won, becoming one of seventeen individuals who were enrolled in the FDA's compassionate cannabis IND program. Now he was coming to help his fellow Montanan cannabis brethren.

The notion of jeopardizing the credibility of our single political patron saint by auctioning off his Montana medical marijuana card to the highest bidder was absurd. I objected until the silly exercise was scrapped.

Then, a few days after the Billings event, Nigel informed me that *Cannabis Now* magazine had just distributed their inaugural issues (ten thousand copies) across the state. Its foldout centerfold showed a Photoshopped medical marijuana card with Governor Schweitzer's name and address printed on the card. It was a funny junior high stunt, except that under the current tenuous political atmosphere, insulting the sitting governor is an egregious mistake. The entire marijuana advocacy scene was beginning to feel like a comedy of errors, although, unlike the Shakespearean play, this was not a comical representation of my reality.

The positive news from the Billings Forum was the event garnered more positive media attention than the one in Bozeman.

But was it too little, too late?

The Midterm Tsunami

The midterm elections were catastrophic for any hope of sane medical marijuana reform.

The Republicans made impressive gains in both the House and the Senate, wiping out the bipartisan parity that had been a generational mainstay in Montana politics. Even President Obama termed the lopsided midterm results a "shellacking" for Democrats. The president reached out to Republicans to come together for the good of the country, believing there was "hope for civility" in dealing with the issues facing the country.[119]

The Montana electorate was rattled by two major factors—the Affordable Care Act and the explosion of medical marijuana. Tea Party representation in Helena restructured the political landscape, with Republicans now holding sixty-seven seats to the Democrats' thirty-three seats. And that was the good news.

The repeal of MT-148 was at the top of the Republican political agenda. For the pro-cannabis folks, there was nothing left to do but regroup and prepare for the political battle that lay ahead. The legislature would convene in nine weeks.

Shannon Bishop, Anthony Gallo's partner, had just opened a business advisory service. During the organization of the Bozeman Cannabis Forum, she volunteered to take care of last-minute details. Shannon asked me if I'd like her to streamline the lab and the clinic.

It was hard to contain my delight. "I would love your help. What do we need to do first?"

"Do you have an employee handbook?"

I replied with a furrowed brow.

"Do you have a policy and procedure manual for either the clinic or the lab?"

"No."

"Do you have a list of the employee job descriptions?"

"Negative."

"I'd be happy to help you with all of this," Shannon said brightly.

"That would be a godsend."

In a matter of days, there were labeled folders, policy manuals, and professional signs on the office doors and walls. The next wave of Shannon's touch included MBA pens, magnets, as well as Christmas cards and fruitcakes for our clients. The icing on the cake was the door sign she placed on the entrance to the lab. In white capital letters against a red rectangular background, the sign read "RESTRICTED AREA."

What Shannon did was miraculous. The moment that she agreed to help me, I felt an enormous weight lift. I confided insecurities as a start-up CEO. Shannon listened with the patience of Job, and I genuinely believe that without her help, I would have lost my mind. Lucky for me, Shannon's arrival coincided with Erin giving me notice that she would begin her Ph.D. program.

Increasing demands from the lab convinced Nigel to resign his NSF fellowship at MSU to devote all of his energy to MBA. I was still working six shifts a month in the ED and was looking for an excuse to leave. Nigel's fellowship resignation and the surge in clinic volume crystallized my decision. I resigned my job in the ED to focus on growing MBA.

Despite the election results, the clinic continued to grow as the demand for medical marijuana continued to rise. I hired Melissa Clark, a physician's assistant, to help me. Melissa and I had a lot in common, and since she was working in one of the local emergency departments, she needed little training.

Melissa performed a complete history and physical, and when I was available, she would give me a brief overview of the patient. I would speak to the patient for a few minutes, ask if they had any questions, and if everything was in order, I signed their physician statement. It was an amicable and efficient system.

It was meaningful that I was seeing repeat patients—individuals I'd seen the previous year. I was grateful that some patients wanted to use me as their family doctor, too. I was comfortable managing their hypertension and diabetes, and even diagnosed a patient with bladder cancer—not bad for a physician maligned as a pot doc.

It was apropos that Anthony Gallo was my first patient renewal. Anthony and I had known each other well for more than a year, and although the relationship had its ups and downs, his kid brother charm always won out. During his follow-up exam, I asked him a few questions.

"Have you noticed anything different in your life since you've received your card?"

Anthony cocked his head. "Absolutely, dude. I no longer wake up at night wondering if I'm going to jail for growing my own cannabis and selling it."

After I signed his physician statement, Anthony grinned. "Alright, my man. I'll see you next year for my renewal."

Before he left, I wanted to ask him something that had been troubling me. "Do you think it's silly that you have to see a doctor for your renewal every year?"

"Do I think it's silly? Yes, I do. But if it's something that keeps the Man off my back, it's a small price to pay for freedom and peace of mind. It's just a political game. No biggie."

The biggest concern I had with the Montana program was its effect on the doctor-patient relationship. MT-148 allowed physicians to recommend marijuana for conditions that only the state approved. Having a legislative body pass laws regarding how a doctor is allowed to prescribe medication borders on tyranny. Thomas Jefferson echoed those sentiments back in his day.

Since Phinney was evicted, opening a dispensary in the Medical Arts Building was something that percolated in my mind, as MBA held the exclusive option for opening a dispensary. Over time, several growers and other interested individuals had approached me about selling or leasing my dispensary option to a third party.

On one such occasion, Mike Singer hosted Nigel and me at his house. He had invited several other potential investors and we discussed my vision of a dispensary in the Medical Arts Building. I considered leveraging some of the revenue from a dispensary into subsidizing a community cannabis health clinic.

Aside from the altruism of running an indigent clinic, there was a larger motive. If the public could observe a cannabis-funded health clinic in action, one that provided a needed contribution to the community's indigent health needs, perhaps the current public fear of cannabis might be stymied.

I worked the numbers after dinner. Even with conservative revenue projections, the community cannabis health clinic was doable. If it was successful, we had a chance to garner favorable media attention that could convince legislators that cannabis wasn't a scourge. Cannabis-subsidized health care might be the key to usurping the political momentum of the anti-cannabis coalition.

Everyone in attendance was excited by the possibilities.

I was reluctantly cautious. "I need to speak with my attorney about this and see how best to proceed."

And that's what I did.

Art Wittich, the local attorney who had facilitated Phinney's eviction, won the Senate seat in the Thirty-Fifth District and had recused himself of personally dealing with clients with political agendas. I was referred to his associate, Colleen, who thought that MBA subleasing a medical marijuana dispensary was a bad idea. "I can't urge you enough to reconsider subleasing a marijuana dispensary in your office space."

It was disappointing to hear Colleen's legal assessment, but Devin had suggested a similar course. The law was just too vague to risk putting a dispensary into the same space as the lab and the clinic. Despite the disappointment, I was excited the lab was having an impact on the marketplace. MBA was on track to turn a profit within its first year of operation. My businesses were firing on all cylinders.

Aside from the midterm tsunami, the future looked bright.

A Really Good Question

Just before Thanksgiving, I received an email from Daubert about an upcoming marijuana conference in New York City. I was indifferent about giving cannabis two more days of my life, as my time back home was precious, but a friend convinced me to attend. The Marijuana Conference 2010: A Forum for Discussion of Business, Legal, & Health Issues was presented by DealFlow Media, a marketing group looking to exploit the impending cannabis explosion. The conference was the next day, so I hastily made plans to attend.

By the time I took the MTA train from Poughkeepsie to Grand Central Station, then walked to the conference hotel in midtown Manhattan, I'd missed most of the first day's speakers. Regardless, I sat in the back of the room and listened to the panelists discuss their outlined topic: Potential Medical Consequences and Societal Issues Related to Legalization. I scanned the room, hoping to see a familiar face, but the large room was comprised of almost entirely well-groomed men in suits—Wall Street analysts and venture capitalists scoping out the pot scene.

Listening to the panelists, I wondered if they would mention testing. The guy from California NORML (National Organization for the Reform of Marijuana Laws) was talking about marijuana approval by the FDA. No one mentioned testing. During the Q&A sessions, I stood up and asked for their opinions regarding cannabis testing and quality control. It was as if I'd asked them to describe, in excruciating detail, the meaning of life.

The frumpy moderator looked perplexed and pulled the microphone closer. "What do you mean by 'cannabis testing'?"

Unexpectedly, my window for influencing and educating a national audience on the importance of cannabis quality control suddenly presented itself. I took a deep breath. "My name is Dr. Michael Geci, and I own a medical marijuana testing laboratory in Bozeman, called Montana Botanical Analysis. We analyze the potency of cannabis for its cannabinoid content by using sophisticated analytical instrumentation—an Agilent 1100 HPLC, to be exact. Our lab brings an element of quality control to an industry whose idea of quality control is lighting up a joint and seeing how high it gets you."

I thought more people would have laughed.

A nervous silence fell over the room while I tentatively continued. "As you know, quality control in the medical marijuana industry is virtually nonexistent. How do you expect the FDA to approve cannabis as medicine if no one knows what cannabinoids are actually in the strain of cannabis you are using?"

The trio of panelists huddled. Next to the moderator was the head of The Hemp and Cannabis Foundation; he bent toward the mic. "That's a really good question. You seem to know a lot about this."

For the next few minutes, I explained the importance of cannabis quality control. I recited my pitch to the attentive crowd. "Why is marijuana the only medicine in the country that is unlabeled for active ingredients? If you are going to call cannabis a medicine, you have to treat it like a medicine. Right?"

"You make some good points, Doctor."

At the cocktail reception that followed, I mingled among the suits, discussing MBA's business model. It was obvious that few people had considered quality control in the cannabis industry.

The next morning, I was present for the opening discussion: Budgetary Implications and Tax Benefits of Legalization. I sat next to a journalist, Ted Rose, who'd heard me at yesterday's Q&A session. We whispered as the Harvard economics professor outlined the potential tax windfall if marijuana were legalized. He quoted a study suggesting the federal government would save $41.3 billion per year in law enforcement costs alone—and that didn't include cannabis sales tax revenues.

Ted seemed interested in what I was doing. "I never thought about testing marijuana for its cannabinoid content."

"That's why there are currently only three labs in the country doing this." I gave Ted my three-minute pitch. He asked if I'd be interested in contributing a paper to an industry marketing analysis for marijuana—a 500-word synopsis on analytical testing in the marijuana industry. I took his card.

The morning presentations were interesting. Yet what struck me was the concluding theme of each speaker: cannabis prohibition was coming to an end, and for those with a taste for risk, it was the next gold rush.

At lunch, a man approached me. "Hi, Dr. Geci, I'm Francis Yang."

I shook his hand and offered him a chair.

"Dr. Geci, I really enjoyed what you had to say at the Q&A session yesterday," he said earnestly. "I'm from Arizona, representing a group of investors, including myself, who are trying to get an Arizona dispensary license. Our group is in the middle of the application process. We've talked about setting up a laboratory within the dispensary as a way of distinguishing ourselves from the other applicants."

"You're looking to set up a lab in Arizona?"

"Yes sir. After the conference was over yesterday, I called my partners and told them about you. We all agreed that we'd like you to help us set up our lab in Arizona."

"Seriously?"

"Absolutely. Dr. Geci, I spent nearly a decade on Wall Street, and during that time I got good at problem solving. I think your ideas regarding cannabis quality control are spot on. Your logic makes perfect sense. Our group would really like to work with you."

I wasn't sure if I should feel flattered or conned. Francis was either the most genuine person I'd ever met, or he was the slickest salesman. For a moment I allowed myself to wander in the land of grandiosity. I currently owned a lab in Bozeman. I was discussing putting labs in California, in Washington, and now, with Francis's Arizona group. It seemed too good to be true.

I took Francis' card and told him I'd be in touch.

Life was feeling surreal.

Damage Control: The MTCIA

For weeks, the fallout from the midterm election reverberated throughout the country and nowhere more dramatically than Montana. Surely, I thought, someone would be organizing a group to address the mounting opposition in the upcoming legislature.

Finally, I heard a rumor.

A group of key players in the industry had been formed to counter the anti-marijuana political machine. They'd scheduled an organizational meeting and I was miffed not to be invited. I'd been a key supporter of the industry, I'd invested my own money into legitimizing the system, and the lab was the keystone to this effort. But after eighteen months of working among these people, I'd become calloused. I wanted a say in how the potheads were going to wage this war. After my morning clinic, I drove up to Helena.

It was another cold and blustery December day when I rolled into town. I texted Daubert for the address, and to my surprise, he promptly replied back. When I walked in, the room was littered with familiar faces slouched in comfortable furniture. A few gave me the "What the hell is he doing here?" look. I found Daubert discussing something with his business partner (and meeting site homeowner) Chris Lindsey.

Chris is an attorney and one of the four partners in Montana Cannabis located on the outskirts of Helena. He's a frail, soft-spoken man with a clear complexion and dark eyes that look out over black horn bill glasses. He said cannabis helped his abdominal pain.

People listened to him because he was the only attorney in the room and had worked to acquit a couple of patients from ridiculous marijuana charges (one of which I'd testified). He seemed nice, but it bugged me that he always referred to me as "Doctor."

I invited him several times to call me "Mike" or "Michael," but he never did. It seemed odd, but I was getting used to dealing with odd.

Beth Thorner, the owner of Cannabinalysis, glared at me. I smiled and waved. She thought I was an ass, and I knew she wasn't as good a chemist as Nigel. Our mutual disdain and mistrust of each other seemed like a great combination to enter the political battlefield against a united foe.

Hiedi Handford, the publisher of the fledgling cannabis-focused magazine *Montana Connect*, was the loudest in the room. A fiery woman in her late forties, she walked with a noticeable limp and wore thick sensitivity stockings on her arms and legs. If you wanted a loud passionate protester, Hiedi was your girl. She was a canna-zealot, an infantry soldier who loved being in the trenches.

Talking to Hiedi was Kristy Fairy, the canna-baker. Her elegant Nordic features contrasted her California sun-bleached skin.

In the corner was a granola blonde reading something on her cell phone. Daubert told me her name was Katrina Farnum, a smart, wicked-funny dispensary owner and herbalist from Missoula. Katrina proved to be a true cannabis warrior.

The final prominent member of the group was John Masterson. He was a founding member and current president of Montana NORML. John is tall with long straight hair and a Jackson Browne way about him. He and Daubert were the two power brokers; they understood the battle we were facing and realized that organizing a group of cannabis activists was going to be like herding cats while riding rogue kangaroos.

Masterson introduced the members of the group and passed around a notebook for contact information. The name of the organization was the Montana Cannabis Industry Association (MTCIA). The primary task of the MTCIA was to re-brand marijuana while regaining the trust of Montanans. He talked about the Herculean job that lay ahead and the need to work together. Masterson understood the struggle facing us. But ultimately, his agenda was different than mine. John's end game was marijuana legalization; mine was protecting patient access to medical cannabis.

The meeting lasted several hours. I was stumped why they were resistant to utilizing the academic capacity of MBA to validate the medical science of cannabinoids. It seemed that the truth was a reasonable tactic to counter the biased Safe Community Safe Kids (SCSK) political propaganda. My proposal to utilize the lab as a talking point to counter the anti-cannabis propaganda was politely declined. Nothing substantive was agreed upon, except that we were all in deep shit if we didn't work together. We agreed to meet again, communicating through Masterson's private web server.

Walking to my car, I felt a stark indifference. The SCSK coalition was well-funded, organized, and passionate about defeating any medical marijuana reform. Additionally, they had significant momentum coming off the Tea Party's resounding victory. The bright spot for our team was that we finally all came together and formed a group to protect the industry in which we all had a vested interest. I hoped it wouldn't be too little, too late.

Ultimately, the political fulcrum of our lobbying effort came down to trust. Daubert was the undisputed leader. He had thousands of members of Patients and Families United (PFU) and had been essentially lobbying the legislature since 1983. He knew all the critical players in the legislature. Daubert was the principal architect of MT-148, and as the industry's sole marijuana lobbyist, no one knew the political waters we were entering better than him.

As much as I liked him, I was suspicious about Daubert's agenda. Obviously, he had a sizable stake in the game as one of the partners of Montana Cannabis. It seemed disingenuous when he would comment that the company was a money pit. From what I'd seen, selling marijuana seemed like a pretty lucrative business. I couldn't believe that being a co-owner in Montana Cannabis could be a bad investment. Maybe he thought I was naïve? Whatever the reason, it didn't add up for me.

Another item that caught my eye was Daubert's relationship with Anthony Gallo. Earlier in the year, Gallo paid for Daubert to attend Hemp Fest, the Seattle-based festival purported to be the world's largest advocacy event for the decriminalization of marijuana. Hearsay rumored that Gallo was paying Daubert for lobbying services. Although I found Gallo charming, he had an agenda, it was all about making as much money as possible. This foggy relationship with Gallo gave me further cause to be apprehensive of Daubert's motives.

And, although I bought Daubert a lot of Guinness and burgers while we talked shop, I never felt like one of his trusted comrades. I wished our relationship could have been deeper and more robust.

With the newly formed MTCIA plotting its strategy, I wanted Sam in the group, too. I thought that having Sam working alongside Daubert would be the one-two punch we needed to defend our cause. But the reality that I was slow to see was the smoldering mistrust between Daubert and Sam. Neither trusted the other more than was required for civility. From my perspective, Tom underestimated Sam's political abilities and he wasn't eager to have her help. And I think that Sam considered Tom to be a self-serving hypocrite.

Despite these private grievances, and much to my surprise, I brokered a deal to have an account created to help fund Sam's lobbying effort. The monies would come from Daubert's war chest, funded in part from NORML and the Drug Policy Alliance.

The agreement between Daubert and Sam bought me time to find a dedicated stream of money to fund MBA's political efforts to thwart repeal. I spoke to Nigel about recruiting our most trusted customers into becoming contributors. I was relieved when a number of them ponied up the initial deposit to keep Sam in the game.

Hiring Bryan

Each month the lab was busier. My informal patient surveys consistently reported that patients would pay more for tested medicine than for untested cannabis. The surveys suggested that cannabis testing gave them a sense of security knowing that their medical marijuana was subjected to some sort of quality control assessment. Since the Rev started marketing his cannabis as being tested and packaged by MBA, his business took off.

It was a huge deal. And as I predicted, it snowballed.

By the end of the week, MBA had secured testing contracts from two other major providers, including the largest dispensary in the state. Locking down these contracts provided the lab with a welcomed infusion of operating cash flow.

Hiedi Handford helped get the news of the dispensary contracts adopted as a press release to the cannabis-friendly news site *TokeOfTheTown.com*. It was the first article about MBA that had a national audience.[120] We were finally making a dent in the insulated bunker of the medical marijuana industry.

MBA began getting requests for testing cannabis from across the country. Federal jurisdiction regarding interstate commerce of cannabis required me to be highly tuned to the sensitivities of the DEA and other law enforcement agencies. Invariably, I politely declined all interstate testing requests.

We received a query from a Canadian hemp company. They were looking to use hemp-based cannabinoids as an herbal anti-inflammatory veterinary supplement. After consulting with Devin, the company sent the required customs paperwork and we had our first international client.

More clients meant more cannabis to run through the HPLC. With Erin's departure, there was no one to help Nigel. If MBA was going to expand, Nigel was the person to make that happen, so I gave him the green light to search for a lab assistant. After a week of reviewing applications, we settled on Bryan, a soft-spoken thirty-something chemist with penetrating eyes. He earned his master's in organic chemistry from Oregon State University. He'd spent the last several years working with a local tech start-up working in nanochemistry. He and Nigel got along well, and each enjoyed the mutual academic stimulation.

Nigel and I had talked about adding a research and development (R&D) arm to the lab. Now with Bryan on board, we were on track to make that happen. Several herbalists were eager to have their cannabis products clinically tested for commercial human use. BioScience Laboratories, one of the largest drug and chemical testing companies in the country, was just down the hall. After discussions with the lab director, we put together our first proposal. The herbalists were excited that their cannabis-infused products could be tested for patient safety. I was excited because this was another step toward validating the medicinal cannabis industry.

Bryan came to our next monthly lab meeting. He was interested in researching novel cannabis delivery systems. Because of the exceptionally high-fat solubility of cannabinoids, it was next to impossible to dissolve them into water-soluble solutions. I understood the clinical and economic significance of an effective water-based delivery system for cannabinoids. In the ophthalmology space alone, the clinical market for CBD-based eye drops would be in the tens of billions of dollars. Diabetic retinopathy and macular degeneration are the leading cause of blindness in adults, and there was research to suggest that CBD could help.[121]

Nigel called me the day after I returned home from the Marijuana Conference I'd attended in midtown Manhattan, excited about a couple of unexpected developments. Bryan's old boss was upgrading a bunch of their laboratory apparatus and offered us some of their old equipment. There were a few handy odds and ends, but the big score was the ventilated lab hood. With a lab hood, we could begin mold testing.

And then came the other unforeseen development, seemingly from outer space: "Hey, Mike, you'll never believe this."

A prominent grower in the central part of the state called to inquire if we would be interested in accepting their donation of a brand-new gas chromatograph machine.

"Nigel, what are you talking about? They want to *give* us a GC?"

"I know it sounds nutty, but that's what the guy said on the phone. I made a couple of calls around, and he sounds legit."

"That's crazy," I muttered.

"I couldn't agree more, but this is what they wanted me to ask you about. It just proves that this industry will never stop surprising me."

According to Nigel, a group of growers/investors decided to start a lab of their own. Apparently, someone in the group had passed general chemistry in high school and recommended that they buy a gas chromatograph to start their new lab. Finally, someone in the group realized that for the purpose of cannabinoid analysis, not only had they purchased the wrong type of analytical equipment (they needed an HPLC), but nobody in the organization even knew how to operate a GC. In exchange for the GC, we would do their testing on a prorated basis. Now we had the analytical tool to perform analysis on cannabis terpenes, too.

On the heels of obtaining the GC, the lab earned itself increased public credibility by an important alignment with the state small business and scientific community. MBA was invited to join the Montana Bioscience Alliance. The alliance offered discounts for lab materials and offered TGIF gatherings where various scientists could talk shop in a relaxed atmosphere. It seemed that whenever cannabis was the topic of discussion, the crowd perked up.

One afternoon while Nigel and I were discussing Francis Yang's Arizona group lab proposal, I noticed his dampened enthusiasm.

"I've been meaning to talk to you about something, Mike."

"What's up?" I asked, curious to hear what was on his mind.

"Since I left MSU, we've been getting our health insurance through COBRA, but that's going to expire soon, and I really need to be able to get health insurance for the family. My wife's been bugging me about it."

I had planned on MBA eventually providing full benefits for its employees, but the company wasn't yet generating enough revenue. Devin suggested deferring health insurance for as long as possible, but it was more important to me to be a good boss.

"How much do you need?"

"About $300 a month, I think."

"I want to make sure you have enough money to get the insurance that you need. You've done a bang-up job here, and I want to keep you happy. But I also want to keep Audrey happy." We both laughed.

By and large, Nigel and I got along exceedingly well. I consulted him about every major decision. When it was time to hire someone to replace Erin, Nigel chimed in about hiring Lori's friend, Annie. Nigel was my confidant about the lab, and he always offered an ear when I needed to discuss any personal issues.

Then one December day, I was skimming through the latest edition of *Entrepreneur* magazine. I turned to a full-page ad promoting an upcoming small business conference co-sponsored by the magazine and UPS. I was always looking for ways of getting MBA into the public consciousness. What caught my eye wasn't the conference itself—a one-day event on small business strategies for growth—but the opportunity they were offering participants:

Give a three-minute pitch to the editors of the magazine about your start-up company. If they like it, they'll do a story about your business in the magazine.

"What a great idea."

Pitching Amy

Once the *Entrepreneur* editorial staff had accepted my proposal, I began working on my three-minute pitch. The night before I flew to Atlanta for the event, I asked Shannon and Anthony to help me with my presentation. We struggled to come up with a catchy pitch that would hook an editor's interest. After a couple of hours of brainstorming, we took a break. Shannon excused herself to fetch us drinks. Anthony used the break to roll a joint from one of the two-dozen different jars of cannabis he stored in his basement.

"Hey, Dr. Mike, you mind taking a look at something?"

"Sure. What do you got?"

Anthony pulled down his trousers and pointed at his thigh. "I've been watching this thing for a couple of weeks. But I'm starting to freak out cuz I think it's getting bigger."

I pulled my reading glasses down from the top of my forehead and crouched closer. "Do you mind if I touch it?"

"Dude, you're the doctor. Do what you gotta do to tell me what the fuck this shit is."

The mass was conspicuous. It was a three-centimeter, minimally tender, non-mobile mass about the size of a large walnut and located on his thigh, about halfway up his leg.

"Does it hurt when I mash on it?"

Anthony grimaced. "It doesn't hurt, but it sure feels weird."

"How long have you had it?"

He shrugged. "Two weeks…maybe a month." He eyed me for a minute. "Why? You think this is something serious?"

"And you think it's gotten bigger?"

"A little, I think."

"Hmmm."

Anthony let out an anxious sigh. "What kind of doctor sound is that?"

"Have you been losing any weight?"

"No."

"That's good. Can you lie back for a second? I want to check the lymph nodes in your groin."

"Dude, it's a good thing I like you." Anthony grinned as he moved over to the oversized leather couch. I palpated his inguinal area, searching for enlarged lymph nodes. I was relieved that nothing felt unusual.

"So, what do you think?" he said nervously.

"Let's wait till Shannon gets back. I want to make sure she hears this, too."

When Shannon returned, I gave them my spiel about the mass. I told them that the likelihood that this mass represented a malignancy was small, but I wasn't in a position to make that diagnosis. I told them it was most likely benign but could possibly be either a leiomyosarcoma or a rhabdomyosarcoma. I urged them to follow up with their primary doctor and get a referral. At a minimum, Anthony needed an MRI and a biopsy of the mass for a confirmatory diagnosis.

"You need to call as soon as possible. The sooner you know what this thing is, the better off you'll be. I'll call you when I get back from the conference in Atlanta."

Driving back to my apartment, I had an idea, and swung by the lab. I found a sheet of extra MBA labels that had been printed off earlier during the packaging and labeling of a batch of tincture. I filled an empty cobalt blue tincture bottle with water, slapped a label on it, and shrink-wrapped the cellophane collar around the cap and bottle. Then I grabbed a tin of an MBA-labeled cannabis-based salve. With product examples in hand, I was ready to take my pitch to Atlanta.

On the afternoon flight to Atlanta, I visualized the editors choosing MBA. My company would be in a national business magazine within a year of its inception. I was hoping not to drown in a pool of grandiosity. To ground myself, I said a simple prayer: a request for wisdom and guidance, and I asked God for a sign.

The morning of the conference I was nervous. I continued practicing my pitch, but the more I practiced, the harder it got. When I arrived at the Omni, it was clear this was a big event. Hundreds of people mingled in the hallways making small talk about their respective businesses. The keynote speaker was the former governor of Kentucky, John Y. Brown Jr. I scoured the audience. On the far edge of the seating area, wearing a spring-inspiring blue flower dress, was the editor-in-chief of *Entrepreneur*, Amy Cosper.

I had a plan.

There was a twenty-minute intermission between the keynote speaker and the first presentation. The individual pitches to the editors would take place right after lunch. As the crowd filed out into the lobby area, I noticed that Ms. Cosper was speaking to a young woman, so I made my move.

Patiently, I waited for the conversation to conclude. Then I stepped up and introduced myself. "Hello, Ms. Cosper. My name is Dr. Michael Geci. I'm the CEO of Montana Botanical Analysis. My company is an analytical testing lab that offers quality control testing in the Montana medical marijuana industry. These are a few examples of the products we help make and test."

I handed her the tincture bottle and the salve tin. She eyed the samples with great interest. Then she looked at me with a huge smile. "I want your story."

"I'm sorry?"

"I want your story, Michael. Your lab sounds like an amazing idea. We're going to do a story about you guys out there in Montana."

"Wow. You're serious?"

"Absolutely."

I was shell-shocked. "You mean I don't have to stand in line to pitch the editors like everyone else?"

"Nope." Then she snuck a glance at her Rolex. "I have to run along. I'll be in touch." She handed me her business card and walked off.

"Thank you very much."

I trembled with excitement. The first person I called was Jacob's mom.

I was overcome with emotion. "They want my story."

"That's fantastic. Congratulations," she said.

I called Sam next, and then Nigel. It seemed like it was all coming together. God had sent me a sign.

A wine and cheese reception followed the conference. My flight didn't leave until the next day, so I was intent on relaxing and mingling with my fellow entrepreneurs. I nursed a glass of Malbec and made small talk with a few of the other participants. Then I began speaking with one of the conference speakers. When I told him about my business, he interrupted me.

"Are you the doctor with the cannabis tinctures?"

"I am, but how do you know about me?"

"Amy has been passing your tincture around to all the speakers. What a great idea."

I was speechless. I later saw Ms. Cosper walking about, and we took a selfie. I thanked her again for her interest in picking my company for their magazine. I even sent her a follow-up email before the reception concluded.

When I got back to Bozeman, I called Shannon to check on Anthony's. After consulting with physicians at the National Cancer Institute, Anthony was flying to Seattle and see a specialist at the Fred Hutchinson Cancer Research Center. He would be evaluated and worked up there. I was glad he was getting the care he needed.

Like a cruel junior high prank, the excitement of being in a national magazine quickly faded. Days turned into weeks, and despite several polite voicemails to Ms. Cosper, I heard nothing from *Entrepreneur*. The experience became yet another lesson that nothing about cannabis is smooth or predictable.

And that signs from God require careful translation.

ACS

The cannabis train had left the station, and I was on board. It had been a surreal ride up to now. Had anyone told me two years prior that I'd own one of the first cannabis testing labs in the country, I would have asked them if they'd suffered some sort of recent closed head injury. This whirlwind journey had taken me places I couldn't have possibly imagined; now the sky seemed to be the limit.

Over time, it was a relief to discover other serious scientists interested in cannabis testing, and Arno was the hub that brought everyone together. Aside from Michelle, I was in contact with several scientists and physicians from California and Hawaii. The goal was starting an organization to advocate for professional standards for cannabis quality control. During our inaugural Skype conference, we each told horror stories about why cannabis quality control was such a vital issue.

One of the Bay Area scientists described the contraband he'd found in the cannabis tested in his lab. "It's surprising how often I find the cannabis cut with sand or these plastic and silica nanobeads. Without our microscope, these contaminants look just like trichomes."

"Why would anyone do that?" I asked.

"First, because they can get away with it, and two, because it's super cheap. You can easily increase the weight of the cannabis by more than 20 percent, depending how much of the crap you sprinkle on." The thought of smoking marijuana cut with millions of microscopic glass or plastic beads made me cringe.

The group was confident that other labs would want to join our organization. Someone asked about an organizational name, and after a moment, I suggested the Alliance for Cannabis Science

(ACS). The name had a ring to it, especially since most of the group had doctorates in chemistry. The irony of our group sharing similar initials to the American Chemical Society wasn't lost to anyone.

During the follow-up meeting, we thought the ACS should have a board of directors that would oversee new membership with strict criteria. With the approval of the other members, Sam received a temporary supporting membership to bolster her credentials for MBA's legislative lobbying effort.

The primary goal of the ACS was to usher an era of professional self-regulation in the newly emerging industry of analytical cannabis testing. Our self-regulatory format would be modeled in the same manner as Good Manufacturing Practices (GMP) self-regulates the United States supplement market. It was clear that many cannabis labs were using bogus testing methodology to convince the public (and their customers) that their results were accurate. Arno wanted the ACS to allow science, not prejudice, to be the referee in deciding the future of analytical cannabis testing.

"Clearly, we cannot force such standards on anyone, but if we get enough attention and enough heavyweight science members, authorities, and leaders in the field will voluntarily adopt our standards. Others will follow," Arno said. "An example is our current involvement with the American Herbal Pharmacopoeia (AHP). If the AHP adopts the HPLC method we currently use as the standard, our position will be strengthened."

The AHP is an educational organization dedicated to promoting the responsible use of herbal products and herbal medicines and is recognized as one of the world's leading herbal research organizations. It has published numerous monographs on plants widely used in alternative and complementary medicine. The monograph for cannabis was finally released in late 2013.

The ACS outlined a two-year plan. First, the ACS wanted to organize at least one annual symposium. Second, the group desired member representation at the most important cannabis-related events such as the Patients Out of Time conference, the International Association for Cannabinoid Medicine conference, and the High Times Cannabis Cup. Our goal was to become the place for credible scientific answers on cannabis issues.

With the launching of the ACS, I hoped that the resumé and experience I'd compiled over the past year would be an asset in our upcoming legislative struggle. I fantasized that science would unveil the myths and misconceptions about cannabis as a tenable societal threat. I truly believed that the truth would speak to those in power, freeing us from the threat of medical marijuana repeal by the religious and right-wing zealots who allowed fear and ignorance to guide them.

I was about to appreciate the extent of my naïveté.

The War Begins

At precisely noon, and pursuant to the Constitution of the State of Montana, the House of Representatives of the Sixty-Second Legislature of the State of Montana was called to order. On this frigid third day of January 2011, the Honorable Linda McCulloch, Montana's Secretary of State, led the assembly in the Pledge of Allegiance and thanked the students from the Montana National Guard Youth Challenge Academy for posting the colors. Across the rotunda in the Senate chamber, Pastor Keith Johnson gave the invocation. After the prayer, Secretary Marilyn Miller called the roll of the newly elected Senators.

In the House, all members were present.

Secretary McCulloch extended greetings to the members on behalf of the State of Montana and then delivered an impassioned speech that far too few heeded. She recalled the opening day of her first session as a house member representing the Seventy-Fifth District, a mere eighteen years ago. Her speech pleaded for the statesmanship of her first legislative session:

> My first session in the House looked a lot like this one. Republicans held a majority over Democrats: 67 to 33. Despite a 2 to 1 stronghold, both parties worked well together. Many of us—on both sides of the aisle—were able to pass our bills with strong support. Compromise happened then, it's happened since then, and you all have the power to ensure it happens in the next 90 days. You are in this room because your constituents believe in your ability to reason, to work through disagreements, and to approach policymaking in a civil manner. Let's start this session on more than just a promise to work together.[122]

With that, she invited every member of the House to walk across the aisle and meet legislators that they had never met. She instructed the group to shake hands or hug at least three legislators, not from their party. After a few minutes of cheerful banter, McCulloch concluded her speech.

The months of anticipation and preparation were over. It was show time. The mettle of the MTCIA was about to be tested. I was confident that we'd win, but was anxious about the battles that lay ahead. As a self-invited member of the MTCIA, I was clearly viewed by many as an outsider; I'm sure many in the group trusted me as little as I trusted them, which is why I was so grateful to have Sam on my team, making sure our interests were being addressed.

After the first installment of Sam's salary was paid, we needed a name for our lobbying group. I suggested using the ACS; I'd already spoken to the guys during our last Skype meeting, and they were fine with the idea. Sam liked the name and appreciated her honorary layperson membership. "We'll need as much firepower as we can muster. And now I got the science boys on my side."

For the past year, Sam and I spent countless hours creating, dissecting, and predicting various contingencies of what constituted fair and reasonable reform of MT-148. Our goal was to construct a medical marijuana program that could be the national model for efficiency and rationality. One afternoon, after writing out the skeleton proposals that would eventually become LC-991 (the Caferro bill), we stopped and looked at each other.

"You think we could really make a difference shaping this industry?" I asked.

"Damn straight, we could."

"What do you think our chances are of pulling this thing off?"

Sam wrinkled her forehead, running her fingers through her shoulder-length hair. "I can't believe our odds are good. But I also don't think anyone else has a really strong bill that could garner the bipartisan support needed to get Schweitzer to sign it."

By now, it was evident that medical marijuana had become the sacrificial lamb for the Tea Party. Several Republican committee chairmen were fanatically anti-marijuana. Representative David Howard, who chaired the House and Human Services Committee, and Speaker of the House Mike Milburn, who sponsored House

Bill (HB)-161, the Marijuana Repeal Bill were the loudest voices in the House, whereas Senator Jeff Essman led the marijuana repeal charge in the Senate.

Without a doubt, MT-148 needed a major face lift. People in the industry wanted loopholes closed, and mostly they wanted clarity regarding what was legal and what wasn't. But with the new Tea Party influence, it was repeal or bust.

Over the summer, the Sand's Committee, a bipartisan group of legislators, formulated what they thought was a palatable reform bill to both Republicans and Democrats and presented it as HB-68. The bill was a consolidation of testimony and recommendations from hundreds of concerned parents, law enforcement officials, teachers, doctors, and local district attorneys. We were encouraged that several ideas in Sam's letter to the committee ended up in HB-68. The bill had the support of several key legislators and rumored to have the support of Governor Schweitzer. Although HB-68 was by no means perfect, this was going to be our best bet to get a reasonable cannabis reform bill through the House.

But that was before the midterm elections.

Years afterward, Daubert noted:

The hang-up with HB-68 was that it would have worked—it would have taken big steps to fix the problems, and in the bargain brought some professional respectability to the "industry." Republicans who controlled the legislature, especially the House, were NEVER going to allow any steps toward respectability.

By the time the 2011 session began, it was far too late. Folks like Jason Christ, and the huge expansion in the number of crazy-behaving patients and caregivers, had created a backlash that doomed us.[123]

HB-68 was roundly supported, except by the extremist members of Safe Community, Safe Kids (SCSK), the group of evangelical Christians from Billings led by Susan Smith. Ms. Smith spoke of the marijuana industry as "preying upon the weak and unsuspecting, to further their agenda, which is to ultimately control the hearts and minds of our precious youth, now and in future generations."[124] Many Republicans had constituents who were SCSK members, turning marijuana repeal into nothing short of a holy crusade. I called them the Repealists. Despite some dramatic and theatrical testimony (on both sides of the issues), the hearing on January 21 for HB-68 went well. But in a telling symbol of his power, Chairman Howard insisted the bill sit in committee until it was formally tabled on March 23, killing any hope we had of reasonable reform.

In my opinion, the Tea Party took aim at marijuana because it was an easy target. Conservative legislators embraced the repeal effort with the passion of the crusaders marching to save Jerusalem. Every flaw in Montana society was blamed on marijuana. Representative Milburn gave a speech on February 2, defending his decision to push forward his repeal bill, HB-161. Milburn, an aging ex-fighter pilot, spoke of medical marijuana as "a scourge" to Montanan society. He categorized the growth of the marijuana industry in the prior two years as "opening the flood gates" of marijuana use, likening the damage in Montana to that felt in New Orleans during Hurricane Katrina. In his words, the only way to control this "out of control" industry was to "shut it down."[125] And that's precisely what they tried to do.

What most offended me was the Repealists' absurd claim that too many Montanans were seeking to use cannabis for chronic pain. There was no denying that more than 85 percent of patients who received their medical marijuana card did so under the auspices of chronic pain. Yet, as I learned through my years as an emergency physician, pain is relative. The hubris of these legislators viscerally offended me—lay politicians dictating who suffers from pain and who doesn't. I felt it was intrusive enough requiring patients to register with the state to get cannabis; now Repealists wanted to legislate the number of citizens who could use cannabis to assuage their chronic pain.

The Repealist leader, Representative Milburn, championed the view that the very cultural identity of Montana—the image of the Homesteader, the cowboy, the logger, the miner, and the rancher—was being eroded by marijuana. In his mind, there was no compromise. His consecrated mission of saving the moral fabric of the Big Sky state was simple: repealing medical marijuana. Period.

Interestingly, Milburn hung much of his rationale for repeal based on marijuana's classification as a Schedule I substance, arguing that since the federal government considered all forms of cannabis illegal, there needn't be further discussion on the matter. I found this an odd twist for a state that deeply prided itself on its independence from elitist bureaucrats back in Washington, D.C.

Not surprisingly, the Repealists simply ignored inconvenient truths like the Ogden memo, the CBD patent held by the NIH, or the federal government supplying Irv Rosenfeld and the other IND patients with their monthly allotment of medical cannabis. I sat next to Daubert at the HB-161 committee hearing and cringed at the acrimony of the testimony. I was gob-smacked by blatantly false statements made by Repealists, declaring that there were no reliable medical studies showing cannabis having any medicinal value.

Although most of what Milburn and his group contended was politically biased and grossly inaccurate, the group made a couple of points that I couldn't dispute, such as medical marijuana having no standards for quality control to ensure safety. I understood the anger of Montanans, many of whom voted for cannabis use for patients that were truly debilitated. There was no question that the original citizens' initiative spurred by Robin Prosser's activism and sacrifice was being abused.

According to DPHHS statistics, the largest age group of medical marijuana card recipients was the eighteen to thirty-year-old demographic. This statistic was probably the most damaging, as this age group was most associated with recreational marijuana use. It was hard to justify debilitation from chronic pain in this age group as well, further fueling the Repealist argument that the program was out of control. Rep. Scott Reichner spoke about the people of Montana being "duped" by MT-148. Because of the abuse I saw with the MCN clinics, I agreed with that assessment, which is why I appealed to the Montana Medical Board to intervene back in November of 2009.

During Chairman Howard's hearing on HB-161, Mark Long, a spokesman of the Montana Narcotics Officers Association, highlighted the problems with MT-148 and testified for HB-161. Mr. Long spoke to the need for reform of MT-148 and was one of the only Repealists who said anything positive about the pro-cannabis activists. "There are good people who are involved in this program…who are trying to do the right thing and are just looking for medication for their problems." Long then spoke about the volume of marijuana being produced by the state's nearly 4,800 licensed caregivers/growers: "Where is all of this marijuana going?" According to his colleagues in neighboring states, he said that Montana was now classified as a "source country" for marijuana production.[126]

When it was time for the pro-cannabis folks to speak, Chairman Howard cut the testimony time. After standing in line for over an hour to give my testimony, I lobbied for physician discretion regarding qualifying conditions. I brought dozens of research papers from prestigious medical journals like *Science*, *Nature*, *NEJM*, and *Cell* that validated cannabis as a medicine, but no Republicans seemed interested. Sadly, the truth ceased to matter.

After the hearings, it seemed that things went from bad to worse. There were credible signs that repeal would pass both the House and the Senate, although the governor's office hinted that he would veto an outright repeal. Everyone I knew who was associated with medical marijuana was visibly stressed by the proposition that a bunch of narrow-minded, maliciously intolerant fascists, under the guise of the Tea Party, was waging war on an entire subgroup of the population. Anyone who declared themselves as pro-cannabis were portrayed as vile and repugnant.

It was a sad thing to behold.

The Logical Ghost: LC-991

For weeks, Sam crafted our version of a reform bill that was going to be presented by Senator Mary Caferro (D-Helena). The proposal took the form of LC-991. It was a reasonable and logical way of bringing order and regulation to the state's Medical Marijuana Program. The bill proposed creating a regulatory structure that promoted a program that was fair, equitable, and conformed to the intent of MT-148.

LC-991 was a multi-year proposal that included transparent licensing standards for caregivers, growers, and dispensaries. The system broke down into four categories of licenses: (1) growers, (2) medical cannabis centers (i.e., dispensaries), (3) manufacturers (i.e., makers of CIPs), and (4) cannabis testing labs. Persons could own more than one license, and patients would be permitted to grow their own cannabis—up to six flowering females at any time.

The Department of Agriculture would enforce regulations on growers, while the Department of Health would have a regulatory domain with the manufacturers and the cannabis testing labs. Any fees generated that exceeded the costs of administering the program would go into a fund designated for community-based senior services and community health programs.

LC-991 also called for the beginning of a marijuana production reporting system. It allowed the state to regulate the amount of cannabis produced and track exactly where the product went, effectively discouraging diversion. Everything cannabis would be accounted for: seedlings, clones, plants in production (both vegetative and flowering cycle plants), trim, product on the shelf, product sent to manufacturers, plants slated for destruction, and perhaps most importantly, total revenues. Yearly (and random) inspections were also accounted for in the first year of the program's implementation.

One of the most progressive innovations of LC-991 was a carbon tax on cannabis. The proposal would tack an 8 percent tax on gross sales of refined products such as CIPs and dried flos, as an attempt to use economic incentives to motivate policy decisions and cultural behaviors. My observations in Humboldt County reinforced my hunch that you could meet the needs of most patients by growing cannabis under natural lighting conditions, either in greenhouses or in outdoor gardens. We proposed cutting the carbon tax by the amount of electricity saved by the percentage of sustainable energy technologies each facility used. Any carbon-neutral grows were carbon-tax exempt.

By the end of the first year of implementation of LC991, several goals were anticipated. First, clearing out the criminals, carpetbaggers, and the incompetent through state licensing. Second, ensuring that all operating businesses meet basic health and safety standards. Third, tracking the flow and volume of all cannabis-related production and sales.

The second phase of our proposed reform assumed an open market. Unlike in MT-148, patients would no longer be tied to a specific caregiver or dispensary; patients would be free to purchase their medicine wherever they wanted—a novel concept called a free market. All patient purchases would be entered into a central database, tracking all sales and production. Further offsetting the risk of diversion, purchase limits were proposed for patients. Our proposal suggested a maximum of three ounces of dried flos and three ounces of CIPs, unless specifically approved by a physician—something I estimated would encompass less than 5 percent of the patient population.

Aside from the regulatory model that we proposed, other items in the bill infused a sense of professionalism and protections to the industry:
1. Medical professionals could no longer deny patients treatment because of their medical marijuana use.
2. Physicians making more than ten medical cannabis referrals a year would need to take a continuing education course in cannabis medicine accredited by the American Medical Association.

3. CIPs would require labeling with the cannabis content listed by weight.
4. Local governments could regulate marijuana businesses for the general health, safety, and welfare of its citizenry, but may not ban them.

Sam knew that the bill proposal was reasonable and progressive, and that its chances of making it out of committee were sheer fantasy. She suggested that I calculate revenue figures that we could add to the bill, to help sweeten the pie.

Merely doubling the annual state-imposed patient renewal fee to $20 would generate almost $600,000 a year. Even without an additional sales tax of all cannabis products, seeking a similarly modest increase in caregiver licensing, depending on the number of patients serviced, would generate several million dollars a year.

Ultimately, our effort went for naught as Senator Caferro's bill, as expected, never made it out of committee.

The Calm Before the Storm

As the new year of 2011 opened, WH&H was enjoying its most profitable month. The lab had a growing list of contracts from growers and dispensaries across the state. Although we were entering into a fierce political battle, I was optimistic that we would persevere because I took solace that the truth would win out over the darkness of repeal.

I followed up with Francis Yang regarding his group's interest in having MBA help secure an Arizona dispensary license. I invited him to bring his group to Montana to visit the weekend of the Citizens for Responsible Crime Policy (CRCP) fundraiser Gala in Missoula.

Devin had been very clear about the caution needed in moving forward with potential investors. He applauded the progress I'd made in nurturing MBA from a wild idea and was committed to protecting what I'd created. Before the group's arrival, I laid down a few ground rules—simple things like signing a nondisclosure agreement before any technical or business discussions about the lab occurred.

I rode to Missoula with Francis and his partners, Terry and Marc. Their excitement about being in western Montana, combined with our discussions of forming a potentially lucrative business partnership had everyone smiling. I was confident Nigel and I could help them secure one of the highly coveted dispensary licenses in what was about to become the second-largest state in the country to legalize medical marijuana. I admired Francis for his ability and insight to see the utility of having a lab associated with their dispensary.

We stopped in Deer Lodge for gas and snacks. Terry was the youngest of the group, a pre-med biology major finishing his senior year at the University of Arizona. Although he looked like he could have been a Navy SEAL, Terry was the science guy and assigned to be the chemist for the proposed Arizona lab.

An hour south of Missoula, Terry leaned forward. "I just want to tell you guys that this is one of the happiest days of my life." Then he turned to me. "This is so cool that we're going up to this event with you, Dr. Mike. I can't wait for us to get this lab going."

"I'm thrilled you guys are here, too. This could be an amazing partnership."

"Arizona Botanical Analysis," Terry smiled.

Francis was typing on his cell phone. "Looks like that domain name is already taken, Dr. Mike," he noted with a hint of disappointment.

"I know. I own the *botanical analysis* domain name for every legal state in the country."

"Dot-com or dot-org?"

"Both."

Francis nodded. "Impressive, Dr. Mike."

As we drove into Missoula, Shannon called to inform me that Anthony had surgery on his leg a few days earlier in Seattle and would be at the event. At the gala, he was wheeled around in a wheelchair by his entourage of support staff. It was good to see him. He looked weak and in a considerable amount of pain. He said the surgeon successfully excised the mass, but it was much deeper than anyone suspected; fortunately, it was benign. It was a humbling experience for all of us.

The gala raised a lot of urgently needed money to combat HB-161. The day after, we toured dispensaries that were MBA clients. The Arizona group met a bunch of intriguing folks and were introduced to a variety of unique products, including a cannabis-infused soft drink, Keef Cola (in a variety of fruity flavors). Upon their return, Francis sent a thank-you note, and generously donated $1,000 to the ACS. He understood our political dilemma and offered his services for anything that we might need. Nigel had thoroughly impressed the group with his ability to pull off the science of the lab, but Francis was suspect of my business acumen.

The Calm Before the Storm

At my next monthly meeting with Devin, he examined the joint venture agreement sent from the Arizona group. "Don't feel forced into signing anything. If you're not completely comfortable, just walk away. Your ripcord can be me. Tell them you can't sign anything until you review the documents with me." My meetings with Devin became a refuge for me—a reliable, safe place for reality checks as i navigated the wacky and turbulent waters of the Montana medical marijuana industry.

Although I understood that the Arizona group had deadlines, Francis called or emailed me a half-dozen times a day. I was happy to lend a hand with a prospective partner, but his frequency of calls and the urgency of the decisions became maddening. To make matters worse, he began probing into my relationship with Nigel, asking me variations on the theme of, "Is Nigel *really* happy?"

Francis was blind to my day-to-day pressures. The extinction asteroid on the horizon was the growing threat that HB-161 would make it to the governor's desk. Despite communicating that, he didn't get it—he just kept pressing and pressing. But the straw that broke the camel's back was the conflict that arose from the logo. I loved the MBA logo. The logo was becoming the Good Housekeeping Seal of Approval for safe cannabis in Montana, and Francis wanted to change it.

Since Francis is a smart guy, I figured that telling him a couple of dozen times how much I loved the MBA logo would make an impression. Yet he persisted, pestering me about "alternative" logo designs for Arizona Botanical Analysis (ABA). His insistence was pissing me off.

Devin and I considered a range of possibilities for Francis's nagging and pestering, including the nefarious idea that he might be looking for ways of usurping my authority and taking over MBA. Devin helped me develop our guidelines of what MBA brought to the bargaining table. MBA provided (1) thought leadership as one of the leading cannabinoid analysis labs in the world, (2) an R&D department working on clinical applications of novel cannabinoid delivery systems, (3) our own marketing material, and (4) a "turnkey" operating model for anyone who was interested in setting up a marijuana testing facility. Above all, MBA was delivering value.

As the winter deepened, Kristy Fairy, MBA's biggest CIPs customer, sent me an email that her landlord was evicting her after renovated her space into a commercial kitchen and dispensary. I felt compelled to help because she was an ally and had volunteered to be the treasurer of the ACS. I told her about a recent vacancy available on the second floor of the Medical Arts Building and asked if she'd be interested in leasing the space.

The lease with the Bozeman Medical Arts Building required that each new occupant sign a non-compete clause, and MBA held the exclusive rights to open a cannabis dispensary. Legally, for her to use the space, I would need to cede my rights of the dispensary. In exchange for the dispensary space, Kristy agreed to send all of her patients to me for their physician statement.

The entire medical marijuana community was in a fight for its survival, so helping a fellow activist who I thought was being unfairly treated was an easy decision. Lending a hand to a colleague in need was the right thing to do, yet the decision proved to be another regrettable miscalculation regarding trusting those in the cannabis industry.

Consulting the HR Book

After nearly two years, the responsibilities of running multiple businesses were evident. I knew what I liked and what I didn't, but for the most part, I found that being a boss is a drag. I'm not someone who enjoys reminding people to do their job. I was tired of asking Nigel to keep the lab tidy. I wasn't asking for surgical suite cleanliness, but the lab often looked as though multiple volatile experiments had gone awry.

Between the lab and the clinic, the businesses were generating enough revenue to warrant having a full-time office manager. Annie, who'd done a great job filling in for Erin, wasn't interested in full-time work. I went back to Craigslist. Nigel and I met with the prospective applicants separately and consulted each other on whom to hire.

One afternoon I was at my office catching up on paperwork after another powder day of skiing the Ridge. I called one of the applicants, Danielle. After a pleasant conversation, I asked if she wanted to grab a bite to eat. She agreed.

The goal of the new office manager was to find an invested caretaker for the lab and the clinic, someone who could give each business the tender loving care each company required. I needed someone dedicated and loyal, who understood how to keep good records and organize the respective messes of two boy geniuses trying to revolutionize the medical marijuana industry. What I didn't need was a beautiful blonde who oozed sensuousness from every pore.

When I pulled into her driveway, Danielle was waiting on the porch. My first impulse when I saw her walking toward my car was to drive back to the office and continue calling applicants. But I didn't. Danielle smiled when she got into the car and shook my hand. Her grip was warm and firm. Wafts of her perfume transported me back to Paris as we drove to a quaint Korean restaurant, I-Ho's, near MSU. I sat across from her, trying to concentrate on job-related questions. About midway through our meal, I couldn't contain what I was thinking.

"Danielle, I owe you an apology."

"Apology? Why?"

"I think you're the wrong person for the job."

"What do mean, Mike? I thought we were getting along great!"

"That's the problem, Danielle. I think you're great. But I think I'd rather ask you out on a date than have you be my office manager."

"Why can't we do both?" she smiled.

Sometimes, understanding your weaknesses doesn't always keep you from making mistakes. I was keenly aware of the importance of hiring a competent person. Yet, I sat across from a woman that seemed as attracted to me as I to her. Shannon would wring my neck—a boss dating an employee was surely a human resource cardinal sin. Plus, how would I explain this to Nigel and Arno?

"I don't know, Danielle. I don't think it's a good idea."

She reached across the table and gently squeezed my hand. "C'mon, Mike. I need a better job. I'll be good. I'll even try not to distract you while we're at work."

"Let me talk to Nigel about it."

And that's what I did.

The next day, I came into the lab and pulled up my favorite stool. Despite my reluctance, I told Nigel the whole story and wanted his approval. I promised I would yield to his decision. "If you get a bad vibe, no worries, end of story. Shannon wants us to start consulting the HR book before we settle on somebody. Otherwise, we'll just keep looking for someone else."

Not unexpectedly, all of Danielle's references were glowing. Nigel said his lunch interview with her had gone well. "I think she'll be fine." Then he directly looked at me and gave me a fatherly look. "Just be careful, Mike."

Danielle was fine with the written job description that Shannon insisted I give her. Danielle's first task was to mail a letter to each WH&H patient (along with a self-addressed stamped envelope) objecting to HB-161. Each patient was to sign it and send it back to their respective House Representative and Senator. Danielle did a great job.

After the first week, Danielle and I went to a music gig in Livingston, where Mike Singer was playing with a new band. On the drive over Bozeman Pass, she began telling me about the people she knew in the marijuana business.

"How did you know Chris Williams?" I asked, a little surprised.

Chris is a tall rock of a man, the Paul Bunyan of Montana medical marijuana. He was the chief grower for Montana Cannabis and was one of the masterminds in pulling off Cannabis Day at the capitol.[127] I found Chris to be an affable guy. He was also one of the featured characters in a Montana PBS–funded documentary on the medical marijuana boom, called *Code of the West*. [128]Unbelievably, the film concluded with a slow-motion pan shot of assault rifles leaned up against the greenhouse wall.

Why would anyone allow weapons to be filmed in their grow?

In the nearly two years that I'd been working in the medical marijuana industry, I'd learned an awful lot about a lot of things. Aside from all the science and political wisdom I'd accrued, I knew that in the eyes of the feds, marijuana is bad, but the combination of marijuana *and* guns is simply catastrophic.

Danielle smiled sweetly. "I dated him for a while.."

It was hard to hide my disillusionment. I wasn't willing to allow myself to become enmeshed in parts of the marijuana culture I had heretofore avoided.

Money Talks

The 2011 ski season at Bridger Bowl was unusually good.

Since the legislative session had started, good snow was one of the few things putting a smile on my face. Skiing fresh powder off the Ridge was my most reliable means of venting the accumulating stresses in my life.

After all my years working in the ED, I wasn't remotely prepared for the level of stress manufactured from the political games playing out in Helena. I could only imagine how exponentially more cutthroat things must be in Washington, DC. Despite the inglorious behaviors emanating from the state capitol building, there were a few bright spots in my life.

The brightest was my son, and it was rejuvenating to see him. I did my best to attend every school event, basketball game, and swim meet. During our weekends together, we'd watch college basketball. As a Christmas gift, I bought tickets to the second and third rounds of the NCAA Basketball Tournament in Cleveland. We couldn't wait for March Madness.

Professionally, the See Change Strategy LLC report *The State of the Medical Marijuana Markets 2011* had just been released and included an article that Ted Rose had asked me to write: "The Role of Analytical Testing in the Medical Marijuana Industry." I was also invited to contribute a column for the inaugural Montana edition of *Kush* magazine, which morphed into a monthly column.

Sam was another bright spot. There were few people I enjoyed spending time with more than her. Her wit and intellect were unmatched, as was her passion for our cause. Perhaps foolishly, we thought that our efforts would make a difference and salvage a marijuana reform bill that would protect patients from fear and prosecution, in addition to providing patients with safe and reliable medicine. I was confident she would put every ounce of her soul into the lobbying effort.

At the beginning of the session, Sam and Daubert worked together, each doing their share to impart a modicum of sense and rationality to usurp the Repealists. But from the beginning, it was a tenuous partnership. Although each respected the other's considerable ability, I can't say they completely trusted each other. If I had to choose between Sam and Daubert, Sam won out. We had a bond, and when we were together, I felt like I was with a Viking queen.

There were a few times when our relationship became strained, and money was invariably the culprit. Perhaps she felt I was taking advantage of her—a doctor from New York looking for a female to help build his cannabis testing empire. Considering the amount of time we'd spent together, and as much of myself as I revealed to her, she still didn't completely trust me. Maybe she didn't completely trust any man. But I thought I'd convinced her that I wasn't like the other men she'd known. Since I didn't have the cash to pay her salary during the session, I promised her a 5 percent stake in MBA stock as compensation for her work.

But as she warned me, more than once, stock doesn't pay the bills. "Money talks."

I understood that Sam needed to be paid, but I didn't have a spare $30k lying around. It was a relief that Daubert had found money to initially help support her efforts, but it was uncertain how long that support would last. Her financial reliance on Daubert made both of us uncomfortable.

Sam and I wanted a bill that would reward quality and weed out the wackos, and that was the problem—there were a lot of wackos. Unveiling our naïveté, we wanted a bill that was logical and did the most good for the most people—a bill that was pure and organic (eventually becoming LC-991). And just like the others vying for a political advantage, we stood our ground to defend our position.

Daubert finally stepped down from his position at Montana Cannabis, and thereby eliminating his conflict of interest. I was glad because Daubert was invaluable. No one knew the politics of marijuana better; he was as tuned in as a flight control operator at NASA. But there was still a lingering undercurrent of suspicion.

After the Sand's bill, HB-68, was buried in committee, a new proposal emerged, termed the "gray" bill because the proposal seemed to have appeared out of the shadows. The bill draft of Senate Bill-154 (SB-154) was submitted by Sen. Dave Lewis (R-Helena) in May of 2010, and the word was Daubert had a prominent hand in writing it. When Sam first caught wind of SB-154, she thought that the timing of the bill draft smelled fishy.

Lewis knew more about medical marijuana than most of the legislators. I'd evaluated one of his family members for their medical marijuana card, and they said that he was sympathetic to the cause. I'd seen Lewis speak at an MMGA medical marijuana workshop, calling the marijuana boom an "industry" publicly.

I suggested to Sam that Lewis appeared to be an ally.

"Don't count on it. He's a politician. He's always sizing things up. He'll say what he thinks he needs to say to get what he wants. Don't ever forget it."

I'm not sure that an educated person could have been more politically naïve than me lulled into believing that facts mattered. I assumed that legislators living in such an incredibly beautiful state like Montana would be immune from the same type of corruption as states like New York and Louisiana. I assumed these elected officials would listen to reason and appreciate the science surrounding cannabis. I thought they'd work toward finding a compromise to best meet the needs of all Montanans.

Sam tried to snap me out of my *Mayberry* world. "This isn't the high school student council. It's the big leagues."

In her not-so-subtle manner, Sam explained the harsh reality: the overwhelming majority of the legislators did what was politically expedient for them and their almighty party. Lewis's bill, SB-154, would set up a marijuana industry that favored a few. Lewis's proposal wasn't the egalitarian plan we'd been discussing for months, and it made us skeptical.

Perhaps if Sam and I had been consulted on the bill, and been allowed to insert some key policy additions, we might have supported it, but we weren't. SB-154 opened a rift between Daubert and Sam that never healed.

I anticipated that Daubert might tamper with Sam's lobbying funding, and when February rolled around, there was suddenly no money available for her. I shook the funding tree with the people I knew, mostly well-banked MBA clients, and pleaded with them to contribute monthly installments through the end of the session. My efforts were successful, but it was well short of what she needed for the entire four-month session.

I encouraged her to continue, despite the financial shortfall. I did my best to convince her how vital she was to the cause and how much folks appreciated her efforts. The MBA clients that donated to Sam's fund received daily email updates and were free to call her with their questions and concerns. With every relevant bill, she briefed us on the nature of the legislation and its status. If a bill was coming up in a committee hearing, or for a vote, we knew about it.

As a last resort, I shot an email to John Masterson, hoping that within his deep network of "banked" local and national NORML contacts, he could find additional funding for Sam. Without Sam, our ability to win this political war would be critically compromised.

I never received a reply. Masterson represented a national organization that advocated for the unfettered legalization of marijuana, not for medicinal cannabis; the issues and the political arguments for each are light years apart. In conservative states like Montana, recreational pot stood no chance of legislative approval without a medical marijuana pathway. Masterson and his colleagues at NORML owed a debt to the heavy lifting that medical cannabis had done for their cause; I expected them to return the favor.

As long as my MBA donors honored their financial pledges to support Sam's lobbying effort, I thought we had a fighting chance.

And then things got exponentially worse.

9:12

The morning of Monday, March 14, wasn't unusually cold, but the dampness in the air was remarkable, penetrating my goose-down parka that heretofore had protected me from such thermal fluctuations. The sky was a milky overcast, and snow squalls hid the tops of the Bridgers. It was surely a powder day up on the Ridge.

The day before, Nigel, Terry, and I went skiing. It was a brilliant bluebird day, with a foot of white crystalline freshness. We skied as long as Terry's legs held up and then headed to Ale Works for après' ski.

Terry was in town to be trained on the HPLC protocols from Nigel. Once he was confident in the technical methodology, he would take what he'd learned back to Arizona to start MBA's first satellite lab, Arizona Botanical Analysis. He was being groomed as the chemist as part of our implicit partnership with the Arizona group. But there was a catch. Despite numerous calls and emails to Francis, there was still no signed contract to cement our business relationship. Devin urged me not to give away our analytical protocols until the contract was signed—a simple command I could easily follow.

Although I was prepared to tell Terry that he wouldn't be permitted to train on the HPLC until I had a signed contract, I got a break from the management gods. The Friday before his arrival, the DAD detector on the HPLC blew. Without the detector, the machine was worthless. Nigel said the device would be inoperable for at least a week until a replacement detector could be shipped and installed.

Earlier in the week, Steph Sherer, the founder of American's for Safe Access (ASA), had flown into Helena to help with a fundraiser, lending her support in rallying the troops during a pro-cannabis rally at the capitol. The mission of ASA was to ensure patients had safe and reliable access to medical cannabis, as well as advocating for increasing cannabis clinical research.

On the day of the rally, there were hundreds of medical marijuana patients who converged on the capitol demonstrating and demanding a pro-cannabis reform bill. It was hard for me to gauge whether the rally helped or hurt our effort. Many of the marijuana supporters looked like they'd just emerged from a month-long squatters' convention—adults with tattered hair, dirty jeans, and T-shirts bearing such endearing phrases as "Fuck you" and "I'm baked, but you're flaked." I appreciated their conviction, and God bless their intentions. Still, if they frightened me, I'm sure they petrified those sunlight-adverse Christians and members of SCSK, validating their crusade to save Montana from these cannabis-loving heathens.

Fortunately, there was an equal number of cannabis supporters who came looking as though they'd come dressed for an Easter service, with groomed hair, bright eyes, and generous smiles. This was my group. We did our best to mitigate the energy of the stoner contingent.

Rumors on the MTCIA list serv suggested that Steph had clashed with influential MTCIA members, including Daubert, and some were furious. There was a sentiment that she didn't clearly understand the nuances and dynamics of our struggle. Despite the rhetoric and egos that were acting out, Steph and her staff at least showed up, which was more than other groups that professed patient cannabis advocacy, like the Marijuana Policy Project, Drug Policy Alliance, or Patients Out of Time. From my perspective, whether or not she stepped on a few toes, Steph had good intentions.

I conveyed the growing unease of the natives to the ASA staff. Steph had planned a rally in front of the governor's mansion the day before Easter. There was near unanimity among the MTCIA that a rally would be a huge mistake. Then it was leaked that ASA had filed for a parade permit to demonstrate at the Governor's mansion, demanding that he provide patients with safe access to cannabis. Some felt that Steph was trespassing, showing up like an uninvited distant in-law trying to take over the show. Ultimately, ASA conceded to local wishes. The parade was canceled, and the rally postponed, but the seeds of mistrust were sown.

Friday evening, Sam hosted a friendly get-together. The parade tensions generated earlier in the week easily dissolved with a delightful offering of good food, alcohol, and potent marijuana. Steph and I mingled. She dismissed the drama earlier and said she'd seen much worse. She also expressed considerable interest in what I had accomplished with the lab; she appreciated the void we were trying to fill in the cannabis industry.

I was flattered. "If you have the time, I'd love to give you a tour of the lab, and you can see it for yourself."

Steph showed up Monday morning at about 8:40 a.m. Nigel introduced himself and gave her a tour of the lab. Steph understood the value in a cannabis market that had reliably dosed products. MBA was offering an element of quality control to an entire industry that had no more QC than moonshiners in Appalachia.

Nigel's phone went off as we were making our way into my office.

"Hey, Mike, it's the Rev. Let me get this, and I'll join you guys in a few minutes."

I glanced at the clock in the lab. It was 9:12.

The Rev was our most important customer. Patients appreciated the variety of labeled strains he offered, many containing CBD. Perhaps most importantly, he had the "golden goose" strain. The Rev had been playing with some breeding and had come up with a 1:1 THC/CBD strain, similar to the strain GW Pharmaceuticals was marketing as Sativex. This strain could be worth a fortune.

Steph asked me what I thought about some of the other cannabis testing labs in the country.

"I think it's safe to say that there's a wide range of competencies out there. I think quality control concern with cannabis is the biggest obstacle…"

"What the fuck?" Nigel's voice rang from outside the door.

I stopped mid-sentence.

"Are you OK?" Nigel asked, as he listened in silently. "The DEA *and* the Sheriff's Department? They're taking everything? Even your lights? Be safe. Call me back when you can."

I felt nauseous. "What's going on?"

Nigel was pale, which made his scraggly red beard look afire. "It's unreal. The Rev says there's dozens of cops and DEA agents at his place, and they're taking everything."

"Holy cow."

I looked at Steph in disbelief.

"Give me your non-dominant arm," she ordered.

Time slowed—of that I'm absolutely sure. Nigel and I obediently followed directions. A black sharpie appeared from Steph's purse, inscribing a ten-digit number on my left forearm.

"What are you doing?" I asked in a numbed monotone.

"This is the phone number for the ASA legal team. You both should be prepared to spend the next three days in jail. We have no idea how big the scale of these raids will be, but we need to be prepared."

"Seriously?"

"Do you have any cannabis in this space?" she asked.

I snickered. "Of course we do; it's a cannabis testing lab."

Steph was matter of fact. "Then, there is a reasonable chance the DEA may come here next."

Nigel stared at me with a deer-in-the-headlights look. "Holy shit. This is serious."

Steph was firm. "You better believe this is serious, Nigel. We found that if we write the number on your forearm, it's easier to remember, and it's easily accessible. Plus, the police can see that you have our legal team's phone number on your forearm. You guys should make arrangements to have your affairs taken care of for the next three days because if the DEA does come here, they will likely be taking you both to jail."

My head spun. I had a flight to catch on Wednesday and was taking my son to the NCAA basketball tournament. Going to jail wasn't an option.

The raid at the Rev's dispensary and grow facility was one of a series of strikes being executed simultaneously by federal, state, and local law enforcement. Everything that the Rev had was confiscated: all of his plants, clones, dried flos, tinctures, edibles, and equipment—hauled off in rented Ryder trucks. Grimly, I thought about the loss of genetic material from his Sativex-like plants—and all the patients who could have been helped by the cannabinoids these plants contained. The expropriated plants became another voiceless victim in the endless and futile war on drugs.

Calls poured in. Nigel fielded questions from MBA clients from across the state, skittish as lost lambs at a wolf convention. Nigel updated us as details of the raids became available.

It was ironic that the raid coincided with the start of a key House committee hearing that was to vote on several medical marijuana reform bills later that morning.

I called Sam. She was in utter disbelief. "This is seriously not good."

The Morning After

Details of the raids continued to trickle in. People called it Black Monday. When the dust finally settled, federal agencies conducted twenty-six raids on medical marijuana facilities in thirteen Montana cities. Armed government agents seized thousands of marijuana plants and froze about $4 million in bank funds.

Hiedi Handford later explained to me that evidence for the raids came from a leak within Montana Cannabis. The DEA was tipped off that all the information needed to secure search warrants for the raids was found within the Helena-based business services company, Anderson ZurMuehlen & Co. The firm had records of all of Montana Cannabis' accounting transactions since 2009. Every grower or caregiver in the state who had done any business with Montana Cannabis was meticulously documented. It proved to be a treasure trove of prosecutorial information.

All the major news organizations covered the raids. *USA Today* reported: "Montana U.S. Attorney Michael Cotter said there was 'probable cause that the premises were involved in illegal and large-scale trafficking of marijuana.'"[129]

I'd heard gossip about marijuana being shipped out of state, as well as rumors of cheap marijuana being flown in from California and Washington—separating fact from fiction was anybody's guess. In this business, truth seemed as elusive as the Holy Grail. There were shadows everywhere; untold nooks and crannies where shards of truth and untruth hid side by side.

The day after the raids, a group of local activists held a rally at the Gallatin County Courthouse in downtown Bozeman. As the snow fell in thick wet chips, assorted protesters stood in the slush disguised as ski bums, holding homemade signs. The signs reminded citizens about the importance of the Fourth

Amendment: *Feds Out of Montana, Bozeman Is Fed Up, Have a Heart, Don't Take Our Medication, Reform NOT Repeal, States' Rights.* [130] Dozens of cars drove by honking their horns in support. The organizer, a thin young man with long hair and an adolescent mustache, explained to the crowd that they would be holding protests every day beginning at 4:20 p.m., culminating in a march down Main Street on Friday.

Hardly anyone took notice.

The morning after, a patient came to see me about donating money to his protest. Carl Smith said he'd just secured a parade permit and was in the process of building 420 plywood caskets to symbolize the death of the medical marijuana program in Montana. He ranted passionately about how he was going to fight this police action for as long as he could. I gave him fifty dollars, applauded his passion, and wished him luck. His ambition to make a statement gave way to reality, and he managed to produce a mere twenty coffins for his solo parade.

I looked for consolation, but little was to be found.

Sam was busy with her legislative agenda and didn't have time for anything but keeping our listing ship afloat. Nigel was silent; he buried himself by catching up on overdue paperwork, as there was no new work since the raids. I was envious. At least he got to go home to his family every night. Mine was thousands of miles away, so I went to the place I considered my second home—Anthony Gallo's place.

Anthony and Shannon welcomed me in to commiserate with them. Anthony was catatonic. "Dude, I just spent a hundred grand on my new place. I think I'm fucked." In just a few months, he turned a drab yoga studio at the end of a strip mall into a dispensary that reminded me of the Bellagio. Dragging hard on an impeccably rolled joint, he blew an enormous plume of smoke toward the ceiling. "I could be next," he said with a slight tremor.

"Hope not." What was there for me to say? I wasn't the only person who wondered why Anthony was spared a visit from law enforcement during the raids. Rumors abounded about his shady business deals and debt. I hoped that if the DEA were coming for Anthony, they'd at least wait for me to leave his house.

After his third joint, Anthony twitched a nervous grin. "Maybe I'll just pack up and leave. Go somewhere safe like Colorado or Arizona."

I wondered if there were any other options left for me, too.

Despite the Black Monday chaos, I had plans. Jacob and I were off to the dance of March Madness at the NCAA basketball tournament in Cleveland. The concept of March Madness seemed to resonate with me on lots of levels. Before I left for New York, I called the Wittich Law Firm and made sure Nigel and Danielle receive proper legal representation while I was away if something happened.

Nigel emailed me later in the week: "People are assuming the sky is falling, and I fear some of them may be right. Pete Jones called me about the Haag memo. These are crazy days. Not very fun."

The "Haag memo" was a little-publicized document written on February 1, 2011, by the US Attorney from the Northern District of California, Melinda Haag.[131] The memo was a response to John A. Russo, the Oakland City Attorney, in response to a request by the Oakland City Council for guidance regarding medical marijuana and federal law. The memo was written with the consultation and approval of US Attorney General Eric Holder.

The "Haag memo" was intended to clarify the 2009 "Ogden memo," which opened the floodgates to the national explosion of medical marijuana expansion. The "Haag memo" clearly stated that the federal government will continue to investigate, arrest, and prosecute medical marijuana dispensaries in every state "regardless of state laws." The memo defined all dispensaries as illegal under federal law, and their prosecution as a "core priority."

Ironically, within four days of the memo's release, the DEA raided four dispensaries in California, followed by the subsequent March 14 raids in Montana. And as a result of the raids, the fate of medical marijuana in Montana was in freefall.

The events of Black Monday put the fear of God into everyone associated with cannabis. The March WH&H clinic was only half full, and appointments for April were sparse. Work at the lab slowed to a trickle. The home equity loan I secured to grow the lab in other states was soon to become my cash-flow lifeline as we all awaited the final political solution.

Despite my years in the ED working under challenging conditions and, at times, enormous stress, I knew that at the end of my shift, I was done. When I walked out of the hospital, I checked out, physically and emotionally. But my concerns with the fate of the clinic, the lab and the legislature's final bill were omnipresent. I was desperate, clinging to the tiniest sliver of hope that the heavens would open, and truth and reason would ultimately prevail. Delusion can be a beautiful thing.

Upon my return from Cleveland, it had been more than five days since I'd heard anything from Nigel. Something was wrong. I also hadn't heard anything from Francis Yang. There was still no signed contract. In my gut, the Arizona deal was dead.

Unexpectedly, the Arizona venture exposed a rift between Nigel and me that apparently had been brewing for some time. Francis had probed the weaknesses in our relationship. Privately Nigel confided that, among other things, he wasn't happy with his compensation. It was always my intention to make sure Nigel was handsomely rewarded for his efforts and loyalty. I spoke to Devin about an equity partnership for Nigel on numerous occasions, and the conclusion was always the same. I was the sole investor and financial risk-taker; at this stage in the business, there was no equity to distribute.

Hidden beneath Nigel's persistently jolly demeanor, a number of percolating issues could no longer be politely packaged—the failed Arizona deal, the stress of the raids, and the precipitous loss of business. But the principle issue was the mounting probability that the very company that we'd developed and nurtured together was going to be suffocated by fanatical political forces completely out of our control.

Upon my return to Bozeman, and in an uncharacteristic display of anger, Nigel finally vented. It was impossible to say what hurt the most—his bitter tone or the precision of his slicing personal jabs. Nigel seethed. He was tired of making excuses for my behavior, pissing off clients with my sarcastic wit and arrogant doctor personality.

As I sat there, I realized that my side of the story was inconsequential, because this was Nigel's reality, and somehow I'd been responsible for enabling it. Maybe I shouldn't have come into work early, cleaning the lab for him, like a pampering parent. Maybe I shouldn't have given him and his family gifts on Christmas, trying to buy my way into his family. And maybe I should have just been his boss, rather than trying so hard to be his friend. It was deeply painful to hear his assessment. I imagined how an angry younger brother, lost in the shadows of an elder successful sibling, might lash out. Then I remembered what Devin had said about Cain and Abel.

The Morning After

A few days later, the final blow was the incident with Danielle.

After Black Monday, Anthony Gallo sowed a seed about Danielle being a plant for the DEA. Gallo brought up her relationship with Chris Williams (who along with Daubert and Lindsey had just been indicted) and asked me if I really trusted her. Gallo's manipulation caught me at a vulnerable time. They sparked a doubt.

I spoke to Nigel about Gallo's accusation and the issues I was having with Danielle's increasingly sloppy work ethic. Nigel was confident that he could talk with her and defuse the situation without my intervention. But instead, I plowed ahead, grossly underestimating how upset Danielle would get when I asked her if she was an informant for the DEA. I thought she would just roll her eyes and ask me where I'd come up with such a crazy idea. Instead, she stormed out of the office, and in tears, she submitted her resignation to Nigel. It was the last time I ever saw her.

Nigel was incensed. He lashed out, insinuating that I'd driven off another office manager, listing off Hillari, Erin, Annie, and now Danielle. Nigel was hurt, too. His dreams were crumbling, along like mine.

"Why couldn't you have just let me handle it, Mike? *Why?*"

I sat in silence. I had no answers.

Perhaps it would have been easier to swallow had I been fed Nigel's complaints in smaller, more manageable bites rather than as one giant suffocating bolus. Even during the bleakest moments in my divorce, I never felt so utterly helpless. My Montana dream was unraveling, and there was nothing to stop it.

The Nuclear Option: SB-423

When it didn't seem like it could get any worse, it did.

With the entire medical marijuana community still reeling from the aftershocks of the raids and arrests of Black Monday, Sam called, her voice strained. "Are you sitting down?"

"I am now. What's up? You sound upset."

"Jeff Essman just submitted a bill draft that will annihilate this industry. No question about it. It's the nuclear option, a fucking direct strike nuclear blast."

"Seriously?"

"This is really bad."

Jeff Essman had been the Republican Senator from District 28 in Billings since 2005, and as a result of the November Republican landslide, he was the new majority leader of the Senate. His bill, SB-423, signaled that rumors from the governor's office regarding Schweitzer's intended veto of HB-161 were accurate. Anticipating the governor's veto, Essman's bill, in essence, was "repeal in disguise"—a Republican contingency plan that would predictably bring the medical marijuana industry to its knees. The bill's first hearing was on March 25.

It didn't give us much time.

On March 30, 2011, Essman began his Senate floor discussion, acknowledging that the Ogden memo had precipitated the explosive growth of marijuana in the state. He talked about the dispensary storefronts on Main Street (one of which he caustically referred to as the "home of the $200 ounce"), along with marijuana advertisements on TV, the radio, and in the newspaper.

Trained as an industrial engineer and later graduating from the University of Montana Law School, Essman is a calculating politician. He outlined the historical circumstances of medical marijuana in the state, providing the context for his legislation in a pedantic monotone that was as deliberate as it was paced.

"The good intention of Montana voters...has been made a mockery, by the system that has grown up here in this state the past year and a half." Essman weighed his words with equal timbre. "The overall arching goal of this bill is to repeal a system that is obviously broken. Cleanse the system out...and restore the Laws of the State of Montana...in a fashion that...will recognize the intent of Montana voters in 2004."[132]

He called on fellow legislators to remove the profit motive from the industry and asked his colleagues to help him reset the clock and take the state back to a time when there were a smaller number of patients who qualified for their medical marijuana card.

"Now what will this bill do? First, with respect to physicians..."

As I listened to the live broadcast, I held my breath.

"It requires the bona-fide doctor-patient relationship of at least four visits, or more, over the last six months."

His suggestion was ridiculous. How does the government find the authority to dictate how often you should see your doctor to obtain permission to use a medication? Allowing the government to pick and choose which medicines and therapies doctors are permitted to recommend to patients threatens the sanctity of the doctor-patient relationship. It was absurd.

Without emotion, Essman outlined the bill's most egregious feature. It required that the DPHHS refer any physician who signed twenty-five physician statements within a one-year period to the Montana Board of Medical Examiners for a thorough licensure investigation, and the physician would bear the full investigative costs.

Essman understood how the system worked. His bill focused, with surgical precision, on the rate-limiting step in the entire system: physicians. This measure in the law was nothing short of a means to threaten and intimidate physicians.

Limiting the number of patients a doctor could evaluate was a stroke of Machiavellian brilliance. First, it curtailed the number of doctors evaluating patients for medical marijuana use. If the number of doctors fell, the number of patients receiving cards would drop precipitously. Secondly, Essman knew that no physician in their right mind was going to knowingly engage in a practice that was statutorily assured to bring an investigation upon them from the Montana Board of Medical Examiners.

I was speechless.

There were other onerous provisions contained in SB-423, although none of them impacted me like the twenty-five-patient limit. The law also outlawed any commercial advertising of cannabis and limited the number of patients that a provider could sell to three. The bill also removed any profit motive for growers, making it illegal to charge patients for cannabis.

Within days of Essman's bill reading, the MTCIA huddled to respond. Without an even remote chance of brokering a political solution, the only option was to seek relief with the courts. The sole hope was to retain one of the most celebrated and respected attorneys in the state, Jim Goetz—a local Bozeman lawyer whose office was just up the street from the Medical Arts Building. If the MTCIA could come up with enough money for a retainer, we stood a remote chance of convincing the judiciary to halt the implementation of SB-423.

Branding Day

On a crisp, sunny April 13th morning, Gov. Brian Schweitzer countered the political theater of the Republicans by having an outdoor press conference. Before a large, friendly crowd, he ridiculed the large number of bills that had been passed by the legislature as "frivolous, unconstitutional, and just bad ideas."[133]

Behind the governor were seven poster-sized representations of the major legislative bills Schweitzer was to veto. The bills were attached to planks of wood that had the bill's name scorched onto them. One by one, Schweitzer (a long-time rancher) took a red-hot "VETO" branding iron from the large propane-powered barbecue and theatrically pushed the glowing iron into each of the planks, the paper bursting into a flash of flame before the wind scattered the charred remnants across the Capitol lawn. Like a public execution, with each bill incinerated, the crowd cheered.

"At an actual branding party, there's usually some castration, but we're not doing any of that today," he mused to the boos of those in attendance. In all, Schweitzer vetoed seventeen bills that morning, including the medical marijuana repeal bill, HB-161. But with Senator Essman's bill, SB-423, making its way effortlessly through both the House and the Senate, Schweitzer's veto of the HB-161 held little importance other than political showmanship.

To my macabre delight, it was reassuring that HB-161 wasn't the only nut-job bill that came up in the 2011 Session. Other notable bills introduced during the session included:
- HB-278 creates fully armed militias in every town.
- SB-279 allows legislators to carry weapons in the capitol.
- HB-382 creates an eleven-person panel with the authority to nullify all federal laws.
- HB-558 allows guns in schools.

- HB-244 eliminates all state incentives for developing wind power.
- HB-205 omitted Barack Obama's name from the 2012 ballot because his father was born outside of the United States.
- HB-174 legalizes hunting with silencers.
- HB-354 eliminates the law that requires landlords to install carbon monoxide detectors.
- HB-384 lifts the prohibition on carrying concealed weapons in bars, churches, and banks.
- Senate Joint Resolution 2 withdraws the United States of America from the United Nations.
- HB-154 eliminates educational requirements for persons seeking the job of state superintendent of schools.[134]

With little resistance, SB-423 made its way to the governor's desk. To my surprise, I received a call from the governor's office asking for my input on the bill. Schweitzer's aide assured me that my input would be given to the governor and used in his decision-making process. I told the aide the law would negatively impact tens of thousands of patients and permanently derail the entire medical marijuana program in the state. For a brief moment, I felt important.

From my perspective, a political miracle was the only hope of usurping SB-423 and maintaining a semblance of my life in Montana. At night I sat in my office and wrote letters. I wrote to Governor Schweitzer, the Montana members of the United States House and Senate, Kentucky representative, and rumored presidential candidate Ron Paul, Senator Essman, the American Academy of Family Practice, the Montana Medical Association, and the American Academy of Cannabinoid Medicine (AACM). I wrote an op-ed piece for every major newspaper in the state.

The response to my letter writing efforts was pitiful. A spokesperson from the Montana Medical Association said they would look into the bill, but they never issued a public comment. To their considerable credit, the AACM graciously agreed to write an amicus brief in support of the MTCIA lawsuit. Many people and organizations talked sanctimoniously about medical marijuana as a sovereign social movement, but in the end, when action spoke louder than words, all I saw was lip service.

Aside from citizen initiatives, which usurp the legislative branch of government, laws in Montana are passed by the legislature and sent to the governor. Once on the governor's desk the bill is signed into law or vetoed. If the governor elects to veto, and the legislature has enough votes, they can override the veto, thus enacting the legislation. Additionally, any bill that sits on the governor's desk after ten days automatically becomes law.

Concerning SB-423, the governor vowed he would not sign such onerous legislation, but not signing the bill boded just as poor an outcome. According to Sam, the political calculus was such that Schweitzer knew that the House had enough votes to override a veto of SB-423. So, to save political face (in light of a rumored US Senatorial bid in 2012), the Governor did nothing, thus allowing SB-423 to become law by default.

And that's what happened. It felt like a bomb had exploded directly over my Montana dream that I'd worked so hard to create.

It took time for things to sink in. I was in denial for weeks, thinking that the MTCIA lawsuit would right this political wrong, but Nigel knew better. After the Black Monday raids, not only did the growers scatter and vanish, but so did the patients. Fear gripped the entire cannabis community. While I brooded on the homestead in New York, Nigel was witnessing the fallout in real time. Day by day, business for the lab completely dried up.

I clearly remember the moment when the reality finally hit me. I was sitting in the lab during our April lab meeting. Nigel and I began going through the "to-do" list. With my MBA notebook open, I sat on the stool and began rattling off questions.

"Any word on the new attorney?" I asked.

"I haven't called yet."

"What about the status for MBA getting state lab certification?"

Nigel methodically blew the steam off the top of his coffee and took a small sip. "They haven't returned my calls."

"Maybe you can call them this week? Did you send the report to the Canadian hemp folks?

I missed the growing tension on Nigel's face.

"I'll get on that today."

"And why haven't I received a weekly business report for the past three weeks?"

Nigel snapped. "Because we haven't had any samples to run, Mike! There's been no new business since the raids; everybody has headed for the hills."

As suddenly as his outburst erupted, so it was gone. The hallmark softness that coddled his voice returned. Nigel mustered a nervous laugh. "I don't know how else to tell you Mike, but we're finished. I get a few calls from folks now and then, but by and large, I'm just catching up on paperwork and a few ongoing projects I had in the works. Nobody is coming in with samples. Nobody is coming in to hang out. Folks are scared to death. And frankly, so am I love what I do and am proud of what we've done with the lab, but I'm not willing to go to jail for cannabis."

The Lawsuit

Once it became clear that the governor was going to allow SB-423 to become law by default, the MTCIA issued a frantic plea to every dispensary and grow operation in the State. Without legal intervention, provisions of the new law would be enacted on July 1. The clock was ticking. Money was urgently needed to secure the services of the Goetz law firm. A $50k retainer was required for the firm to take the case. I wondered how many people would continue to pour money into the sinking ship.

Fortunately, Goetz accepted a reasonable deposit on the pledge that the remaining retainer money could be secured in a timely manner. On May 13, 2011, the MTCIA filed suit against the State of Montana.[135]

I, too, was faced with some harsh realities. MBA's revenues were near zero, and my clinic's revenues were barely paying for my travel from New York. It was time to consider Plan B, and that meant going back to work in the emergency department. Although not my preference, working in the ED would provide a stable and predictable income. Heavy with resignation, I made a few phone calls and started to look for a job.

Still, I clung to the thin thread of hope that radical legal action could somehow end this nightmare. I'd invested so much into this dream over the past three years that it seemed reasonable to tap into my home equity loan to keep operations going for a couple of months until we received a preliminary ruling from the court. A ruling on the case was expected before the July 1 deadline. It was impossible to discern the line between hope and delusion.

My spirits lifted when I received a call from Mr. Goetz, asking me if I'd consider being a plaintiff in the suit. Although honored to join the fight, I wanted to speak with Mr. Goetz about the professional implications of being a plaintiff in the case. I sought some assurance that I wasn't taking my medical career and walking off the plank. Late one afternoon, I headed south on Willson Avenue to the beautifully restored three-story Victorian mansion that served as the office of Goetz, Gallik, & Geddes.

The receptionist smiled. "Mr. Goetz is waiting for you in the conference room."

Jim Goetz is the John Wayne of Montana defense attorneys and considered a legend by many prominent constitutional attorneys. He secured stream access for Montana fisherman and sued the State over unfair school funding practices. And most impressively, he had argued several cases before the US Supreme Court. Goetz was the man.

He sat in the middle of a long wooden table. His thick head of rumpled gray hair sparkled in the sunlight. Black rectangular glasses framed his square face. A loosely buttoned yellow western-style shirt poorly hid a white V-neck T-shirt. There were different stacks of papers strewn before him. Three walls were lined with volumes of hardbound legal books. Pictures of Goetz with celebrities and dignitaries abounded in the room. I felt out of my league. Goetz was absorbed, writing something in a legal pad when the receptionist introduced me.

"It's a pleasure to meet you, Dr. Geci. Devlin will be down in a few moments," he said, looking up and firmly shaking my hand. "Please have a seat. I'm glad you are willing to speak to us about this suit."

"It's my pleasure, Mr. Goetz. I think it's criminal what's happening to patients."

"I agree. It's one of the reasons I took the case. My wife would have killed me if I turned it down," he said with a snicker. "And, please, you can call me Jim."

I was impressed that he was such a down-to-earth guy. I grinned. "And, please, call me Michael."

Goetz looked up as he heard his associate Devlin Geddes walking down the wooden hallway, sporting a smartly cut brown Italian suit. Devlin was much taller than his sixty-nine-year old senior partner, and easily two decades younger and slimmer.

For the next hour, we talked about the case and how I could contribute. I shared my 2009 letter to the Montana Board of Medical Examiners and gave them a copy of the white paper I'd written. I explained the function of the lab and discussed my medical training and credentials.

Geddes asked, "Doctor, roughly how many patients have you evaluated for medical marijuana since you opened your clinic?"

I estimated I'd evaluated over a thousand patients, which seemed to deem me as a credible witness. Devlin outlined the case. Goetz would be the head coach, overseeing the strategy of the case as Geddes formulated the specific questions for the hearing. At the meeting's conclusion, I thanked Mr. Goetz for inviting me.

"I want to do everything in my power to help you guys defeat SB-423."

"I appreciate that, Doctor. We'll be in touch."

My Final Plea

A few days before the Black Monday raids, I received a call from a woman from DealFlow Media about speaking at an upcoming event. The Marijuana Conference, 2011 was to be held in mid-June in San Francisco—the marketing event for marijuana business investment was similar to the event I attended in NYC in November of 2010. The topic I was requested to speak on was "Cannabis Testing: Bringing Standards and Consistency to the Industry." The details about the conference would be enclosed in a forthcoming email invitation.

When I opened the email, I thought it was a little odd that speaker travel information wasn't mentioned. Conference speakers are frequently paid an honorarium, but invariably, travel expenses are reimbursed without fail. I called the conference registration number to clear up my confusion.

In quick fashion, a woman with an unmistakable Long Island accent told me that all of the speakers were responsible for their travel arrangements.

"I'm sorry. You're telling me that I'm supposed to pay to come out and speak at your conference?"

"Yes."

I was perplexed. "You do know I'm one of the invited speakers?"

"Yes."

"And that doesn't matter?"

"No," the woman said impatiently. "Listen, Doctor. This is an opportunity for you to showcase your expertise and plug your business to a national audience. That type of marketing isn't free."

The thought of paying my way to speak at a national marijuana conference was insulting. I asked her if I could have some time to look at my schedule availability.

"That's fine, Doctor, but I'll need your answer by the end of April."

As the deadline for the conference neared, I was awaiting word about securing shifts at a rural hospital in eastern Kentucky where a friend of mine worked. September was the earliest I could expect an income again. I was broke and living off my home equity credit line that was being uncomfortably stretched larger each month. It seemed my career in the cannabis industry was over. There was no incentive for me to speak at the conference and no reason to go deeper in debt.

But then I had a dream. I awoke with a strident clarity that I had an obligation to go to California and tell everyone in the cannabis movement what was happening in Montana. I would have a platform to explain our plight. I wrote a single-page fact sheet explaining the situation the MTCIA was facing. I planned to distribute the fliers to the audience before my Friday panel discussion. In my delusion, I thought I could help raise money for the MTCIA suit, a last plea for help. So, like in Dr. Seuss's classic tale *Horton Hears a Who*, I thought that I could take on the role as the very small shirker, JoJo, let out a loud "Yopp!," and somehow save the day. It would be my final plea for help.

Determined to make this trip happen, I found an inexpensive Airbnb in Berkeley, and the host gave me a coupon for a weekend BART pass. I used frequent flier miles for my plane ticket. I was traveling on a shoestring.

The Friday morning of my discussion panel, the sun was warm and bright as a breeze gently blew in from the bay. The walk to the North Berkeley station twisted through eclectic neighborhoods, cool houses with enchanting arrays of blooming gardens. The BART station was half-full—a mix of students, commuters, and tourists—as I boarded the train for the ride to Embarcadero Station

Heather, a friend who'd helped me after Danielle left, mentioned that she and her husband were also going to the conference. When I arrived in the conference hall, Heather and Bobby were sitting at a table; we caught up on our progress with the lawsuit before passing out the MTCIA flyers to everyone in the auditorium. Then I took my position on the panel discussion.

The moderator of the panel was Steve DeAngello, the founder of Harborside Dispensary. The other panelists were Anna Rae Grabstein, who managed Steephill Laboratory Services; Matthew Cohen, a laboratory technician at MendoGrown; and Dr. Robert Martin, the director of CW Analytical Laboratories in Oakland and the only chemist on the panel.

After DeAngello's opening comments, each speaker was asked their opinion of cannabis quality control. I was the third panelist to speak.

"Good morning. My name is Michael Geci. I'm a physician and founder of Montana Botanical Analysis in Bozeman, Montana—one of the first labs in the country to offer cannabinoid testing of medical marijuana products. Before I begin, I want to bring your attention to something very important. A few colleagues just passed out a flier. I would encourage you to read it, take it with you, and share it with all of your friends. For those of you who don't know, Montana has just passed the most restrictive medical marijuana reform bill in the country, SB-423. This bill is nothing short of repeal in disguise."

There were few concerning mumblings from the crowd.

"The Montana Cannabis Industry Association is a non-profit trade association dedicated to promoting professionalism, credibility, quality, and vitality in the medical marijuana industry among all of its members.

"On May 11, I joined several other plaintiffs in suing the State of Montana over the egregious restrictions that SB-423 places upon patients who have been deemed qualified to use medical marijuana by physicians. The MTCIA hired the Goetz Law Firm to represent the organization to fight this outrageous violation of a patient's civil liberties.

"What happens in Montana affects the entire nation. If SB-423 is fully enacted, it will cripple the whole industry and jeopardize the ability of tens of thousands of law-abiding Montana citizens access to medical marijuana. Your brothers and sisters in Montana need your help. We are waging an expensive legal battle to protect the rights of patients to use cannabis as a medicine.

"Any contributions you can make would be immensely appreciated."

And then, I gave my spiel on why analytical testing should be mandatory for any state medical marijuana program. The panel discussion was lively, and the panelists made a strong case that quality control needs to be an essential component of every state marijuana program.

Boarding the plane back to Bozeman, I knew I'd done my best. I'd hoped that I'd been the Who that Horton had finally heard. Now the fate of medical marijuana in Montana rested in the hands of Judge James P. Reynolds. Our hearing would begin on Monday.

Later, I asked Heather how much money the MTCIA received from out-of-state contributors.

"Nothing. Not a dime."

From the Witness Stand

Testimony day had finally arrived. It was June 20, and in 10 days, SB-423 would become law. Sam and I got breakfast at the No Sweat Café. We kept the conversation light so i could stay loose. I was as prepared for this testimony as I'd been for anything in my life. When we got to the courthouse, I spoke briefly with Mr. Goetz and Devlin before we found our seats at the back of the courtroom.

The court was called to order. I sat in the First Montana District Courtroom eagerly awaiting Mr. Goetz to set the stage for a case that would stretch on for the next five years, eventually making its way to the US Supreme Court.

Since our team had brought the petition against the State, we went first. All quotations are taken directly from the official court transcript, cited at the end of the chapter. Goetz slowly ratcheted himself to a remarkably upright posture and began.

"May it please the court, this is a motion for preliminary injunction to enjoin the implementation of SB-423, which is scheduled to go into effect July 1.

"We have raised a number of constitutional deficiencies with this statute, ranging from warrant-less searches to the blanket proscription against medical use of marijuana for probationers, and undue intrusions on the doctor/patient relationship. But the key issue here, I think, your honor, is the virtual complete denial of access to medical marijuana. And that's the heart of our case, and that's what we'll be emphasizing today."

Goetz laid the legal groundwork with a mustered flair that would have made Clarence Darrow proud. "I urge your Honor to re-look—and I'm sure you're familiar with Article II, Section 1—the Declaration of Rights of the Montana Constitution. And what that says is that all rights are derived from the people. This case is about the fundamental right in Article II to health, to the pursuit of good health. And good health is not a matter of governmental largess, and this case is about the fundamental right to personal privacy.

"And the right of personal privacy is not a matter of the government's grace. And this is also about the right to personal dignity. And they're not a matter of grace by the State."

With each eloquent sentence, Goetz painted another layer of legal logic highlighting the bill's threat to personal privacy and individual liberty—our right to make health decisions without the permission of the State. "And that is what our case is about. It's about excessive government interference in the personal lives of Montanans."

Goetz took a sip of water and checked his watch. "And our proof will show that marijuana, while not completely harmless, is remarkably safe. And it has proven medicinal qualities. If a Montana citizen in consultation with his or her doctor wishes to have access to medical marijuana, that person should have such access without undue governmental restraint. The State will fall back on its general police power, which obviously it has, and upon the fact that marijuana is in this day and age —I might say bizarrely—still a Schedule I substance under the Federal Controlled Substances Act.

"There are real problems with this law. It's so arbitrary. It denies substantive due process. And this access thing is just so difficult to fathom. It's either that the law was so messily drafted that they have all of these catch-22s in it; or, as the history shows, the majority of the legislature initially tried to eliminate medical marijuana entirely. So, we are having to face an archaic system with these myths about marijuana, which we will dispel in our case."

As I sat, I wondered if people really wanted to hear the truth about cannabis. Americans like believing in myths. For the last three years, I had been advocating for a more rational policy toward medical marijuana, yet few legislators cared to shift their position from a state of fear and emotion to one of practicality and facts. Surely Judge Reynolds would see the lunacy of Essman's bill and halt the implementation of SB-423 before the July 1 deadline.

Goetz' opening statement concluded:

"The makers of our Constitution conferred, as against the government, the right to be left alone—the most comprehensive of rights and the right most valued by civilized men. To protect that right, every unjustifiable intrusion by the government upon the privacy of the individual, whatever the means employed, must be deemed a violation of the Fourth Amendment."

The lead attorney from the State Attorney General's Office, James Molloy, was next to present the State's opening statement. He was matter of fact in his opening remarks, pointing out that SB-423 still allowed for patients to access medical marijuana without eliminating any of the conditions that the State had approved in MT-148. From his perspective, the MTCIA suit was about something other than patient's getting medicine:

"And so, your Honor, this is a case, make no mistake about it, about this question: Must the State of Montana allow a commercial marijuana industry to exist in the State?" Molloy paced in front of the plaintiff's table. He outlined how the growth of the State's medical marijuana law had sputtered since its inception in March of 2005 until the beginning of the Obama administration when the program grew exponentially.

"But the real story here lies in the illegitimate increase. And that was through the promotion of cattle-call, mass-traveling clinics where patients literally walked into a room, got signed off by a doctor they had no relationship with, a doctor that was being paid by, quote, 'caregivers,' traveling around and putting people into the system for no legitimate bona fide reason."

I agreed with Molloy, Essman, and the SCSK coalition about the need for change; I lobbied hard for reasonable and appropriate reform. What I vehemently opposed was the putative and heinous nature of the SB-423 reform package.

The morning testimony began with several teleconferencing sessions. The first witness was Jack O. Henshold MD, a triple-boarded hematologist, medical oncologist, and internal medicine specialist from Deaconess Hospital in Bozeman. Dr. Henshold made it clear that he was speaking about his personal opinions, not those of the hospital.

Goetz asked Henshold about recommending medical marijuana. "I think only a slight hesitation," alluding to the issue of the lack of cannabis quality control. "There's always an effort to try to use other methods first where I know exactly what I'm prescribing."

"Are you aware of any other area of the medical practice where you have to get a second opinion for prescribing for chronic pain?"

"In my practice, I'm not aware of that."

One of the pillars of Goetz's case was that SB-423 was a significant liability to physicians wishing to help their patients who might benefit from using medical marijuana.

"Now, finally, Doctor, is there any doubt in your mind that marijuana has important medicinal effects?"

Hensold wasted no time. "I think marijuana does have effects that are beneficial for symptom management of our patients. That's correct."

The next expert witness to testify, Dr. Lester Grinspoon, MD, Associate Professor Emeritus of Psychiatry at Harvard Medical School. Grinspoon was a senior psychiatrist at the Massachusetts Mental Health Center in Boston. Goetz invited Grinspoon to remind the court of the historical background of this case.

"I, at that time, concerned about so many young people using the terribly dangerous drug marijuana, I decided to go into the Harvard Medical School Library and see if I could write a reasonable—reasonably objective—paper on the science that underlays this severe prohibition. And to make a long story short, I had to confront my own ignorance about this. I had been brainwashed, the best word I can think of, like so many other citizens in this country, into believing that this was a very toxic drug.

"I discovered that just the opposite is true. That the most toxic thing about marijuana was not any psycho-pathological property of the drug, but rather the way we as a society were dealing with this problem, by arresting and criminalizing so many young people.

"But in a perfectly rational society, I would say it [cannabis] should be as available as aspirin."

Then Goetz asked, "Now, Doctor, have you observed marijuana clinically?"

Grinspoon shared a story that touched everyone in the courtroom.

"Yes. I first observed it firsthand with my son. He, like so many people, suffered from that awful nausea and vomiting. The nausea went right down to the fingernail. He was ten years old when he was diagnosed [with acute lymphocytic leukemia]. And at the time, the cancer chemotherapeutics that he had to use were ones which led to a great deal of nausea and vomiting. He was about thirteen or fourteen. He got to the point where he just—as many of these kids do—to a point where they just dread getting it. And some of them just refused. So, he had to have a lot of coercion to take the cancer chemotherapeutics.

"And he told them that he had smoked marijuana in the parking lot twenty minutes before the injection. Dr. Frei never had any difficulty with him again. They were astonished. I became an advocate on the day I saw my son get the relief he did. I have devoted a lot of my time and energy to [medical cannabis]. I do a lot of the clinical stuff. I feel very good about this because, eventually, marijuana is going to be recognized as a wonder drug, just like penicillin was in 1941."

Goetz finished with his distinguished witness. "Thank you, Doctor."

I was the first witness after lunch. It was one of those Rod Serling moments. You wake up from a dream, and you're sitting next to a State District Judge pleading your case for tens of thousands of patients who are in jeopardy of losing access to medicine that helps them feel better.

Devlin Geddes began. "Going back to medical school, what do they teach you about cannabinoid medicine in medical school?"

"I knew nothing about cannabinoid medicine in medical school because the endocannabinoid system was not discovered until 1993, when I graduated [from medical school]."

"And if you can, will you give us a short description of what you mean by the *endocannabinoid system*?"

"Sure. I think most of us are familiar with the fact that we make our own opiates; that we have our own system of pain relief. It's a system called endorphins and enkephalins, which have been described and accepted in the literature for dozens of years. The endocannabinoid system parallels that—we make our own cannabinoids. We have our own cannabinoid receptors. They are found in practically every cell in our body and are responsible for the myriad of cellular and biochemical controls within our body."

Geddes stepped toward me. "OK. So, in layman's term, our bodies produce cannabinoids naturally, and we have a system that accepts those naturally?"

"Absolutely."

"How did you learn about the system and cannabinoid medicine?"

"One of the things that they are adamant about in medical school is to let us know that there will be things that will be discovered, and we'll need to keep abreast of the current medical literature. I have taken a few courses in cannabinoid medicine. But by and large, pretty much self-learned by going to the literature and reading it."

Devlin glanced down briefly at his legal pad. "Do you have a professional medical opinion as to whether marijuana has true medical benefits?"

"There's no question in my mind that medical cannabis has medical benefits."

"And that's to a reasonable degree of medical certainty?"

"It's as clear a certainty as saying that aspirin is effective."

Devlin continued. "Is it fair to say you were upset that the Board of Medical Examiners didn't do anything about the caravan clinics?"

"I didn't think it was responsible. I was quite disappointed that they weren't more effectual."

"Do you believe if the Board of Medical Examiners had done something about it back then, that we wouldn't be here today?"

"I absolutely believe that."

When Devlin finished, I sat at the witness stand and looked out over the crowd. Molloy and J. Stuart Segrest talked among themselves. Mr. Molloy was intimidating; I was sure he was going to interrogate me and go for my jugular. Segrest seemed much more like a passive-aggressive second lieutenant. I closed my eyes and offered up a prayer. So, when Segrest stood up, I knew the cannabis gods were with me.

Mr. Segrest approached me for the cross-examination. Cold sweat dripped down my arms. Segrest took little time to try to discredit me.

"You mentioned that you were no longer board certified in emergency medicine; is that true?"

"I let my Board Certification in Emergency Medicine expire."

"Why is that?"

"Because I, like many [other] emergency physicians, feel that the new recertification process is a bit onerous. And so, I just keep up with literature. I do my CMEs, but—"

"You are not a fan of the certification process?" Segrest interrupted.

"I didn't say that. I said that I found the American Board of Emergency Medicine pathway to recertification to be onerous. I felt angry when I took my boards [the first time]. I felt like I was being pimped. And after having spent seven years of medical training, I was tired of being pimped around."

Segrest ignored any transition. "And there's disagreement among physicians about marijuana's benefit and use, isn't there?"

"Yes, sir."

"And, in fact, doctors in thirty-four states without medical marijuana law are able to care for their patients without marijuana, right?"

"That's correct."

"And you were able to do so, I presume, in the states that you practiced in that didn't have a medical marijuana law?"

"That's correct."

Segrest paced the brightly polished courtroom floor as he contemplated his next question. "And contrast to those thirty-four states where marijuana is still completely illegal, under SB-423, which I realize you have some significant problems with, but even under that law, a doctor can still authorize marijuana, right?"

I qualified his statement. "Up to the twenty-five-patient limit."

"Well, they can authorize it after that."

I inhaled deeply to settle my growing discontent with his questioning. "Would you be willing to voluntarily go before your state bar for potential disciplinary reasons just because you saw twenty-five pedophile clients?"

Mr. Segrest wasn't impressed with my answer and, for a moment, stopped his pacing, staring at me with a hint of scorn. "We're not talking about me here, nor the state bar. We're talking about the state law. And I understand that at twenty-five, the Board of Medical Examiners will have to conduct an examination. But it's not true that you would have to stop authorizing it at that point."

"You're absolutely correct. I would not have to stop. But it would put undue pressure and put me in a position of potential duress, which I don't think is appropriate."

"And under the new law, patients can still grow their own if they choose to do so?"

"That's correct. But I think you heard extensive testimony by numerous individuals today that it's..."

"That it might be difficult," Segrest interrupted.

"That it could be incredibly difficult."

Segrest wandered over to the defendant's table, glancing at his notepad. "You noted that there were these traveling clinics that were signing people up willy-nilly that you seem to have a significant problem with?"

"Yes, sir."

"So, you would agree, then, that some reform, at least, of the old law was needed?"

"Absolutely."

"In fact, you said that people felt duped by that kind of service?"

"I said that I felt that the clinics represented duping of the people of Montana for their overwhelming support of this act in 2004. That's correct."

And then Segrest pivoted closer. "And were you aware that eighteen- to thirty-year-olds with chronic pain make up the largest portion of marijuana cardholders?"

"I'm not aware of that, sir."

"Does that surprise you?"

I straightened my posture. "It's not reflective in *my* practice."

Segrest stepped closer. "Is it who you would expect to be the largest population that would need medical marijuana?"

"No, sir."

"So really from what I can gather, you believe it's essential that there's a commercial marijuana market?"

I was struck at the randomness of his questions, and by the amount of sweat that continued to drip down my shirt. "I never said that I thought it was essential that there was a commercial marijuana market. I think that it's essential that there's some [market]. I think it's essential that patients have reliable access to safe…"

Segrest cut me off again. "And you feel that the only reliable way for that to happen is through commercial caregivers?"

"I don't think that it's the only way it can be done. But I think that's the way that the State has allowed this to take place for X number of years. And it seemed to be going along OK until these carnival clinics started, and people saw this as an opportunity. There were a lot of caregivers who were construction workers who were losing their jobs in the housing implosion, and they became caregivers. And so, it's…it's had an impact on a lot of people. And I don't think anybody could have anticipated the chaos that ensued."

"You mentioned that the number of caregivers has also exploded. Does that raise in your mind any kind of problems with quality control of the product?"

"That's why we started the lab because we wanted to implement a semblance of quality control. Because heretofore, there [were] no standards, no independent professionals that could give people credible, accurate information to make informed decisions. That's why I made the comment about cannabis being the only [medical] substance in the country that's unlabeled."

Tapping his index finger on his chin, Segrest pondered. "Right. And so that's one of the things that's different about marijuana than your typical prescription. One of them would be quality control?"

"Correct."

"Another would be dosage control?"

I saw an opportunity. "Correct, once you know what's in it. That was one of the services we provided people is that we could dose the cannabis; you would know that this brownie contained X milligrams of THC or CBD or THCV or whatever. You would get a sense of how strong the dried leaf or the bud was based upon its THC and CBD percentages. And, again, [before the lab] that was nonexistent."

Segrest took a second to digest what I'd said. "And you would acknowledge that marijuana is illegal under the federal law, right?"

"Yes, I will."

"And, otherwise, illegal under Montana law except as provided, before in I-148 and now in SB-423?"

"Yes."

"Do you know of any medical treatment or modalities that involve an illegal activity?"

It was time to go on the offensive.

"No, I don't. But what I need to say about that is that there is a program by the federal government that permits medical cannabis to be used by certain patients. It's all part of the Investigational New Drug program, which cannabis was a [part of]. It began, as I'm sure you know, in the late seventies, early eighties. The IND program for cannabis got as large as thirteen patients. And then—I believe it was the FDA that shut the program down for what appeared to be arbitrary reasons. And there are still patients that receive medical cannabis from the federal government, every month. You're aware of that, right?"

Segrest deflected nicely. "To some degree, yes—maybe not the specifics. But in general, though, it is illegal under federal law, with perhaps those minor exceptions for those…"

"Well, I think that if the federal government gives cannabis to patients in the IND, then what's legal? And what's illegal? Because if the federal government is *giving*…"

"I'm sorry," Segrest said with a bow of his head.

"I'm not an attorney. But if the federal government is providing medical cannabis for patients in the United States, are they doing something that's illegal? I mean, this is one of the things that's so oxymoronic about this whole subject, and it just doesn't make a whole hill of beans of sense."

Then Segrest threw me a curve ball. "And you have moved around quite a bit in your career, right?"

I looked at Devlin for help. "I'm not sure what you mean by that."

"Well, you've practiced in a lot of different places and in a lot of the different clinical settings?"

Then it dawned on me.

I leaned forward and looked squarely at Segrest. "Yeah. I decided that I wanted to have more career flexibility. And so, I began doing locum tenens. There are recruiters all over the country looking for doctors to fill spots. And [locums] gives me flexibility with my time and schedule. I was able to coach peewee football with my son because I said [to the recruiters] I'm not available. So yeah, I've worked in a lot of different places. But it's also given me a tremendous breadth of experience. So, I look at it as a positive, actually."

But Segrest persisted. "So, since 1993, roughly eighteen years, you have been practicing. As I counted on your resume, you've practiced in about twenty-two different clinical settings. Does that sound right?

"Yeah, I'll accept that. Did you also note that I was invited to be on the clinical faculty at three medical schools as well?"

"Didn't note that," Segrest shrugged.

"You might want to check that, too."

After the State's cross-examination, Devlin redirected on a few questions, and then Judge Reynolds excused me from the stand.[136]

I was grateful that I'd held my own.

Returning to my seat, Sam leaned over and whispered. "I knew you were going to crush it, but nothing like that. You were great."

The Verdict

On June 30, 2011, Judge James P. Reynolds blocked only four portions of SB-423, allowing the rest of the provisions in the bill to become law.

The portions of the bill blocked included:
1. The prohibition on advertising
1. The prohibition on providers receiving compensation for services
1. The three-patient maximum for providers
1. The requirement that doctors be investigated for recommending more than twenty-five patients in a single year[137]

Although the ruling could have been worse, it was bitterly disappointing. The Reynolds decision put the Montana medical marijuana program on life support, dissolving any remaining wisp of hope that a semblance of normalcy could return to the program. The ruling cemented my decision; it was time for me to leave.

In less than three years, the once bright and promising landscape of developing Montana's medical marijuana industry into a national example of American entrepreneurship and innovation was decimated. What remained of the industry seemed more reminiscent of the zombie apocalypse. It was every man for himself.

The collective stress of Black Monday and the adoption of SB-423 snapped the delicate fabric of trust and camaraderie among many in the industry. Prior to the Reynold's decision, I discovered that Kristy Fairy was hosting cannabis clinics at her dispensary in the other end of the Medical Arts Building. We had agreed that in return for freely giving her my dispensary lease option, she would channel all of her patients through WH&H. So much for honorable expectations. I wasn't in Kansas; this was the face of integrity and respect in marijuana land.

When I confirmed what she had been doing, I calmly walked up to her office. Sitting across from me at her desk, Kristy eked out a frail confession, suggesting that I was overreacting. "Michael, you were in New York. I had patients that needed to be seen. This won't be a problem in the future, I promise."

A promise from someone in the marijuana industry…

I should have had her evicted the moment she acknowledged she was violating the no-compete clause of the lease. Despite my complaints to the building manager, Kristy's cannabis clinics continued. If the political and legal calculus of the situation had been different, I would have been more aggressive. But as it stood, I was utterly spent. Protecting my dying practice was secondary to saving my life.

As the dust from Judge Reynold's decision settled, it became clear that MBA would be one of the many victims of Essman's bill. In my final business meeting with Devin, he suggested that I categorize the political catastrophe of SB-423 as part of the "act-of-god" disaster provision in the lease. I tried to negotiate a zero-penalty exit, but the building manager refused.

With my thirty-day security deposit as leverage, I had until the end of July to leave the Medical Arts Building or come up with another creative solution. In a final attempt to salvage my cherished clinic space, I lobbied a handful of remaining friendly growers and dispensary owners, proposing that they help subsidize my rent for Suite 105. The logic was if WH&H stayed open, there would be a cannabis-friendly physician to see patients and sign physician statements, but no one was interested. Only Nigel knew I'd been keeping the clinic s open by borrowing money. And that had to end.

Mr. Goetz petitioned the State for an exemption for MBA, considering the vital service it provided to the medical marijuana community. The Attorney General's office conceded that MBA was an honorable business venture, but the State declined to award an exemption.

And with that, the lab was dead.

After the Dust Settled

Those who planned the strategy torpedoing of MT-148 should get an award for their Machiavellian achievement. As a result of the Reynold's decision, much of the remaining cannabis industry went underground, closed, or left the state for friendlier pastures. The State's commercial and warehouse real estate space that had been turbocharged by the demand from the cannabis industry collapsed. SB-423 was an economic death sentence for almost everyone involved in any aspect of cannabis.

By April, interest for medical marijuana cards shriveled, and patient demand for legal cannabis dropped dramatically. Patients told me they were afraid and opted to either stop using cannabis or go back to the underground sources they'd relied upon before getting their card.

The political calculus for derailing the Montana medical marijuana program was enormously effective. As a consequence of the Black Monday raids and the passage of SB-423, numerous individuals were arrested, indicted, and some eventually went to prison, while countless individuals declared bankruptcy.

I was one of the lucky ones.

One of the most appalling examples of the personal costs incurred by cannabis entrepreneurs is the story of the four founders of Montana Cannabis. Tom Daubert, Chris Lindsey, Chris Williams, and Richard Flor were charged with conspiracy to produce marijuana, conspiracy to maintain drug-involved premises, conspiracy to sell marijuana, money-laundering, and weapons in the presence of illegal drugs.

The four partners all faced federal minimum drug sentencing of at least eighty years in federal prison. Lindsey and Daubert accepted plea agreements, avoiding jail, but were required to testify against Mr. Williams, who steadfastly maintained his innocence. He was the only person in Montana to go to trial as a result of the Black Monday raids and serve prison time. Faced with a sentence of up to eighty years, Williams eventually had his time reduced to five and a half years in federal prison.

Richard Flor, the sixty-eight-year-old silent partner of Montana Cannabis, pleaded guilty and had the unfortunate luck of receiving a Reagan-appointed judge rather than the Obama appointee (who presided over the other three Montana Cannabis defendants). Mr. Flor, who was also Montana's first registered caregiver under MT-148 and was responsible for providing Robin Prosser her effective strain of cannabis, pleaded guilty to the charge of conspiracy to maintain drug-involved premises. He was sentenced to five years in prison. After spending six months in a private state prison in Nevada while awaiting a bed in a federal medical prison for the treatment of his dementia, diabetes, depression, osteoporosis, and hepatitis C, he suffered a heart attack, was placed on life support while awaiting transport, and died on August 12, 2012, shackled to a gurney. Flor's wife and son were also sentenced to prison for terms of two and five years, respectively.

Additionally, the Flor's forfeited their family home, six vehicles, and were ordered to pay a $288,000 monetary judgment. The others also faced financial penalties. Lindsey forfeited $288,000, and Daubert was fined $55,000. Williams was initially fined $1.7 million, but as a result of his plea deal, the fines were dropped.

Williams was ultimately released from prison in June of 2017. As evidence of the injustice of the government's war on drugs, the US District Court judge, Dana Christensen called the sentencing of Williams "unfair and absurd", stating that his hands were tied during his sentencing by federally mandated minimum drug sentencing. And in a fitting bit of irony, Williams, the cannabis grower for Montana Cannabis was assigned as the gardener during his prison stay.[138]

No statistic bears out the impact of SB-423 more than this: By the second quarter of 2011, at the peak of the Montana medical marijuana expansion, there were 30,036 registered patient cardholders along with 4,848 registered growers. By November of 2012, the number of qualified patients had dropped to 8,404, a 72 percent decline. The number of growers had sunk to 293, an astounding 94 percent loss.[139]

Sadly, before I'd made my final departure back to New York, I'd overheard several people in Bozeman say, "What difference does this law [SB-423] make? It's just a bunch of potheads." Unfortunately, in the minds of many, anyone using cannabis or marijuana is just a "pothead" or a "doper." The anti-marijuana propaganda will take decades to fade, although if racism is an example, this "pothead" mentality will never die.

A suggestion might be for pro-cannabis groups to better organize and assert themselves like other segments of society marginalized due to race, religion, sexual orientation, gender identity, and the like. One thing is certain, if the constitutional rights of patients using medical marijuana are usurped, your constitutional rights are at risk, too.

I'll refer you to the epic poem by the German pastor Martin Niemoller, "First They Came for the Communists":

First they came for the Communists,
and I didn't speak up,
because I wasn't a Communist.
Then they came for the Jews,
and I didn't speak up,
because I wasn't a Jew.
Then they came for the Catholics,
and I didn't speak up,
because I was a Protestant.
Then they came for me,
and by that time there was no one
left to speak up for me.[140]

It took time for me to come to terms with the aftermath of Judge Reynold's verdict. Despite the letters I'd written, it was disappointing that so few national marijuana groups came to our aid (not that anything but the second coming of Christ could have prevented what happened); groups like Drug Policy Alliance, Marijuana Policy Project, and NORML gave us little or no public support in our fight. Montanans were left to deal with the mess on their own. After the full implementation of SB-423, I had tearful mothers call me about securing cannabis for their children with intractable seizures. I told them to move to Colorado.

As I prepared my exit strategy, I became oddly philosophical. What did the implementation of SB-423 say about the sanctity of patient rights? Does the State dictate medical care, or do physicians? If the State determines the who can use medical cannabis, then will it next determine which patients have access to diabetic or hypertensive medicine? Who receives a breast augmentation? And who should have access to the latest advances in chemotherapy? Should patients taking narcotics need a special card from the State to get their prescription filled? Why is discrimination of patients using cannabis tolerated? And why is medical marijuana treated differently from other medicines?

To these questions, I still don't have satisfying answers.

As a physician trained in both the traditional allopathic method as well as in alternative and integrative perspectives, it seems that we have been brainwashed, as a culture, into believing that if it's not a pill or in a syringe manufactured from a pharmaceutical company, then it can't be a medicine.

Citizens should be allowed to grow their own cannabis (marijuana and hemp), just as they are permitted to home brew beer, make cider and wine, or tend a garden. Patients having access to the medicine of their choice is no different than patients being able to choose their own doctor. Regrettably, as long as medical marijuana is still perceived as "pot", then civil rights of persons using cannabis as a medicine just don't matter. But they do.

In my opinion, the biggest issue regarding the medical acceptance of cannabis is its Schedule I designation under the Controlled Substance Act. Not until the FDA removes cannabis from its Schedule I designation will the plant finally be free to be studied objectively and be eligible for federal medical research funding.

Doesn't it make sense that we would want to know as much about the most abused illegal substance on the planet as possible? Without non-biased research, policy decisions are based on nothing more than emotions, myths, and fears—something I thought we'd abandoned when we exited the Dark Ages.

5A

Nigel graciously accepted the unenviable task of removing everything out of the lab that he and I had so proudly built less than a year before. He said he'd keep the HPLC in storage until I could sell it. I drove out to his house to say good-bye before I caught my final afternoon flight back to New York. Pulling into Nigel's driveway, the weight of my sadness settled upon me, and walking up to his front door was an unexpected effort.

We greeted each other with our customary brotherly granola hug. We talked about our kids and summer vacation; then, I told him I'd soon be starting an ER job in rural Kentucky. "It'll give me an opportunity to get back on my feet again and not think about all of this."

"Right on."

"What are you going to do?" I asked with resignation.

"I picked up some roofing jobs. I did it during my summers as an undergrad. I'd rather be in the lab, but it pays the bills for now," he said cheerily. "I'm also going to do some mining analysis for a team of prospectors in Nevada. Things are picking up."

There was a long, dreadful pause. The time had come for the moment I'd never imagined would happen. "Well, I guess I better be going. I hope you know how much I wish things could have been different."

Nigel reached out and we hugged again. "No worries, Mike. I know."

And with that, I drove off. I felt numb, but there were still a few more loose ends that needed to be tied.

My flight to Denver was leaving in three hours.

A friend helped me haul the remaining boxes of books, charts, and assorted collected memorabilia out of Suite 105, storing them in a spare room at his place. My footsteps echoed behind me as I closed the office door for the final time.

There were a few folks in the Medical Arts Building who I wanted to see before I left.

Dr. John Tkach, a dermatologist, was in the next office down. I'd seen him a few times for sun-related skin issues. He's a truly distinguished physician from the Greatest Generation, bearing testament to the dignity and respect all physicians once bestowed upon every patient. During my visits, we talked about his tenure as the personal physician for President Dwight D. Eisenhower and he would quietly ask me about the struggles I'd incurred trying to legitimize medical marijuana. After one of our appointments, he leaned forward, placing his hand on my shoulder, and looked at me square in the eye. "You know, son, you're making history."

I was humbled. It was an honor that someone like Dr. Tkach got it.

Agnes, his receptionist, welcomed me with her usual bright smile and informed me that Dr. Tkach wasn't in. I was bummed, but I left him a note.

"I'll be sure Dr. Tkach gets this. I know he'll miss his chats with you."

Down the hallway, I stopped to bid farewell to the pharmacists, Joe and Barry. On occasion, I sent patients there to get prescriptions filled. Over the past year, we'd had a couple of interesting conversations about various applications of cannabis as medicine. We shook hands, and they wished me well.

My final act as a tenant of the Medical Arts Building was sliding the keys to Suite 105 under the building manager's door. Mike Tweeters had been replaced. I was glad the woman who replaced him wasn't in her office. Rounding the corner, I took one last peek at the building directory and felt a swell of emotion; she'd already removed the plastic letters that I'd been so proud to have displayed: Suite 105...Montana Botanical Analysis.

I walked into the bright July sunshine choked by sadness; it was my last day as a pot doc.

Walking to my Subaru, I was grateful I had a plane to catch—someplace else to go. The distraction of making my flight kept me from drowning in my grief of the present. I felt like a refugee fleeing a still-smoldering homeland. Yet, even when things were bleakest, simply being in western Montana was better than being most anywhere else.

As I made my way toward the airport, I called Lori and thanked her for everything. "Aren't you glad you listened to me and didn't buy a house?" she joked.

Somehow I found the humor of her comment. "Yeah, I'm glad I listened. But I wish were hadn't been right."

I turned off Jackrabbit Road into the potholed, gravel parking lot of Mike Singer's dispensary, Sensible Alternatives. I placed the last box of alphabetized patient charts in the corner of a large locked closet—boxes holding hundreds of stories of people who chose to use cannabis as a medicine. As I closed the door, I thought of Hillari's fateful tap on my shoulder three years ago. It seemed like just yesterday.

As he'd done numerous times before, Mike gave me a lift to the airport. He pulled up to the curb at the Bozeman-Yellowstone International Airport, handed me my overstuffed Osprey pack, and bear hugged me.

"Take care, brother."

"Thanks for everything, dude. Be well."

As I walked through the sliding glass doors into the foyer of the airport, I was glad to be going home, back to my place on Crumhorn Mountain. With no line at security, I felt my karma changing. Passengers muddled about the gate area. I wondered where they were going. What had brought them to western Montana? Fly-fishing on the Stillwater? Spying packs of wolves in Yellowstone? An enchanting evening at Norris hot springs? An epic bike ride on the Going-to-the-Sun Road? Everyone had a story.

I waited in silence for the start of boarding. I would miss this place that had changed my life, this wonderfully beautiful place with the enchanting name: Montana.

When my zone was called, I took my time walking down the jet bridge. I was in no particular hurry. I wanted to soak in every last moment of this place. The smiling flight attendant welcomed me aboard and checked my boarding pass.

"5B, sir."

I thanked her and scanned the overhead bin for the seat number.

Looking up from seat 5A was an angel with golden hair draped over delicately tanned shoulders. She introduced herself as Rebecca Layman, and after a few pleasantries, I felt my sadness beginning to lift.

"So where are you traveling on this beautiful bluebird day?"

"Back to New York. This is my last trip out here. I'm not sure when I'll be back."

"That sounds pretty heavy. If you don't mind me asking, what happened?"

"What happened?" *Did she really want to know*?

As coincidence would have it, Rebecca's ex-husband was a grower; she said she'd heard about my lab. "A couple of my girlfriends got their card from you, too." We talked until we landed in Denver. Deplaning, we exchanged business cards and said good-bye.

It was great to be back home—the place where I could begin to forget about the devastation created by SB-423. I rode my bike hundreds of miles a week and spent countless hours in my garden. I frequently picked my son up after school, helped him with his homework, and shot hoops in the driveway, playing endless games of H-O-R-S-E. At night, to help me fall asleep, I'd don earphones and listen to endless replays of a couple of Patty Griffin songs, "Long Ride Home" and "Useless Desires." The soulful resonance of her voice struck a chord; it soothed me like a mother's embrace.

One afternoon, the sheriff pulled into my driveway. My initial thought was that I was being named in a malpractice suit since that's the method used by the court to deliver such good news to expectant doctors. It had only happened twice—a reasonably low number, considering my specialty and the number of years I'd practiced. Still, an anxiety raged inside of me wondering what court action was being taken against me now.

I signed for the letter and opened it.

In a macabre way, it was a relief to see that the building manager had filed suit against me. I guess her Christian kindness had run out when the MBA July rent was due. I'd done what I thought was the responsible thing—giving her months of warnings that my businesses were likely to become insolvent if we didn't get relief with the court. But business is business, even though I'd invested tens of thousands of dollars into renovating the barren space two years ago, she wanted her money. It was almost laughable.

I walked back to my house and called the Goetz law office. Mr. Geddes kindly assigned me one of his associates to untangle the legal mess with the Medical Arts Building. After a couple of weeks of lawyer haggling, the suit was dropped. My sleeplessness abated.

Rebecca and I finally reconnected. She flew out to see her sister living outside of New York City and suggested that we get together. We met in the city on a crisp September Saturday. She gave me hope that emotionally healthy and attractive women still inhabited the planet. Perhaps most importantly, she showed me I was worth loving.

I would not have returned to Montana had I not sat in 5B. I stayed in touch with Mike Singer, even after he sold my car. He offered me a room in his space to do a monthly clinic. Mike promised he'd make sure it was worth my time. It was an offer I couldn't resist, with Suzanne always at the airport waiting to pick me up.

By the spring of 2012, marijuana-friendly people in the state were still scared, patient numbers continued to dwindle, and I was barely covering my travel expenses. Although it was always a blessing to be in Montana, it just seemed like it was time for me to move on. On my final trip in April, Rebecca took to me Chico Hot Springs, an upscale spa-resort at the base of Emigrant Peak on the western edge of the Absorka Range. The spa is nestled in the Paradise Valley, just north of Yellowstone National Park, and one of the most magical places I've had the privilege of visiting. It was one of the best birthdays ever.

Gratitude is a wonderful thing.

After months of slogging through the rural ED in eastern Kentucky, I'd paid my lingering Montana debts and worked off the home equity loan. I eventually found an ED position less than an hour from home and gladly gave up the commute to the Bluegrass state.

I'd survived my own version of the perfect storm. From the refuge of my home on Crumhorn Mountain, I could now watch things in Montana unfold from a safe distance.

The Final Demon

SB-423 was an egregious injustice for tens of thousands of Montanans. In the movement to stop it, I found myself in the center of a righteous battle and became an outspoken advocate for medical marijuana. But this time, the good guys didn't win; we got clobbered.

By the summer of 2011, almost everything I'd worked to develop over the past three years was lost. Unlike the Andrea Gail, the perfect storm that I tried to circumvent was political, not atmospheric, and rather than going to the bottom of the North Atlantic, I found myself back where I'd started this journey, Crumhorn Mountain. Without an income, my only viable option was packing my bags and returning to my prior life, my Montana dream was dead.

For most of my life, I've powered through difficult situations with shear will and hard work. Finishing med school and completing my residency vouched for my ability to gut it out when the going got tough, but sometimes you just have to walk away because some things are out of your control. Leaving Montana was not unlike how I felt when my marriage ended—a form of emotional amputation. And similarly, walking away from what I'd created within the walls of Suite 105 made me feel a little like the classic Monty Python character, the Black Knight, although the pain I was feeling was clearly more than just a flesh wound.

Once I was back on Crumhorn Mountain, I had time to heal. Friends called to update me on the continuing chaos, the efforts to raise money for the lawsuit, and the accusations that some made about me abandoning the ship. One disgruntled dispensary owner suggested at a meeting that I should be killed. What was most hurtful about hearing that some pothead threatened my life from 1,800 miles away, wasn't the empty threat, but rather that Sam sat next to the guy and said nothing in my defense.

Over the years, the demon that persisted was my severed relationship with what had been my first officer, my business partner, colleague, and friend, Nigel. Ours was a relationship that sprang from our mutual love and curiosity of a plant, and we dared to dream big together. I provided him the training to become one of the most accomplished and respected American cannabinoid chemists. I loved him like a brother.

And like many stories of brothers, I envied him. Not because he was smarter, or better looking, or because he was our parents' favorite; I envied Nigel because he was still dabbling in cannabis. To his considerable credit, his expertise and talent were appreciated as the cannabis industry continued to grow. People offered him jobs, and he became the go-to expert that I wanted to be.

Oh me, the jealous mentor.

Over the years, numerous groups approached me, picking my brain about starting an analytical cannabis laboratory. Their interest temporarily made me feel important and assuaged my damaged ego. Despite my desire to stay relevant in the industry, my participation in cannabis-related projects yielded a single cameo event, participating as a biochemistry subject-matter expert evaluator in the state of Maryland's medical marijuana program.

A few years ago, and out of the blue, I got a call from Pete Jones, who wanted to know if I still had my HPLC for sale. I told him I'd make him a good deal. It gave me an excuse to call Nigel.

After discussing the physical condition of the machine and Jones's offer, the call provided me an opportunity to grow up and move "onwards" as Daubert would say. I told Nigel I was happy for his success, and I shared with him my petty jealousy regarding his ascendancy in the cannabis world. And, most importantly, I told him I missed his friendship and was sorry for how things ended.

A few weeks later, I got an email from Nigel:[141]

Hey Mike—

Glad we can chat. Like you said, it's strange making such a tight bond—then having things be blown into such chaos. It was a wild ride for sure.

I hear your feelings with what went down. I continue to try to understand where you are coming from; I know it was a challenging situation for everyone. When the shit hit the fan, it was more than just ceasing the work in the MT lab and trying to make sense of our lives—it was seeing friends and colleagues go to jail. That time was beyond what I ever thought I'd be involved with, legal and emotionally. I have many regrets about my actions, but those were situations I never imagined for me or my family.

I don't want to rehash the past, but when we decided to not do the lab anymore, I was essentially unemployed for six months. I was helping a friend do roofs in Bozeman (waiting to fall off and break my back) and trying to do mining consulting. When I got an offer to do R/D on cannabis again, it seemed like a no-brainer. No regulatory oversight, homework, low stress—it was clear to me. I understand how you feel/felt; I would have too.

But, to address your comments—on paper, it would appear I'm doing good. I've set up, from scratch—a certified lab in Colorado, something Cannlabs and Steep Hill haven't even been able to do. I've won the ASA Researcher for the year award (thanks Steph, Jahan and Michelle!) and our lab is getting more work. In lieu of all this, I'm choosing to resign from this job and move on. I've already submitted my letter of resignation and our transition is in place. We are currently interviewing for my replacement, which is strange for me. But my choice is made, I'm not a QC chemist. I'm done. So now, me and Ash are looking to the next step. It's weird, but it's happening.

I have options to continue in this industry, in non-QC regards. I may do so, I may not. But my current goal is to leave my current post and get back to the life that lets me be a dad for my kids (Oliver and Sadie are really good skiers), a husband for my wife, and a friend to myself. Right now, I'm working 12-hour days and I'm turning my hair gray by the day. QC chemistry in Colorado is stressful. It's interesting, but stressful.

I agree about our past. Brothers in arms that were put in situations that caused (at least me) to go kind of insane. It's a bummer, I really liked having you as, and being a friend to you. When shit went crazy, I lost my ability to cope. For this, I'm sorry!

I look forward to talking and being able to work past all this. I will always thank you and attribute my successes after post-doc to your trust and faith in my ability to do good work. I know I wouldn't be here today without you. Thank you.

Best Regards! All respect.

N

The note was a gift from God. Now I could move on. Nigel was the only person who truly understood my loss and could make me whole. The load I'd carried for so long was gone, vanishing into the infinite nothingness.

When the tears stopped, I smiled with the blessing that things were finally right with Nigel. His forgiveness allowed me to finally put this fantastical experience to rest.

In the end, I found my way back to a life of joy…a life more interesting because I dared to be a pot doc.

The Crumbling Wall

Despite the setback in Montana, the wall of marijuana prohibition continued to crumble. Without a doubt, the sentinel moment was November of 2012, when Colorado passed Amendment 64, pot's Pandora's Box, making it the first state to legalize marijuana for recreational use.[142] Soon after, Washington state passed I-502, opening the door to begin marijuana for recreational use in July 2014.[143]

In 2013 Vermont decriminalized cannabis while New Hampshire and Illinois passed medical marijuana legislation.

The year 2014 saw a flood of state legislation passing varying forms of medical cannabis, including Maryland, Missouri, Utah, Minnesota, Wisconsin, Florida, Mississippi, Alabama, Iowa, Kentucky, New York, South Carolina, and North Carolina. Missouri and Maryland also decriminalized marijuana, while the legalization of recreational marijuana was passed by voters in both Alaska and Oregon.

2015 saw more medical cannabis legislation in Louisiana, Virginia, Georgia, Oklahoma, Texas, and Wyoming. Delaware passed a decriminalization bill.

In 2016 Pennsylvania, Arkansas, North Dakota, and Ohio legalized medical cannabis, while Illinois decriminalized marijuana. Through ballot initiatives, recreational marijuana legalization was approved in California, Nevada, Maine, and Massachusetts.

2017 saw West Virginia and Indiana joining the growing club of states approving medical cannabis, while New Hampshire decriminalized the plant.

The crumbling wall of cannabis prohibition continued. In 2018 saw Vermont become the first state to legalize cannabis through the state legislature. Kansas legalized CBD use. Michigan, Missouri, and Utah all approved the legalization of marijuana through ballot measures.

In 2019 Hawaii, New Mexico, and North Dakota decriminalized cannabis, while Illinois legalized cannabis through state legislative action.

And numerous municipalities, such as Atlanta, Nashville, New Orleans, Pittsburgh, Chicago, New York City, and Philadelphia, have decriminalized cannabis ahead of state legislative efforts.[144]

The shackles of cannabis prohibition are loosening internationally as well. In 2014 Uruguay became the first country to legalize marijuana,[145] followed by Canada in 2018.[146]

Despite the steady march of states legalizing cannabis for medicinal use or marijuana for recreational purposes (or both), one simple fact lingers: as long as the FDA maintains marijuana as a Schedule I substance, individuals will never be completely safe from the unpredictable wrath of federal prosecution. Although it's unlikely that any US Attorney General could be as vehemently anti-cannabis as former AG Jeff Sessions, considering the current political climate, nothing would surprise me.

In the summer of 2009, not a single soul in Montana's medical marijuana industry could have possibly imagined the apocalyptic landscape they would be facing a mere two years later. But ultimately, what torpedoed mine, and all of the other marijuana-related businesses in the state, had nothing to do with a failing economy, poor business decisions, or a product that wasn't in high demand; what sunk the medical marijuana industry in Montana was the government. What the Montana legislature did to its constituents should be a lesson for every citizen in every state where cannabis is legal. Don't think it can't happen in your state.

Cannabis sativa has thrived for millennium and will continue to do so regardless of what administration resides in the White House or who heads the Department of Justice. Cannabis isn't an ideologue, nor does its use break along party lines. Cannabis is neither red, nor blue nor purple; it's just a misunderstood plant that wants to do what all living organisms do—simply grow and thrive.

We've reached the tipping point with this wonderfully useful yet misunderstood plant. We can never go back to the way things were. The genie is out of the bottle. We can only press onward.

Epilogue

Since June 30, 2011, the injunctions to SB-423, as imposed by Judge Reynolds, remained in place, offering cannabis patients and businesses a rice paper-thin veil of legal protection. The legal status of SB-423 hovered in limbo until February 25, 2016.

And as the universe would have it, that was on that the same day that I finished the first draft of this manuscript. I called Anthony asking for permission to use his name. We called each other periodically to catch up on things. He'd closed up shop in Bozeman and moved his family to Arizona where he was looking for his new cannabis niche.

"Dude, did you hear the news?" he said excitedly.

"What news?"

"Dude, google 'Montana medical marijuana.'"

I typed in the phrase, hit return, and waited. "We finally won?" I asked, as Anthony's tone suggested that our legal victory against the State had just been announced. For a moment, as I waited for the topic to appear on my laptop, I felt a thrill of excitement that justice was served.

"Dude, they got clobbered. 6-1."

"Seriously?" I was stunned.

The information finally popped up on my laptop: *The Montana Supreme Court ruled to uphold SB-423 in its entirety.*[147] I was breathless.

"Yeah, man. I've been getting calls from folks all day. Lotta sad people there right now."

"Wow."

"And folks thought I was crazy for leaving the state when I did."

The implications of the full implementation of SB-423 were chilling. Many of my friends were in complete disarray after the ruling. Few rational people thought that the court would uphold such an egregious infringement on personal liberty, let alone by a 6-1 decision.

Tirelessly, on June 14, 2016, the MTCIA filed a brief with the Supreme Court of the United States (SCOTUS) to appeal the Montana Supreme Court decision.[148] They also filed for a stay on the Montana Supreme Court's decision to allow SB-423 to go into full effect on August 31, 2016. The stay was requested until SCOTUS resolves all matters related to the case, or until a new citizen's initiative (I-182) was decided by voters in November 2016. The State of Montana conceded that they were willing to wait for the SCOTUS decision, but objected to the stay extended to the November election.

Unfortunately, the Supreme Court declined to hear the case. Regardless, being party in a legal case that was argued all the way to the Supreme Court of the United States is among the proudest accomplishments of my life.

Happily, on November 8, 2016, Montana voters approved I-182 by 57.8 percent,[149] paving the way for citizens to regain reliable access to medical marijuana. In 2017, the legislature passed SB-333 a reform measure to the Montana Medical Marijuana Act,[150] and in 2019 the Act was further amended with SB-265.[151]

Tom Daubert had his day in court. In September 2012, Daubert was sentenced to five years' probation for maintaining drug-involved premises. His attorney, Peter Lacey, asked friends and colleagues to write on Daubert's behalf as testimony of his exceptional character. By the time of sentencing, the judge commented that this was the largest outcropping of support for a sentence he had seen in all his years on the bench.[152]

Daubert later petitioned the court to be released from probation early so he could rebuild his career and visit his ailing mother without travel restrictions. In 2014 US District Judge Dana Christensen denied his request because Daubert didn't "meet the exceptional circumstances required for early termination." Christensen noted that Daubert was granted leniency in his original sentencing and that he can still obtain permission to travel to Pennsylvania to care for his mother.[153]

Tom is happily living a full life in Philadelphia. He and I have nurtured a friendship that I wish I could have appreciated during my time in Montana. Without his support, friendship, and assiduous help with details of this text, this book might never have seen the light of day. His story of his involvement in the medical marijuana movement is fascinating, but his recovery journey of how he healed himself from being a victim of the capricious government cannabis policy is truly remarkable. I hope he'll write his story someday.

Jason Christ, the person I hold personally responsible for SB-423, remains an enigma. Because of the nature of his personality, I thought I'd let the press reports do the talking. Perhaps if law enforcement had been more aggressive in restricting his ability to work seamlessly within the entire medical marijuana industry, I'd be writing a different story. As early as 2010, Mr. Christ was convicted of intimidation and threatening to blow up a Missoula Verizon Store.[154] A Missoula judge found Christ in contempt of court for three different violations.[155] He was banned from the University of Montana campus after allegedly smoking marijuana in the law school.[156] Some things you just can't make up.

Yet, in the interest of fairness, Christ did allow for his boundary-less behavior to serve some good. He was the first known person to openly board a commercial aircraft with medical marijuana, flying from Missoula to Seattle., setting a precedent for other medical marijuana patients. In a YouTube video that has since been removed, he showed TSA staff his medical marijuana card, along with his stash of medical marijuana and his vaporizer. After passing through security, he then vaporized at the gate area. Perhaps Christ helped move the bar, as TSA now allows medical marijuana on both checked and carry-on bags.[157]

Pam Likert is still providing quality family medicine care to the under-served of Missoula.

Jerry Taylor lives with his family to Havre, Montana, and is still providing outstanding medical care to the people of Montana. He remains one of my most admired friends.

Pete Jones continues to push the boundaries for marijuana reform. Spared from the wrath of the federal raids, he has run marijuana operations, on some level, in at least five states. He also threatened me with legal action if I used his real name. Duhhh!

Epilogue

Katrina Farnum has continued being a cannabis warrior, serving both on the board of directors and as president of the MTCIA. She was instrumental in helping to formulate and pass I-182 and worked diligently to affect the current medical cannabis legislation, including SB-333 and SB-265. Katrina owns the Garden Mother, an herbal store in Missoula.

Samantha Kovak left politics to pursue a career as a writer. Sam went back to working for the MTCIA and helped coordinate the effort to pass I-182. Although I doubt that I'll ever see her again, I still have warm thoughts about the magical times we spent together.

Hiedi Handford continues her advocacy. She is Founder of two successful businesses My Medicine Consulting and Terpene Healer located in sunny South Florida. She was one of six authors in the political collaborative Sensible Florida, drafting the first adult-use petition for marijuana (Regulate Florida) to reach the Florida Supreme Court.

Chris Lindsey is now the Director of Government Relations at the Marijuana Policy Project, which works to change cannabis laws both at the state and federal levels. He wrote Illinois' current legalization law, which MPP helped pass in 2019.

Chris Williams as former US Marine, he was the only member of Montana Cannabis to plead "not guilty". A jury found Williams guilty of eight felony counts and faced a mandatory minimum sentencing of 80 years in prison. Fortunately, supporters posted a White House petition that called to "Free Chris Williams" with over 27,000 signatures. Ultimately, all but two charges against Williams were dropped. His prison sentence was commuted to five years and the $1.7 million forfeiture requirement was waived. Freed from prison, there is now a movement to support clemency for Williams (https://mychronicrelief.com/free-christopher-williams/) He lives happily in Bozeman.

Lori Bedford is still active in the Bozeman film community, and we have dinner when I'm in town. Unfortunately, her sister lost her long battle to breast cancer in 2015.

Hillari Kennedy is still living outside of Bozeman with her family. She teaches herbal medicine workshops, hula dancing classes, and has launched a successful line of natural skincare products: Recherche Organics. I will always smile when I think of her.

Mike Singer is still playing banjo and is the sole proprietor of Sensible Alternatives in Belgrade. He recently was married and had a child with his amazing wife, Ellie. We remain friends, and I hope to see him on the big stage playing bluegrass sometime soon. He remains someone I can honestly say is truly "living the dream."

Arno Hazekamp is still involved in cannabis research. He resigned from his position as Head of Research and Education at Bedrocan BV and now has his own cannabis consulting company, Hazekamp Herbal Consulting. He continues to operate an annual educational workshop Masterclass Medicinal Cannabis that he teaches in Leiden. Whenever his travels take him to New York City, I make an effort to take the train downstate.

Anthony Gallo was a friend when I needed one. He was given the opportunity to write his own epilogue but opted to stay anonymous due to his continued involvement in the medical marijuana industry. Suffice to say, he is doing well and feels grateful not to have been one of those indicted after the March 2011 raids.

Michelle Sexton, ND, is living in the San Diego area with her partner and surfing whenever Gaia permits. She continues working as a naturopathic doctor as a faculty member at the University of California–San Diego Medical School as well as a medical cannabis consultant both for private industry and several national cannabis foundations. We remind each other of the lunacy that continues to permeate the medical cannabis industry.

Nigel Plumer was dubbed the 2014 Medical Cannabis Researcher of the Year by Americans for Safe Access (ASA).[158] Nigel served as director of research and development at PalliaTech, a phytomedical technology company dedicated to unlocking the therapeutic potential of cannabis. In 2015 Nigel was named Chief Scientist for Mary's Medicinals directing and managing all research, development, and testing for current and future cannabis products. He is one of the foremost authorities on cannabis chemistry in the United States. He and his family remain in Bozeman. We remain friends, and I will always consider him to be my brother from another mother.

Jacob Geci has turned into a fine young man heading off to college. Our relationship has endured the test of adolescence and I am full of gratitude that neither of us gave up on the other.

CITATIONS

1 http://norml.org/component/zoo/item/part-i

2 http://norml.org/component/zoo/item/part-i

3 "The role of cannabinoid system on immune modulation: therapeutic implications on CNS inflammation." Mini Rev Med Chem. 2005 Jul.; 5(7): 671–5. Correa F, Mestre L, Molina-Holgado E, Arévalo-Martín A, Docagne F, Romero E, Molina-Holgado F, Borrell J, Guaza C.

4 https://missoulian.com/news/opinion/editorial/crucial-care-deniedbackward-federal-laws-prevented-robin-prosser-from-using/article_7a119713-d6b5-548d-ba4d-de9035b9f4e7.html; https://www.justice.gov/opa/blog/memorandum-selected-united-state-attorneys-investigations-and-prosecutions-states

5 https://www.justice.gov/opa/blog/memorandum-selected-united-state-attorneys-investigations-and-prosecutions-states

6 https://www.bozemandailychronicle.com/news/network-helps-patients-get-medical-marijuana-info/article_86c26f36-8489-505b-8c9e-6319b2f04e0a.html

7 "Cannabis sativa: The Plant of the Thousand and One Molecules." Front Plant Sci. 2016; 7: 19. Andre CM, Hausman JF, Guerriero G.

8 "Cannabinoid receptors: where they are and what they do." J Neuroendocrinol. 2008 May; 20 Suppl 1: 10–14. Mackie K.

9 "The invertebrate ancestry of endocannabinoid signalling: an orthologue of vertebrate cannabinoid receptors in the urochordate Ciona intestinalis." Gene. 2003 Jan. 2; 302 (1–2): 95–101. Elphick MR, Satou Y, Satoh N.

10 "Cannabinoid receptors: where they are and what they do." J Neuroendocrinol. 2008 May; 20 Suppl 1: 10–4. Mackie K.

11 "The endocannabinoid system as an emerging target of pharmacotherapy." Pharmacol Rev. 2006 Sept.; 58(3): 389–462. Pacher P, Batkai S, Kunos G.

12 "Efficacy and safety of the weight-loss drug rimonabant: a meta-analysis of randomized trials." Lancet. 2007 Nov. 17; 370(9600): 1706–13. Christensen R, Kristensen PK, Bartels EM, Bliddal H, Astrup A.

13 "Antineoplastic activity of cannabinoids." J Natl Cancer Inst. 1975 Sept.; 55(3): 597–602. Munson AE, Harris LS, Friedman MA, Dewey WL, Carchman RA.

14 "Cannabinoid-induced autophagy: Protective or death role?" Prostaglandins Other Lipid Mediat. 2016 Jan.; 122: 54–63. Costa L, Amaral C, Teixeira N, Correia-da-Silva G, Fonseca BM.

15 "Cannabinoids as therapeutic agents in cancer: current status and future implications." Oncotarget. 2014 Aug. 15; 5(15): 5852–72. Chakravarti B, Ravi J, Ganju RK.

16 "The antitumor activity of plant-derived non-psychoactive cannabinoids." J Neuroimmune Pharmacol. 2015 Jun.; 10(2): 255–67. McAllister SD, Soroceanu L, Desprez PY.

17 "Cannabinoids as therapeutic agents in cancer: current status and future implications." Oncotarget. 2014 Aug. 15; 5(15): 5852–72. Chakravarti B, Ravi J, Ganju RK.

18 "Cannabinoids for nausea and vomiting in adults with cancer receiving chemotherapy." Cochrane Database Syst Rev. 2015 Nov. 12; 11. Smith LA, Azariah F, Lavender VT, Stoner NS, Bettiol S.

19 "Pathways and gene networks mediating the regulatory effects of cannabidiol, a nonpsychoactive cannabinoid, in autoimmune T cells." J Neuroinflammation. 2016 Jun. 3; 13(1): 136. Kozela E, Juknat A, Gao F, Kaushansky N, Coppola G, Vogel Z.

20 "Composition and antimicrobial activities of lippia multiflora moldenke, mentha x piperita l. and ocimum basilicum l. essential oils and their major monoterpene alcohols alone and in combination." Molecules. 2010 Nov.; 15(11): 7825–39. Bassolé

IHN, Lamien-Meda A, Bayala B, Tirogo S, Franz C, Novak J, Nebié RC, Dicko MH.

21 http://www.psychiatrictimes.com/articles/efficacy-psychiatric-drugs

22 http://www.cchprint.org/psychdrugdangers

23 "Mental Health Policy and Psychotropic Drugs." Milbank Q. 2005 Jun.; 83(2): 271–98. Frank RG, Conti RM, Goldman HH.

24 "Cannabidiol in humans—the quest for therapeutic targets." Pharmaceuticals (Basel) 2012 May; 5(5): 529–52. Zhornitsky S, Potvin S.

25 "A critical review of the antipsychotic effects of cannabidiol: 30 years of a translational investigation." Curr Pharm Des. 2012; 18(32): 5131–40. Zuardi AW, Crippa JA, Hallak JE, Bhattacharyya S, Atakan Z, Martin-Santos R, McGuire PK, Guimarães FS.

26 "Impact of marijuana legalization in Colorado on adolescent emergency and urgent care visits." J Adolesc Health. 2018 Aug.; 63(2): 239–41. Wang GS, Davies SD, Halmo LS, Sass A, Mistry RD.

27 "Weeding out the truth: adolescents and cannabis." J Addict Med. 2016 Mar.–Apr.; 10(2): 73-80. Ammerman S, Tau G.

28 https://www.nytimes.com/2019/06/16/opinion/marijuana-brain-effects.html

29 "High times for cannabis: epigenetic imprint and its legacy on brain and behavior." Neurosci Biobehav Rev. 2018 Feb.; 85: 93–101. Henrietta Szutorisz H, Hurd YL.

30 "An evidence based review of acute and long-term effects of cannabis use on executive functions." J Addict Med. 2011 Mar. 1; 5(1): 1–8. Crean RD, Crane NA, Mason BJ.

31 "Functional MRI of inhibitory processing in abstinent marijuana users." Psychopharmacology (Berl). 2007 Oct.; 194(2): 173–83. Tapert SF et al.

32 https://medicalxpress.com/news/2013-12-heavy-marijuana-users-abnormal-brain.html s

33 "An evidence based review of acute and long-term effects of cannabis use on executive functions." J Addict Med. 2011 Mar. 1; 5(1): 1–8. Crean RD, Crane NA, Mason BJ.

34 "An evidence based review of acute and long-term effects of cannabis use on executive functions." J Addict Med. 2011 Mar. 1; 5(1): 1–8. Crean RD, Crane NA, Mason BJ.

35 "Persistent cannabis users show neuropsychological decline from childhood to midlife." PNAS. 2012 Oct. 2; 109(40): 2657–64. Meier MM et al.

36 "The influence of marijuana use on neurocognitive functioning in adolescents." Curr Drug Abuse Rev. 2008 Jan; 1(1): 99–111. Schweinsburg AD, Brown SA, Tapert SF.

37 "Effects of cannabis on the adolescent brain." Curr Pharm Des. 2014; 20(13): 2186–93. Jacobus J, Tapert SF.

38 "Delta-9-Tetrahyrdocannabinol induces neurogenesis and improve cognitive performances of male Sprague Dawley rats." Neurotox Res. 2018; 33(2): 402–11. Suliman NA et al.

39 "Non-medical cannabis self-exposure as a dimensional predictor of opioid dependence diagnosis: a propensity score matched analysis." Front Psychiatry. 2018; 9: 283. Butelman ER et al.

40 http//www.youtube.com/watch?v=ddhwldQShk

41 "Marijuana dependence moderates the effect of post-traumatic stress disorder on trauma cue reactivity in substance dependent patients." Drug Alcohol Depend. 2016 Feb. 1; 159: 219–26. Tull MT, McDermott MJ, Gratz KL.

42 http//www.denverpost.com/2016/05/20/u-s-house-votes-to-allow-va-doctors-to-talk-medical-marijuanawith-patients/

43 "Stress as a common risk factor for obesity and addiction." Biol Psychiatry. 2013 May 1; 73(9): 827–35. Sinha R, Jastreboff AM.

44 "Early adverse experience and substance addiction: dopamine, oxytocin, and glucocorticoid pathways." Ann N Y Acad Sci. 2017 Apr.; 1394(1): 74–91. Kim S et al.

45 "Addiction and the brain: the role of neurotransmitters in the cause and treatment of drug dependence." CMAJ. 2001 Mar. 20; 164(6): 817–21. Tompkins DM, Sellers EM.

46 "Cannabinoid-dopamine interaction in the pathophysiology of CNS disorders." CNS Neurosci Ther. 2010 Jun.; 16(3): 72–91. Fernandez-Ruiz J, Hernandez M, Ramos JA.

47 "Introduction: addiction and brain reward and anti-reward pathways." Adv Psychosom Med. 2011; 30: 22–60. Gardner EL.

48 "Environmental factors, epigenetics, and developmental origin of reproductive disorders." Reprod Toxicol. 2017 Mar.; 68: 85–104. Ho SM et al.

49 "Proenkephalin mediates the enduring effects of adolescent cannabis exposure associated with adult opiate vulnerability." Biol Psychiatry. 2012 Nov. 15; 72(10): 803–10. Tomasiewicz HC et al.

50 "Nicotine and Δ9-tetrahydrocannabinol withdrawal induce Narp in the central nucleus of the amygdala." Synapse 63(3): 252–55. Reti IM et al.

51 "Introduction: addiction and brain reward and anti-reward pathways." Adv Psychosom Med. 2011; 30: 22–60. Gardner EL.

52 "Delta 9-tetrahydrocannabinol induces dopamine release in the human striatum." Neuropsychopharmacology. 2009 Feb.; 34(3): 759–66. Bossang MG, et al.

53 "Reducing cannabinoid abuse and preventing relapse by enhancing endogenous brain levels of kynurenic acid." Nat Neurosci. 2013 Nov.; 16(11): 1652–61. Justinova Z et al.

54 "Preclinical studies of cannabinoid reward treatments for cannabis use disorder, and addiction-related effects of cannabinoid exposure." Neuropsychopharmacology. 2018 Jan.; 43(1): 116–41. Panlilio LV, Justinova Z.

55 "Cannabis addiction and the brain: a review." J Neuroimmune Pharmacol. 2018; 13(4): 438–52. Zehra A et al.

56 "Cannabinoid and heroin activation of mesolimbic dopamine transmission by a common mu1 opioid receptor mechanism." Science. 1997 Jun. 27; 276(5321): 2048–50. Tanda G, Pontieri FE, Di Chiara G.

57 "Leveraging user perspectives for insight into cannabis concentrates." Am J Drug Alcohol Abuse. 2018; 44(6): 628–641. Cavazos-Rehg PA et al.

58 "From first drug use to drug dependence; developmental periods of risk for dependence upon marijuana, cocaine, and alcohol." Neuropsychopharmacology. 2002 Apr.; 26(4): 479–88. Wagner FA, Anthony JC.

59 "DSM-5 cannabis use disorder in the National Epidemiologic Survey on Alcohol and Related Conditions-III: Gender-specific profiles." Addict Behav. Jan.; 76: 52-60. Kerridge BT et al.

60 "Delta-9-Tetrahydrocannabinol (Δ9-THC) induces neurogenesis and improve cognitive performances of male Sprague Dawley rats." Neurotox Res. 2018; 33(2): 402–11. Suliman NA et al.

61 "Cannabidiol, a nonpsychoactive Cannabis constituent, protects against myocardial ischemic reperfusion injury." American Journal of Physiology—Heart and Circulatory Physiology. 2007 Dec. 1. Vol. 293. Durst R et al.

62 http://www.epilepsy.com/information/professionals/about-epilepsy-seizures/overview-epilepsy-syndromes/unverricht-lundborg

63 https://clinicaltrials.gov/ct2/show/NCT02397863

64 "Therapeutic potential of non-psychotropic cannabidiol in ischemic stroke." Pharmaceuticals (Basel). 2010 Jul. 8; 3(7): 2197–212. Hayakawa K, Mishima K, Fujiwara M.

65 "Cannabis, cannabinoids, and cerebral metabolism: potential applications in stroke and disorders of the central nervous system." Curr Cardiol Rep. 2015 Sept.; 17(9): 627. Latorre JG, Schmidt EB.

66 "Sleep quality moderates the relation between depression symptoms and problematic cannabis use among medical cannabis users." Am J Drug Alcohol Abuse. 2013 May; 39(3): 211–16. Babson KA, Boden MT, Bonn-Miller MO.

67 "Endogenous and synthetic cannabinoids as therapeutics in retinal disease." Neural Plast. 2016; 8373020. Kokona D, Georgiou PC, Kounenidakis M, Kiagiadaki F, Thermos K.

68 "Diabetic retinopathy: Role of inflammation and potential therapies for anti-inflammation." World J Diabetes. 2010 Mar. 15; 1(1): 12–18. Liou GI.

69 "Prenatal exposure to drugs: effects on brain development and implications for policy and education." Nat Rev Neurosci. 2009 Apr.; 10(4): 303–312. Thompson BL, Levitt P, Stanwood GD.

70 "'A little dab will do ya' in: a case report of neuro-and cardiotoxicity following use of cannabinoid concentrates." Clin Toxicol (Phila). 2017 Nov.; 55(9): 1011–13. Rickner SS et al.

71 "'To dab or not to dab': rising concerns regarding the toxicity of cannabis concentrates." Cureus. 2017 Sep 11; 9(9): 1676. Alzghari SK.

72 "Neuronal substrates and functional consequences of prenatal cannabis exposure." Eur Child Adolesc Psychiatry. 2014 Oct.; 23(10): 931–41. Calvigioni D, et al.

73 "Short-term exposure and long-term consequences of neonatal exposure to $\Delta(9)$-tetrahydrocannabinol (THC) and ibuprofen in mice." Behav Brain Res. 2016 Jul. 1; 307: 137–44. Philippot G, Nyberg F, Gordh T, Fredriksson A, Viberg H.

74 "Neuronal substrates and functional consequences of prenatal cannabis exposure." European Child and Adolescent Psychiatry. 2015 Jun. 8. Calvigioni D et al.

75 "Prenatal exposure to cannabinoids evokes long-lasting functional alterations by targeting CB1 receptors on developing cortical neurons." Proc Natl Acad Sci USA. 2015 Nov. 3; 112(44): 13693–98. de Salas-Quiroga A et al.

76 "High times for cannabis: epigenetic imprint and its legacy on brain and behavior." Neurosci Biobehav Rev. 2018 Feb.; 85: 93–101. Szutorisz H, Hurd YL.

77 "Use during pregnancy: pharmacokenetics and effects on child development." Pharmacol Ther. 2018 Feb.; 182: 133–51. Grant KS, et al.

78 "Maternal marijuana use has independent effects on risk for spontaneous pre-term birth but not other common late pregnancy complications." Reprod Toxicol. 2016 Jul.; 62: 77–86. Leemaqz SY et al.

79 "Maternal drug use and risk of childhood nonlymphoblastic leukemia among offspring: an epidemiologic investigation implicating marijuana (a report from the Children's Cancer Study Group)." Cancer. 1989 May 15; 63(10): 1904–11. Robison LL et al.

80 "Maternal use of recreational drugs and neuroblastoma in offspring: a report from the Children's Oncology Group (United States)." Cancer Causes Control. 2006 Jun.; 17(5): 663–69. Bluhm EC et al.

81 "Higher incidence of clear cell adenocarcinoma of the cervix and vagina among women born between 1947 and 1971 in the United States." Cancer Causes Control. 2012 Jan.; 23(1): 207–11. Smith EK et al.

82 "Marijuana use by breastfeeding mothers and cannabinoid concentrations in breast milk." Pediatrics. 2018 Sept. 142(3). Bertrand KA et al.

83 "Cannabinoids for medical use: a systemic review and meta-analysis." JAMA. 2015; 313 (24): 2456–73. Whiting P et al.

84 "The effect of medicinal cannabis on pain and quality of life outcomes in chronic pain: a prospective open-label study." Clin J Pain. 2016 Feb. 17. Haroutounian S, Ratz Y, Ginosar Y, Furmanov K, Saifi F, Meidan R, Davidson E.

85 "Long-term health outcomes of childhood abuse: an overview and a call to action." J Gen Intern Med. 2003 Oct.; 18(10): 864–70. Springer KW, Sheridan J, Kuo D, Carnes M.

86 "Evaluating the effects of gamma-irradiation for decontamination of medical cannabis." Front Pharmacol. 2016; 7: 108. Hazekamp A.

87 "Fatal aspergillosis associated with smoking contaminated marijuana, in a marrow transplant recipient." Chest. 1988 Aug.; 94(2): 432–33. Hamadeh R, Ardehali A, Locksley RM, York MK.

88 "A total synthesis of DL-Delta-1-Tetrahydrocannabinol, the active constituent of hashish." J Am Chem Soc. 1965 Jul. 20; 87: 3273–75. Mechoulam R, Gaoni Y.

89 https://www.dea.gov/controlled-substances-act

90 http://patft.uspto.gov/netacgi/nph-Parser?Sect1=PTO1&-Sect2=HITOFF&d=PALL&p=1&u=%2Fnetahtml%2FPTO%2Fs-

rchnum.htm&r=1&f=G&l=50&s1=6630507.PN.&OS=PN/66305 07&RS=PN/6630507

91 https://archive.fortune.com/magazines/fortune/fortune_archive/2009/09/28/toc.html

92 "The effects of cannabinoids on the endocrine system." Endokrynologia Polska. 2018; 69(6): 705–19. Borowska M et al.

93 "Cannabis exposure and the risk of testicular cancer: a systematic review." BMC Cancer. 2015 Nov. 11; 15: 897. Gurney J, Shaw C, Stanley J, Signal V, Sarfati D.

94 "Role of cannabinoids in the development of fatty liver (steatosis)." AAPS J. 2010 Jun.; 12(2): 233–37. Purohit V, Rapaka R, Shurtleff D.

95 "Prenatal exposure to cannabis and maternal and child health outcomes: a systematic review and meta-analysis." BMJ Open. 2016 Apr. 5; 6(4). Gunn JK et al.

96 "Comparative assessment for hyperaccumulatory and phytoremediation capability of three wild weeds." Biotech. 2014 Dec.; 4(6): 579–89. Girdhar M, Sharma NR, Rehman H, Kumar A, Mohan A.

97 http://www.bozemandailychronicle.com/news/taking-the-mystery-out-of-marijuana/article_d5ff2830-9358-11df-a697-001cc4c002e0.html

98 https://www.washingtonpost.com/archive/local/2001/06/08/activist-robert-c-randall-dies/05578bc8-7e8d-42f8-8857-f3e469bee388/

99 https://aliceolearyrandall.wordpress.com/about/

100 http://www.druglibrary.org/schaffer/Library/studies/YOUNG/index.html

101 http://irvinrosenfeld.com/

102 https://www.justice.gov/opa/blog/memorandum-selected-united-state-attorneys-investigations-and-prosecutions-states

103 http://missoulian.com/news/state-and-regional/great-falls-puts-moratorium-on-medical-marijuana-shops/article_131f67a4-10da-11df-a35c-001cc4c002e0.html

104 http://helenair.com/news/state-and-regional/towns-react-to-marijuana-biz-with-bans-moratoriums/article_9a67cca4-6ba9-11df-b463-001cc4c03286.html

105 http://www.kmud.org/programs-mainmenu-11/specials/item/583-cannabis-chronicles.html

106 https://cannabisscience.com/2010/307-governor-schweitzer-s-visit-to-cannabis-science-acquisition-montana-pain-management-draws-extensive-media-coverage-governor-impressed-by-the-sophistication-of-operation-model-for-new-state-regulations

107 https://cannabisscience.com/2010/318-montana-pain-management-in-breach-of-non-disclosure-non-circumvention-agreement-with-cannabis-science

https://money.cnn.com/news/newsfeeds/articles/globenewswire/199685.html

108 "Association between cannabis use and schizotypal dimensions—a meta-analysis of cross-sectional studies." Psychiatry Research. 2014; 219(1): 58–66. Szoke A et al.

109 http://www.dailyinterlake.com/members/arrest-total-hits-four-in-murder-case/article_c5a226cc-5343-11df-a59e-001cc4c03286.html

110 https://www.washingtonpost.com/wp-dyn/content/article/2010/05/10/AR2010051004566.html

111 http://newstalkkgvo.com/billings-bans-storefront-sale-of-medical-marijuana/

112 http://flatheadbeacon.com/2010/04/20/council-votes-to-prohibit-medical-marijuana-businesses-in-kalispell/

113 https://montanafesto.wordpress.com/2011/03/23/the-truth-behind-safe-community-safe-kids/

114 https://www.youtube.com/watch?v=eFBMAtUFDJo

115 "Medical marijuana for epilepsy?" Innov Clin Neurosci. 2016 Mar.–Apr.; 13(3–4): 23–26. Kolikonda MK et al.

116 "Efficacy and safety of cannabinoid oromucosal spray for multiple sclerosis spasticity." J Neurol Neurosurg Psychiatry. 2016 Sept.; 87(9): 944–951. F Patti et al.

117 "Taming THC: potential cannabis synergy and phytocannabinoids-terpenoid entourage effects." Br J Pharmacol. 2011 Aug.; 163(7): 1344–64. Russo EB.

118 "Chemical characterization and evaluation of the antibacterial activity of essential oils from fibre-type cannabis sativa L. (Hemp)." Molecules. 2019 Jun.; 24(12): 2302. Iseppi R. et al.

119 http://www.washingtonpost.com/wp-dyn/content/article/2010/11/03/AR2010110303997.html

120 http://www.tokeofthetown.com/2011/01/montana_lab_contracts_to_test_medical_marijuana_pr.php

121 "Diabetic retinopathy: Role of inflammation and potential therapies for anti-inflammation." World J Diabetes. 2010 Mar 15; 1(1):12-8. Liou GI.

122 https://leg.mt.gov/bills/2011/HJrnl/HJ0001.pdf

123 Personal communication, August 6, 2018.

124 https://www.youtube.com/watch?v=Bdk1t9NfhtA

125 https://www.youtube.com/watch?v=wRKzhiAnsJI

126 https://www.youtube.com/watch?v=lQYp3sMlTQs

127 https://www.bozemandailychronicle.com/news/cannabis-at-the-capitol/article_08373406-1e8c-5af2-9921-f0f45bb91196.html

128 http://www.codeofthewestfilm.com/

129 http://usatoday30.usatoday.com/news/nation/2011-03-18-medmarijuanaraids18_ST_N.html

130 https://www.bozemandailychronicle.com/news/warrants-issued-in-monday-pot-raids-remaining-businesses-vow-resilience/article_df545e30-4f66-11e0-ade4-001cc4c03286.html

131 http://www.cannabistherapyinstitute.com/legal/feds/doj.haag.memo.pdf

132 https://www.youtube.com/watch?v=4QVm-REdJOk

133 http://billingsgazette.com/news/state-and-regional/montana/schweitzer-fires-up-branding-irons-to-veto-bills/article_801bce1a-6601-11e0-b3ab-001cc4c002e0.html

134 http://www.dailykos.com/story/2011/2/17/946428/

135 http://leg.mt.gov/content/Committees/Interim/2011-2012/Children-Family/Meeting-Documents/June-2011/sb423-legal-action-overview.pdf

136 Transcript of Proceedings on Appeal, Montana Cannabis Industry Association, Mark Matthews, Shirley Hamp, Shelley Yeager, Jane Doe, John Doe #1, John Doe #2, Michael Geci-Black, M.D., John Stowers, M.D., Point Hatfield, and Charlie Hamp vs State of Montana [pages28-54, 57-119, 191-246], Montana First Judicial District, Case # DDV-11-518 (2011).

137 https://www.bozemandailychronicle.com/montana-medical-marijuana-changes-cause-confusion/article_56b0b22c-a42a-11e0-9cb2-001cc4c03286.html

138 Personal communication, July 15, 2019.

139 https://dphhs.mt.gov/Portals/85/qad/documents/LicensureBureau/MarijuanaProgram/MMPStatsbyQuarterthruSept2016.pdf?ver=2016-11-02-140718-047

140 https://allpoetry.com/First-They-Came-For-The-Communists

141 Personal communication, 2015.

142 http://www.huffingtonpost.com/2012/11/06/amendment-64-passes-in-co_n_2079899.html

143 http://www.liq.wa.gov/mj2015/faqs_i-502

144 https://disa.com/map-of-marijuana-legality-by-state

145 https://www.reuters.com/article/us-uruguay-marijuana-vote-idUSBRE9BA01520131211

146 https://www.nytimes.com/2018/10/17/world/canada/marijuana-pot-cannabis-legalization.html

147 http://missoulian.com/news/local/missoula-medical-marijuana-providers-react-to-supreme-court-decision-with/article_340b5e9e-2d13-54c0-855f-39ae600195c1.html

148 https://www.mtcia.org/mtcia-files-appeal-to-scotus/

149 https://ballotpedia.org/Montana_Medical_Marijuana_Initiative,_I-182_(2016)

150 https://leg.mt.gov/bills/2017/billpdf/SB0333.pdf

151 https://leg.mt.gov/bills/2019/billpdf/SB0265.pdf

152 https://missoulian.com/news/local/medical-marijuana-activist-daubert-gets-probation-in-federal-drug-case/article_e279b332-f850-11e1-abe0-0019bb2963f4.html

153 http://www.washingtontimes.com/news/2014/jan/15/judge-denies-dauberts-request-to-lift-probation/

154 http://missoulian.com/news/local/jury-Jacob-christ-guilty-of-intimidation-for-threatening-missoula-verizon/article_7b903edc-a88d-11e2-8d9d-0019bb2963f4.html

155 http://www.nbcmontana.com/news/judge-sentences-Jacob-christ-to-jail-for-contempt-of-court/21454516

156 http://missoulian.com/news/local/medical-marijuana-advocate-christ-banned-from-um-campus/article_8d9c3176-1d73-11e2-b40f-0019bb2963f4.html

157 https://www.tsa.gov/travel/security-screening/whatcanibring/items/medical-marijuana

158 https://ir.curaleaf.com/press-releases/detail/5/palliatech-scientist-named-medical-cannabis-researcher-of

CPSIA information can be obtained
at www.ICGtesting.com
Printed in the USA
BVHW091124301220
596710BV00002B/3